STUDIES IN

AFRICAN AMERICAN HISTORY AND CULTURE

D0081962

edited by

GRAHAM RUSSELL HODGES
COLGATE UNIVERSITY

A GARLAND SERIES

THE ASSERTIVE WOMAN IN ZORA NEALE HURSTON'S FICTION, FOLKLORE, AND DRAMA

PEARLIE MAE FISHER PETERS

GARLAND PUBLISHING, Inc.
A MEMBER OF THE TAYLOR & FRANCIS GROUP
NEW YORK & LONDON / 1998

Library of Congress Cataloging-in-Publication Data

Peters, Pearlie Mae Fisher, 1947–
    The assertive woman in Zora Neale Hurston's fiction,
folklore, and drama / Pearlie Mae Fisher Peters.
        p.   cm. — (Studies in African American history and
culture)
    Includes bibliographical references and index.
    ISBN 0-8153-2888-5 (alk. paper)
    1. Hurston, Zora Neale—Characters—Women. 2. Feminism
and literature—United States—History—20th century. 3. Women
and literature—United States—History—20th century.
4. Assertiveness (Psychology) in literature. 5. Afro-American
women in literature. 6. Women—United States—Folklore.
7. Afro-Americans in literature. 8. Afro-Americans—Folklore.
9. Women in literature.   I. Title. II. Series.
PS3515.U789Z8 1998
813'.52—dc21
                                                            97-38425

Printed on acid-free, 250-year-life paper
Manufactured in the United States of America

This book is dedicated to Boley, Charles Etta, Dexter, Maurice, Lucille, Johnetta, Betty, Charles, Ralph, John, Herbert, William C. Fischer, Lyle Glazier and Bruce Jackson.

And to Zora Neale Hurston wherever she may be lurking and sharpening her own oyster knife without fear and tears in the cosmos . . .

Contents

Acknowledgments

Grateful copyright acknowledgment is extended to the following sources: Harper Collins Publishers for permission to reprint excerpts as submitted from *Their Eyes Were Watching God* by Zora Neale Hurston. Copyright © 1937 by Harper & Row, Publishers, Inc. Renewed 1965 by John C. Hurston and Joel Hurston. Reprinted by permission of Harper Collins Publishers, Inc.; excerpts from various stories as taken from *The Complete Stories* by Zora Neale Hurston. Introduction copyright © 1995 by Henry Louis Gates, Jr. and Sieglinde Lemke. Compilation copyright © 1995 by Vivian Bowden, Lois J. Hurston Gaston, Clifford Hurston, Lucy Ann Hurston, Winifred Hurston Clark, Zora Mack Goins, Edgar Hurston, Sr., and Barbara Hurston Lewis. Afterword and Bibliography copyright © 1995 by Henry Louis Gates. "John Redding Goes to Sea" originally published in *Stylus*, May, 1921, and was reprinted in *Opportunity,* January, 1926. "Spunk" was originally published in *Opportunity*, August, 1926. "Sweat" was originally published in *Fire*, November, 1926. "The Gilded Six-Bits" was originally published in *Story,* August, 1933. "Uncle Monday" and "Motherine Catherine" were originally published in *Negro: An Anthology*, collected and edited by Nancy Cunard, published by Wishart in 1934. Copyright © 1934 by Zora Neale Hurston. "Story in Harlem Slang" was originally published in *The Southern Literary Messenger,* July, 1942. "The Conscience of the Court" was originally published in *The Saturday Evening Post*, March 18, 1950; *Color Struck: A Play* was originally published in *Fire!!*, 1 (November, 1926); excerpts from *Mules and Men* by Zora Neale Hurston, copyright © 1935 by Zora Neale Hurston. Copyright renewed 1963 by John C. Hurston and Joel Hurston. Reprinted by permission of Harper Collins Publishers, Inc.; excerpts as submitted from *Jonah's Gourd Vine* by Zora Neale Hurston. Copyright © 1934 by Zora Neale Hurston. Copyright renewed © 1962 by John C. Hurston. Reprinted by permission of Harper Collins Publishers, Inc.; excerpts from *Mule Bone* by Langston Hughes and Zora Neale Hurston. Copyrigt © 1931 by Langston Hughes and Zora

Neale Hurston. Copyright renewed 1991 by George Houston Bass and Henry Louis Gates Jr. Reprinted by permission of Harper Collins Publishers, Inc.; excerpts as submitted from *Dust Tracks on a Road* by Zora Neale Hurston. Copyright © 1942 by Zora Neale Hurston. Copyright renewed © 1970 by John C. Hurston. Reprinted by permission of Harper Collins Publishers, Inc.; excerpts from *Tell My Horse* by Zora Neale Hurston. Copyright © 1938 by Zora Neale Hurston. Copyright renewed © 1966 by Joel Hurston and John C. Hurston.; excerpts from *Moses, Man of the Mountain* by Zora Neale Hurston. Copyright © 1939 by Zora Neale Hurston. Copyright renewed © 1967 by John C. Hurston and Joel Hurston. *Polk County: A Comedy of Negro Life on a Sawmill Camp.* Play in three acts written with Dorothy Waring, 1944. Reprinted with the kind permission of the estate of Zora Neale Hurston. Excerpt from *The Color Purple*, copyright © 1980 by Alice Walker, reprinted by permission of Harcourt Brace & Company. Excerpt by Roger Abrahams reproduced by permission of the American Anthropological Association from *Journal of American Folklore* 88:347, January–March, 1975. Not for further reproduction. Excerpt from *Invisible Man* by Ralph Ellison. Copyright © 1952 by Ralph Ellison. Vintage Book, March, 1989 Edition by Random House, Inc. Excerpt from "Recent Books" by Ernest Kaiser in *Freedomways*, Second Quarter 1978 reprinted with the permission of Ester Jackson, Managing Editor, *Freedomways*. Reprinted by permission of the Modern Language Association an excerpt from "Are You a Flying Lark or a Setting Dove?" by Robert Hemenway in *Afro-American Literature: The Reconstruction of Instruction*, edited by Dexter Fisher and Robert Stepto, 1979. Excerpts from *Seraph on the Suwanee*, Scribner's 1948. Reprinted with the kind permission of the estate of Zora Neale Hurston.

Special thanks are extended to Rider University for its generous support of my research and scholarship projects with a sabbatical and summer research fellowships.

Gracious appreciation with bountiful gratitude is echoed to Kristi Long, Rebecca Wipfler, Alan Brown, and Graham Hodges.

Introduction

As individual, writer, and socio-political spokeswoman, Zora Neale Hurston was one of the most assertive voices of her time. In personal demeanor as well as in professional and artistic deportment, she was a loud voice to be heard and reckoned with by her intellectual peers and by other social acquaintances. Her creative talent, or natural skill at talking, at articulating her views in a confident and bold voice, was the key element in her early rise as a successful anthropologist and literary artist. On the verbal turf, she was free-spirited and existed with the contention that she had the law of authority in her mouth as she aspired to jump at the sun in the fulfillment of her ambition and natural drive to succeed and to make something of herself. She had no reservations about either expressing her naturally Southern and folk-spirited self, or of articulating her unorthodox views on such touchy subjects as race, integration, the separate-but-equal doctrine of Jim Crowism, marriage and careless love, historical Black colleges, politics and voting rights, no matter how controversial or absurd they may have sounded to her staunchest critics.

If anything, Hurston was a mischievous verbal imp who gloathed mirthfully at the fury she generated amongst her critics and colleagues of the Harlem Renaissance and Depression Era. At the same time, however, she was amply prepared to put on a serious and mean face and stand her ground in verbal defense as critics stabbed at her personal integrity and professional reputation as a Black artist. In such an orbiting and self-made existence of talking and fighting to find her way in the world, she indeed loved herself when she was laughing and then again when she looked mean and impressive. Surely she was an intellectual rebel and woman of verbal spunk as she expounded her unorthodox ideas.

In the vernacular of Southern Black folk speech, Hurston's motto of existence in the artistic and intellectual world of the often revered urban North—New York, the Promised Land—seemed to rest in the old-time Negro proverb, "Don' say no mo' wid yo' mouf dan yo' back kin stan." A bold fighter and defender of her identity and philosophical viewpoints, Hurston was not only ready and eager to speak her mind, but she was also prepared to physically battle, to fight blow for blow, and stand her ground on a contentious point. Talking, and, if need be, fighting, became essential forms of self-defensive weaponry paramount in her personal survival plan as a woman and as a professional creative writer and anthropologist. As her career progressed, Hurston became very competitive and combative in her ambitious drive to reap fame and national recognition as a talented and serious-minded artist. She wisely used aggressive Black speech styles of expression, such as the dozens, bulldozia (intimidation), and signifying as part of her verbal arsenal of defensive strategy to confront her intellectual battles, in print or in conversation, as when she ridiculed Alaine Locke for his negative critique of her most famous novel, *Their Eyes Were Watching God* (1937). Her words were so inflammatory and damaging to her adversary in battle that they might, to illustrate a measure of their effect, be equated with the stinging knockout blow that one of her punches might have landed on Locke's face. For Hurston, then, talking and fighting—in whatever form she employed these survival forms to illustrate her aggressive or combative style with a foe—were dual entities in her style of existence.

Hurston's survival strategies were dually influenced by her presence in a Southern community that relied on the Black oral tradition as its prime way of existence and by her presence, upon the death of her mother at age eight, in predominantly white communities which taught her the value of the written word as a vehicle for survival and advancement. Hurston, the unusual woman that she became, bridged these teachings about the Black oral vernacular and the standard American English lexicon into her combative stance as assertive and aggressive individual. In conversation (including professional debates) and in print, Hurston demonstrated how crucial the oral vernacular of the American South, individualistic spunk, and the traditional or more formal Standard English of the urban North were unique components in her survival plan. On language communication alone, she easily existed in both the white and Black worlds of the South and North without difficulty. In other words, Hurston possessed an indelible assertive personality and a mastery of essential communicative skills that enabled her to exist in either environment without fear of danger or harm.

Hurston's assertive individualism was initially instilled in her during her upbringing in the all-Black community of Eatonville, Florida, where individual character is largely demonstrated through speech interaction and skillful manipulation of various verbal forms of expression for pleasure or for serious combat. Frontier-spirited in nature, (very much reminiscent of Mark Twain's Hannibal and

Dawson's Landing, small and close-knit communities on the Mississippi River), the town stressed the importance of individuality and the defense of one's self identity and respect through the medium of folk speech in all of its varied manifestations. This philosophy of self-defense through verbal power was therefore ingrained in Hurston from several prominent Eatonville sources. For example, on the home front she was encouraged to assert herself by a strong and verbally efficient mother and other female relatives, the most memorable of which was Aunt Caroline. Her father's public oratory as preacher at Macedonia Baptist Church and as mayor of Eatonville, as well as his defeat in verbal squabbles in the Hurston family home with the fiery-tongued Mrs. Lucy Hurston, gave Hurston the impetus to assert herself, to speak her mind in all endeavors, be they of a playful or serious nature. Surprisingly, a friendly white man also inspired her to speak her mind as an individual and not as a Black person conditioned by the indignities of Jim Crow restraints. On the social and cultural front in the Eatonville community at large, the townsfolk and their verbal comradeship in storytelling and lying contests, performed almost exclusively by men congregated on Joe Clarke's storeporch, the heartbeat of the town, also affected her verbal creative fancy and genuine love of the folktale and Black storytelling. In due time, she became a gifted storyteller and imaginative creative voice like her oral mentors— the storeporch talkers or big liars. From these talkers, she learned that language is empowerment and this philosophical wisdom becomes a pervasive theme in her life and in her art. To a large degree, it may be argued that Hurston's lively and amusing folksy personality, and her early professional years as talented short story writer and folklorist, were largely influenced by the big talkers or liars of her native Eatonville. Beyond doubt, the words of the Eatonville folk marked the early beginnings of Hurston, the assertive woman of words.

In post-Eatonville years which she describes in her autobiography, *Dust Tracks on a Road* (194) under the chapter heading, "Jacksonville and After," there were other oral influences shaping Hurston's assertive individualism. During her years spent in Jacksonville and after, Hurston was exposed to several benevolent white people who nurtured her assertive voice and instructed her to speak and to be her natural self, as opposed to her adhering to the ethics of living Jim Crow in a manner which fostered fear, hate and racial protest in a fellow Southerner like Richard Wright. Around white people, she was, therefore, her natural folksy self when she spoke and dramatized her blackness and Southern down-home roots. She did not speak with a Black voice knowledgeable of racial politics, but rather she spoke as an individual attuned to the problems and experiences that all people undergo in the life experience.

Her novels, folklore, and socio-political essays in later years would be created on this same premise.

Additionally, Hurston's exposure to the numerous styles of Black expressive speech designed either for amusement or for serious verbal conflict and self-defense, in such diverse Black cultures as Polk County, New Orleans, Harlem, Jamaica, and Haiti, left an imprint on her assertive individualism. Out of these experiences, which she witnessed first hand as objective scientist and participant, Hurston's assertive voice on the intellectual front further took shape. The variety of speech styles of which she availed herself, especially in the cabarets and on the streets of Harlem, and in the jook joints of Polk County, would form the basis and stylistic format for many of her controversial socio-political essays where her verbal demeanor, as narrator of persuasion, enabled her to discuss, with facility and tact, volatile issues which Black peers and outspoken race leaders such as Roy Wilkins, A. Philip Randolph, and Walter White, avoided. What other contemporary of her time had the finesse and verbal skill to speak to both Black and white audiences about such inflammatory issues as the pet Negro system, vote peddling, integration, and Communism without being physically harmed?

Oddly enough, Hurston's folksy humor and shrewd oratorical skill made her survival possible in a volcanic climate of verbal road mines. Orally, her assertive individualism gave her what it took to make it, it appeared, in both worlds. It is, therefore, from the perspective of a viable and confident individual voice that happened to be Black, in texture and style, that she spoke, wrote, and developed her analytical views, many of which seemed, to many Blacks, to be anti-Black.

An examination of Hurston's professional emergence reveals that her assertive individualism, as early as the late 1920s when she first entered Harlem with a show of her Southern folk character and downhome metaphorical speech mannerisms, caused her hardship and led to great controversy about her racial allegiance and sincerity as legitimate Black artist. As she confronted the racial politics infringing on her professional and personal lives in the widely publicized sex scandal of 1948, Hurston's voice grew silent, and, in uncharacteristic Hurston behavior, lost its verbal spunk and vitality. After 1948, Hurston no longer exemplified an assertive spirit and combative style in the defense of her stance on controversial topics. At best, a startling portrait of Hurston emerges as a result of her being emotionally battered and spiritually bruised by the New York media, African American community leaders, and residents of the Harlem tenement building where she resided when the alleged sex scandal took place. In the eye of the storm, Hurston retreated back to her native South, succumbing to relative obscurity and wretched poverty. At this point of submission to defeat at the hands of the media and legal system, she no longer appeared, even in her old age, to represent the assertive Black woman she aspired to be. There was no impetus to address herself to the evil forces of racism and sexism as they caught an unrelenting foothold on her personal integrity and professional reputation. As Robert Hemenway states in *Zora Neale Hurston, A Literary Biography* (1977), Hurston felt that her professional nemeses were out to BLOCK THAT ZORA NEALE HURSTON, whatever the cost.

Hurston's assertive individualism, it may be said, caused her to travel on a rocky, tumultuous road of human existence—a road which eventually enables the modern Hurston scholar to peer cautiously at her life and to ponder the pros and cons of the question as to whether or not a Black woman should rely on a Black consciousness survival plan, or a rigid assertive individualistic posture as the ticket to survival and success in the American mainstream. Hurston's life suggests the latter, even though she failed to employ it during the most crucial personal crisis in her life. Had she employed her assertive and combative voice in the 1948 sodomy charge made against her, she might have won and, thus, re-established her professional career. Unfortunaely, Hurston reached a verbal lull in a verbal wasteland and retreated South in most uncharacteristic fashion. All of her assertive individualistic training, and her competitive spirit were thrown out "the back door" without a sigh, somewhat like the useless and dirtied wash water of her assertive and fictional heroines, the likes of Grandma Potts and Delia Jones. Hurston had a pure and innocent voice as she matured and prospered as anationally known writer; somehow in the whirlwind of her stance as an assertive and combative Black woman, she lost her voice and never totally regained it. Hence, as contemporary scholars Mary Helen Washington and Alice Walker suggest, Hurston was indeed a woman half in shadow. Her assertive personality and art are so complex that they warrant future critical study that would explore the mystique of Hurston, the assertive woman. One initial gateway to an understanding of Hurston, the mouthy Southern Black woman and writer, is her unforgettable assertive female characters who have the tendency to speak no more with their mouths than their backs can stand. None of these women of word might succumb to verbal defeat in the talking game.

This book examines Hurston's style of assertive individualism as it may be applied to her female characters in selected works from the fiction, folklore, and drama. My contention is that even though Hurston personally failed to demonstrate the total validity and practicality of the assertive individualistic approach in her own professional life as a Black woman, especially after the 1948 sodomy charge which caused her to retreat into obscurity in the South and to grow silent as poverty and ill-health overwhelmed her once-spirited nature, she artistically succeeded in revealing the usefulness of it in her depiction of assertive female characters she admired. The positive fruition of this phenomenon of the assertive Black woman is, therefore, evident in the non-professional Southern Black folk woman confined most predominantly to the rural communities of Florida. These women are viewed through the medium of folk speech—or oral discourse, the tangible symbols of their empowerment—as they talk and negotiate for respect in a traditionally male-dominated verbal culture where Black men act, in the talk arena, as verbal power lords (or gods as Jody proclaims in *Their Eyes Were Watching God* with the affirmation, "Ah god").

In the fiction, folklore, and drama, Hurston's emphasis is not simply on the diverse images of the varied Black women who populate her artistic landscape, but rather her stress is on their metaphorical folk speech patterns and verbal behavior used in social and communal rituals of church and storeporch, or in intrafamilial feuds with men in the privacy of the home, or on very rare occasion (as is the case with Big Sweet, Janie, Lucy, and Laura Lee) in interracial encounters with whites who normally are situated at the periphery of her art so that Blacks have the freedom to interact amongst themselves without the gaze of the oppressor. How women project themselves orally—by demonstrating the essence of their personality, and moral, spiritual and religious value system with the posture of bold talkers and skillful fighters and not necessarily how well they look in the beauty contest category—is the important point here. Women in individual conflict, generated and then resolved through the medium of dialogue initiated in a verbal bout with a spouse or external foe, where they become the verbal victors, are the yardsticks or reflective mirrors for evaluating character and human worth in Hurston's art. It is largely how women speak, and not how they look, which strikes Hurston's literary fancy. Strong female characters in her art are notably assertive and individualistic. Empowerment is manifested largely in their strong, assertive voices which often resound in *Mules and Men*, for example, with the declaration: "Ah got de law in my mouth."

Throughout Hurston's works, there is a recurring pattern of development in her portrayal of the assertive woman. Hurston habitually uses male-female relationships in a courtship or a marriage situation to stress the importance of spoken language or folk speech in conveying one's sense of worth and self-resepect. For Hurston, dialogue is the vehicle for depicting individual character development. The drama of an oral confrontation or argument between a man and a woman—that sometimes erupts in physical violence with the woman holding her own—is a salient element in Hurston's art, as is the talk motif which is a characteristic trademark of her short stories, novels, folklore, drama and socio-political essays. The judgmental eyes and voices of the townsfolk, who function as watchers, listeners and gatekeepers in the dramatic world of the folk, are also vital ingredients in Hurston's recreation of the world of the Black oral tradition and the assertive woman's place in it.

Hurston utilizes the vehicles of women and words to imply much about her concepts of Black manhood in folk cultures which have traditionally been misrepresented in the works of other Southern literary giants such as Ernest J. Gaines, Richard Wright, Sterling Brown, Mark Twain, William Faulkner, J. Mason Brewer, Julia Peterkin, and Joel Chandler Harris, to name a few. In light of Hurston's innovative work in a renewed depiction of Black manhood through the eyes and voices of Black women, it will therefore be the overall intent of this book to emphasize the importance of oral discourse in reflecting character and social values in Hurston's fiction, folklore, and drama. How Black women manipulate speech in a variety of talking styles so that they serve as functional expressions of self-identity will be of paramount concern. Such female figures as Big Sweet, Laura Lee, Leafy, Janie, Delia, Pinkie, Missie, Lucy and Amy are embodiments of the ideal representation of the assertive Black female voice Hurston wanted to emphasize in folk literature. Assertive folk women succeed in home and in community as a result of their wise utilization of their creative oral talent. Our last image of them as they are observed functioning in their verbal environments is a triumphant one where they are accorded respect for their speaking skill. This is very much unlike the failed image we are left with when observing Hurston's true-to-life exploits with her assertive talent, a talent which she personally preferred not to draw upon during the critical period of her personal life in 1948. Thereafter, during the fifties and until her death in 1960, she became a recluse and a non-assertive voice who left behind a marred and shattered image of the orally gifted Southern Black woman. In large part, then, it is to the images of the noble verbal warriors she recorded for posterity in her art that we must turn to observe the positive ramifications of the phenomenon of assertive individualism, particularly as it applies to Black women.

It is hoped that this critical analysis of women in her art who fully represent the ideal standards of assertive individualism will stimulate more scholarly interest in her life and work in Black folk culture. A major influence on her life and philosophical views which many scholars have overlooked in their condemnation of her assertive individualism in public life is that of the Black oral tradition and its impact in shaping her character. It is the factor which caused her to speak out in a bold manner on a range of controversial topics. Many scholars, especially those in the anti-Hurston camp, should note that in the artistic field Hurston was not alone; some of the Black race's other

strong female leaders of diverse professions and backgrounds, such as
Ida B. Wells, Harriet Tubman, Sojourner Truth, Fannie Lou Hamer,
Barbara Jordan, Patricia R. Harris, and Rosa Parks, the mother of the
Civil Rights movement, spoke with loud, assertive voices that were
indeed influenced by the Black oral tradition and its stress on assertive
individualism and human dignity, factors that were not limited by
Southern Jim Crowism. Is it not logical for a Black professional
woman to utilize her own creative talent in the talking arena and say
what she feels? It seems Hurston was penalized for her talking talent
and combative and aggressive stance. Ironically, she spoke with a
thunderous and insightful voice for all Blacks and whites to hear, but
her message was totally ignored or shunned by even popular leaders
such as Roy Wilkins, W.E.B. DuBois and Walter White. No one took
her unorthodox views seriously even though they were prophetic and
offer "food for thought" in modern Black America of the nineties. She
has remained, up until the revival of interest in her during the seventies,
one of the least well known and studied artists of her generation. And,
the lack of serious interest in her from some contemporary critics may
also be due to the still prevalent antagonism generated by her
conservative political stance on race matters. Such sentiment has been
most detrimental to her overall professional image and it may have also
swayed many scholars away from serious study of any of her works. A
clear, poignant example of such resistance, mainly to her socio-political
views, is evident in the commentary about her by the late Ernest
Kaiser, who served as associate editor of *Freedomways* magazine and
staff member of the Schomburg Center for Research in Black Culture.

In his critical review of Hemenway's widely acclaimed literary
biography of Hurston, Kaiser is adamant in his antagonism toward
Hurston and virulently denies that her socio-political ideas have positive
nationalistic implications for Black Americans. Rather, her politics, he
adamantly maintains, were basically harmful. Consider his following
unfavorable picture of her:

> Hemenway calls Hurston a Republican conservative and an
> early black nationalist. She wrote some of the most vicious,
> anti-Black political articles for the *American Legion Magazine,
> American Mercury* and other publications during the 1930s and
> 1940s. She was anti-New Deal and against helping black
> people mired in poverty. I don't see how people with any
> social consciousness can admire Hurston. She did black people
> a lot of harm. Where was her humanity? Oppression had done
> Blacks no harm and those who protested were sob-sisters, she
> seemed to say. Then her fiction and other writings set forth a
> lot of stereotyped black characters.[1]

Contrary to Kaiser's negative assessment of Hurston, I feel she represents something positive—her assertive individualism to confidently articulate her ideas however discordant they sounded to the Black race leaders and intellectuals—that the unbiased and open-minded Black scholar can admire. In light of this perspective, I believe that now is the time for Hurston and her socio-political views to be heard and studied, not only for their political merit, but also as evidence of the positive illustration of the workings of her assertive individualistic posture as opposed to the Black consciousness stance of race protest and social politics which she abhorred. Now is the time for her to be judged and studied from within the bounds of her assertive individualistic philosophy, the main principle by which she existed as both woman and creative artist. Was she verbally true to herself when she left all-Black oral communities and ventured, rather carefreely, into predominantly white cultures where she endured, up until 1948, almost insurmountable tests of her life's motto: "Dont say no more with your mouth than your back can stand"? It is the folk women in her art who articulate in their simple, down-home vernacular the characteristics of assertive individualism which Hurston valued and practiced to the fullest extent during the most productive and controversial years of her career.

The Assertive Woman in Zora Neale Hurston's Fiction, Folklore, and Drama

. . . . how women assert their image and values as women is seldom found in folklore literature. We know even less about the verbal traditions of black women in particular.

Roger Abrahams, "Negotiating Respect: Patterns of Presentation among Black Women," *Journal of American Folklore*, 88 (1975), 58.

The Black woman affirms herself in Hurston's fiction because she has the courage and the verbal techniques to establish herself in something other than a dependent relationship with a man. It is one reason both *Jonah's Gourd Vine* and *Their Eyes Were Watching God* present such strong women; the biographical facts of Hurston's life confirm that this verbal skill was one of the dominant characteristics of her own personality.

Robert Hemenway, "Are You a Flying Lark or a Setting Dove?" in *Afro-American Literature: The Reconstruction of Instruction*, edited by Dexter Fisher and Robert B. Stepto (New York: The Modern Language Association of America, 1979), 145.

Chapter 1

"Ah got de law in mah mouf": Negotiating Respect in the Hurston Mold

The assertive woman stands out as a main characteristic figure in Hurston's fiction, folklore and drama. This woman's omnipotent presence is felt largely because of the profound sense of individualism she conveys in crucial scenes of dramatic verbal confrontation. The talking skill the assertive woman exhibits in verbal interchange casts an indelible sound on the reader's ear. There are, echoed in her folk speech, rumblings of rebellion and independence as she addresses herself to the verbal inequalities sounded out by her male adversary. An able and pugnacious verbal warrior in the face of oppression, she is not to be intimidated into silence. Her voice asserts itself most predominantly in the pages of Hurston's art, echoing the positive and admirable virtues of Black womanhood in folk culture. Through her oral disposition in common, everyday speech relations, we see mirrored the individualistic qualities and human virtues which place her at the center of Hurston's folk milieu.

This woman of words is indeed nourished by her verbal durability and vitality. Her very social existence and individuality are influenced in large part by the value system inherent in the Black oral tradition. To be human, to be a person of courage and substance, is to talk effectively, to orally project a positive sense of self and well-being. Effective talking is valued by her as essential to social cohesiveness and personal survival. Squaring off against an adversary is an acceptable manner of affirming her self-identity, of negotiating respect for herself as woman and person. Talking, the utilization of folk speech in verbal performance in the home or community, is self-revealing for her.

Talking, furthermore, is also a drama in itself, the external expression of the internal elements of which she is made.

The assertive woman's personality—in fact, her entire being—is articulated through Black folk speech rendered in a variety of speech styles. In a serious verbal feud, she may draw upon specifying, signifying, playing the dozens, loud talking or shaming to convey a point. In less serious situations, such as the verbal rituals of courtship or play acting, she may employ the exaggeration of lying or woofing to outwit a competitor and generate laughter and respect from a crowd of onlookers. These two types of talk situations reveal that she is also gifted at adorning her verbal style with non-verbal body language or mannerisms in order to convey a more effective message. Her physical gestures evoke drama and expression, accentuating her verbal power. For example, when talking, she might use such non-verbal techniques as eyeballing, hand gesturing, hip swaying, adopting a particular body stance or walking style to drive home her verbal point. The best illustration of this technique occurs in the autobiography, where Hurston refers to it as "putting your foot upon a person's doorstep."[1] In this instance, she is stressing the point that speech and body pose work in unison so as to communicate Big Sweet's ideas.

Looks or physical beauty are secondary elements in the self-identification process, for the assertive woman carves out what is essentially a verbal identity, established primarily through the drama of speech interaction. Her first priority and standard of judgment is word power, a kind of word beauty exemplified in the oral tradition. As she strives for verbal satisfaction, she is hardly concerned about beauty as understood in the Anglo-Saxon context. Words shine and radiate her inner personal beauty. Through the talk experience, she articulates her individualistic virtues of honesty, loyalty, faithfulness, kindness, perserverance, spunk and stoicism, in conjunction with the sorrows and troubles of her intra-familial or intra-racial social existence. She desires full and equal participation in the often male-dominated speaking arenas of storytelling, woofing and lying. She, too, is capable of creating on-the-spot "crayon enlargements of life" in the jook or on the storeporch. In serious confrontations, the capacity to talk effectively enables her to challenge a foe (usually a man) on his own turf and in his own terms. Aggression and rivalry can be channelled into a verbal tug of war rather than into a physical battle of the sexes where she by nature is the weaker of the two. (Of course, it must be interjected here that Big

Sweet and Laura Lee Kimble, strong fighting women, are exceptions to this limitation.)

As her experience unfolds, the assertive woman becomes independent in being able to draw upon whatever verbal assets she requires to achieve self-affirmation. The reader of Hurston's fiction observes the Black woman undergoing a verbal metamorphosis, a kind of self-rejuvenation, as she attains a greater level of maturity and understanding. Verbally, she matures while sorting out the entanglements and complexities of her life. Such experiences, and the consequent stages of change she personally undergoes on her journey of life, are all recorded in her folk speech. What becomes available to the reader is a verbal portrait of her that captures her assertive disposition in its varied forms and moods. As her relationship with a verbal foe or amiable talking friend changes, so does the nature of her speech. She may have to utilize the inflammatory language of the dozens in an oppressive and violent environment, or she may talk in rhyme and rhythm in order to realize a totally cohesive verbal union of equality, love, and cooperation.

Think, for example, of Lucy Pearson's verbal metamorphosis from innocent girl-bride to mature, devoted mother and then embittered wife. Initially she is John's equal verbal partner in realistic and playful courtship talk. She guides him with words of love and encouragement as he prospers in the community. But by the end of the fifteen-year marriage, she toils miserably, especially during abandonment in childbirth, as a result of John's infidelity. Her dissatisfaction with him becomes most apparent during the decaying stages of the marriage in her altered verbal rapport with him. As she forcefully reprimands him for his sins, she becomes more than his verbal equal. He might excel with the word in the pulpit, but not in verbal discourse on the home front with Lucy. In the crucial conversational scenes of Chapter Sixteen of *Jonah's Gourd Vine,* there is an obvious verbal rebirth in Lucy. She is now a fluent and scornful critic, asserting herself with a ferocity which John cannot equal. Her tongue-lashing is so severe that he is eventually reduced to beating her in an attempt to silence her and to soothe his own guilt. He prays that she and her accusing tongue and sharp eye will quickly die. But, to his humiliation, Lucy remains assertive even as death approaches and the marriage disintegrates beyond repair. Death, not John's physical intimidation of his frail wife, is the superior force which finally silences Lucy's bold voice of moral and religious truth.

The reader might also think here of another assertive woman, Janie from *Their Eyes Were Watching God,* whose personality and verbal metamorphosis unfold differently than Lucy's.[2] Janie Killicks Starks Woods, after two failed marriages, finally grows to experience meaningful love with Tea Cake. Her efforts to find love, to talk of love in the sweet springtime images of budding trees and plants, and to secure the husband most symbolic of fulfilling her love dreams, are all recorded by the talk she engages in with a marriage partner. She is surely a woman of change in the talk experience. Her growth from ignorance and innocence to philosophical enlightenment and personal contentment after overcoming a catastrophe is apparent even in widowhood—the stage of life experience she is in when we initially observe her in the novel.

The talk experience is a cleansing process, a verbal ritual of "self revelation" (*TEWWG,* 10) for Janie as she orally re-creates and analyzes her experiences for Phoeby in a storytelling narrative. At its end, she and Phoeby both gain understanding about her past and a sense of optimism about her future as a contented widow. She can proudly assert without hesitation, "Ah done been tuh de horizon and back and now Ah kin set heah in mah house and live by comparisons. Dis house ain't so absent of things lak it used tuh be befor' Tea Cake come along. It's full uh thoughts, 'specially dat bedroom" (*TEWWG,* 158).

The talking process not only illustrates Janie's verbal and spiritual growth through marriage and subsequent widowhood, but it also serves another thematic purpose for Hurston as she moves away from an emphasis on the marriage relationship in the novel. Indeed, Hurston's portrayal of the assertive woman's speech experience shows that she is interested in the sisterhood that develops between trusted female friends. Janie calls this type of verbal union between women a "kissin'-friends" (*TEWWG,* 11) experience in which the assertive woman confides in her confidant with the belief that "mah tongue is in mah friend's mouf" (*TEWWG,* 9). Mutual trust, loyalty and understanding have closely bonded Phoeby and Janie for twenty years, and Janie has no qualms about engaging in real and purposeful talk with Phoeby. This is an attachment that is far removed from the vindictive gossip that greets her on return to Eatonville after the death of young Tea Cake, fifteen years her junior. The tongues of other less intimate female friends are cocked and loaded like killing tools for slaughter when she remains publicly silent about her marriage to Tea Cake. Of these women's assertive but evil voice, Hurston writes: "A tongue cocked and loaded is the only real weapon left to weak folks" (*TEWWG,* 10). Janie (and even Hurston herself in real-life verbal relationships) finds such gossiping, false friends to be despicable, just as she does another type of female adversary who stands in opposition to her not so much because of their lack of verbal self disclosure, but because of the hate and animosity generated from a rivalry for the affection of a man. Like Hurston's female ancestors who boldly announced ownership claim of their men, Janie stands by her man and battles the other woman, Nunkie, *(TEWWG,* 113–114), who aims to steal her husband.

For Hurston, then, verbal skill, whether in serious conflict or in play acting, is a main determining factor in the character development of her heroine. Her female character is to be evaluated by how well (or in some cases, as with Arvay, how ineffectively) she asserts herself, and by how proficiently she uses word power in a given situation. The reader must ask about Hurston's assertive woman: Can she talk effectively or does she appear to be a mealy-mouth rag doll? What are the detailed and intricate workings of her verbal portrait in encounters with a man, a trusted confidant or a fierce rival? What points are on her score card for using the dozens or other highly skilled verbal techniques to combat male verbal supremacy? How crafty is she when a man engages her in the old Negro courtship ritual with the leading phrase, "Are You a Flying Lark or Setting Dove?" Words, when utilized shrewdly and judiciously, are one of the basic survival tools a woman requires to be individual and personal, especially amongst her own Black folk. Words are a mirror of her true self, symbols of truth and wisdom, which constitute a functional language of reality as opposed to the unreal, playful talk of men on the storeporch.

The assertive woman is not a maudlin, sentimental person. She doesn't cry, rather she shouts out words of wisdom and morality. She is an indivdual to be respected because she is a bearer of the truth, a talker who rightfully can claim, as Big Sweet does, "Ah got de law in mah mouf."[3] Above all, she is at the center of talk, meriting attention because she is a perceptive voice of reality and authority. Her verbal proclamations ring in the ears of her spouse with accuracy and sensitivity. In verbal squabbles, that perceptive voice methodically strips away a man's composure with direct and purposeful talk, far removed from the realm of exaggerated speech he feels most secure with on the storeporch or in the pulpit. Indeed, she tends to exhibit truth and power to a point where she becomes the rightful possessor of all the keys to the kingdom of Black domestic life (*M&M,* 52–54). As the stomp knocker's sermon suggests (*M&M*, 178–192), all is well in the family structure when she is recognized in an equal partnership with her man—like Missie May and Joe or Janie and Tea Cake. Her verbal keys to the bedroom, kitchen and cradle unlock doors of verbal cohesiveness and union. Her pointed fluency allows her to reign at a level of respect to be reckoned with by all Black men, as even John Pearson (a gifted preacher with the straining voice) acknowledges: "Jes' 'cause women folks ain't got no big muscled arm and fists lak jugs, folks claim they's weak vessels, but dass uh lie. Dat piece of red flannel she got hung between her joints is equal tuh all de fists God ever made and man ever seen. Jus' take and ruin a man wid dey tongue, and den they kin hold it still and bruise 'im up jus' ez bad."[4]

Additionally, the storeporch talkers also attest to the woman's verbal prowess: "Don't you know you can't git the best of no women in the talkin' game? Her tongue is all de weapon a woman got" (*M&M*, 88). Such is the case of the Black woman throughout Hurston's art which Henry L. Gates describes as being the speakerly text. The woman's tongue is part of the weaponry of survival she needs in home and community. Through various speech styles, she builds her image and credibility and gains respect from her judgmental audience. This is clearly the case for Janie, Lucy, and Big Sweet, women who earn respect from the community primarily on the basis of their verbal projection of self and moral value system. Unlike their male counterparts, who employ talk most frequently for pleasure and to avoid dealing with serious personal predicaments in marriage and home life, these women consider talk an essential aspect of their total sense of being. It is not only the foundation of their personal appearance, but it is also a free-flowing base from which they confront the real experience of existence which they call life.

Because the assertive woman might ignite hostility and precipitate physical violence through her aggressive verbal stance, when the need arises, she will require an additional survival tool. A bold demeanor is needed to work as a conjunctive agent to her talking prowess. As the old folk saying goes, she must be mindful not to get biggity with nobody and say more than her back can stand. When she talks, she must be prepared for imminent danger and she must not be inhibited by the fear of physical violence, as is the case with the assertive Amy who is not intimidated by Ned's awesome bullwhip once she is inclined to speak the truth about his business dealings with Beasley (*J'sGV*, 17–22). Amy is courageous and spunky, a "fighting dog," and she is ably prepared to face the consequences of her words in the face of impending male opposition. For her, then, talking and fighting, or verbal and physical violence, may sometimes function as twin necessities in her survival plan, even on the home front. Other examples of women who possess these twin qualities are Big Sweet (considered by her associates at Polk County work camps to be two women and half a man) and Laura Lee Kimble (called a man-killing bear cut of a woman). Each of these women holds her own verbally in conversation and in physical combat as her probing words evoke opposition or direct violence from her rival. The nobility and magnitude of each woman's talking and fighting ability are measured by the community in words of admiration and praise.

As words move from the realm of pleasure and entertainment to a level of serious conflict, they may become so inflammatory that the assertive woman must avail herself of direct physical action with her fists or weapons of cold steel (i.e., knives or guns). There is an intricate relationship in rugged, individualistic cultures like Polk County and Eatonville between talking and fighting, or the word and the act. Here the individual has the mind to solve his or her own problems without resorting to the law or police, and does not show any restraint about settling a verbal war of words on the spot with fist or weapon. Clearly, then, talking and fighting become a part of the code of ethics and, in such a milieu, the assertive woman is obligated to secure a place for herself. She will not be a silent victim of wife-battering and verbal abuse. In the context of this survival strategy, she is aware that she must be an effective talker and a skilled fighter prone to direct action if necessary. A discriminating display of such combined expertise does not show her to be a super woman or bully, exploiting and trampling on an underdog. Rather, it proves her to be a woman with the courage to speak her mind and demonstrate her Christian virtues without deliberately precipitating unnecessary violence just for the sake of exercising it.

But, like the instant flip of a coin, she also recognizes that violence—especially when it occurs in a frontier-spirited lawless culture like Polk County where minds are quick to anger as they are to sunshine—cannot always be avoided. Violence sometimes drives home a point, as Big Sweet intends it to do when she metes out her own brand of justice. Even in an unhappy marriage, such as that of Ned and Amy or the one of Delia and Sykes, the assertive woman is bound to generate violence when a husband finds that he is verbally out-witted and shamed by her quick and wise tongue. His only source of power for combating her truthful and emphatic talk is retaliation by physical abuse. But she in turn stands her ground by nobly fighting back with her gun, fists or skillet, even if a man is victorious in beating her unmercifully as the cowardly Ned does when he initially attacks Amy on his tip toe with a cowhide whip normally used for thrashing his horse or beast of burden. Even though physically defeated at times, the assertive woman of small, physical stature, in contrast to the robust Big Sweet or Laura Lee, remains resilient and steadfastly prepared, with courage and fortitude, for her next battle. Big Sweet's talking and fighting skills serve as an illustration of the more successful union of the assertive woman's verbal and physical stamina. She is a very efficient talking and fighting warrior in the lawless Polk County where carrying a gun or switchblade is a natural part of daily existence. Big Sweet has no misgivings about asserting herself and then backing up her words of intimidation, if need be, with physical might and with weapons of cold steel. Maiming or killing an opponent is no unusual happening once verbal fireworks have been launched. She feels as free and confident in this aspect of her survival struggle as she does in the pleasant experiences of the jook. Talking and fighting are natural attributes of her will to survive and be her sweet and strong self.

In the autobiography, Hurston reveals the juxtaposition of talking and fighting in the life of Big Sweet. At first, Big Sweet is depicted confidently playing the dozens with a verbal opponent in public because she knows the range of both her talking and fighting competencies. She articulates, what is locally called in Polk County lexicon, a "reading" (a word borrowed from the fortune tellers, *DTOR*, 186), outlining in lurid detail a character sketch of her foe, "bringing him up to date on his ancestry, his looks, smell, gait, clothes and his route through Hell in the hereafter. Big Sweet broke the news to him, in one of her mildest bulletins that his pa was a double-humpted camel and his ma was a grass-gut cow, but even so, he tore her wide open in the act of getting born, and so on and so forth. He was a bitch's baby out of a buzzard egg" (*DTOR*, 186–187). When her rival does not take up the challenge implied in the insults, Big Sweet further baits him by engaging in what is termed "putting her foot upon her opponent's doorstep," sounding him out and low-rating him and his family as she physically positions herself on the doorstep of his home, his castle, the private domain where he is supposed to be a superior figure of authority to outsiders. As she usurps his private territory, she is amply prepared to back up her insults of the dozens verbal ritual with a fist fight or with weapons. Self-confidence is the driving force behind such a daring and brazen act, as Hurston elaborates in the following cautionary words about the dual process of playing the dozens and "putting your foot on your enemy's doorstep": "If you are sufficiently armed and know what to do with your weapons after you git 'em, it is all right to go to the house of your enemy, put one foot upon his steps, rest one elbow on your knee and play in the family. That is another way of saying play the dozens, which also is a way of saying low-rate your enemy's ancestors and him, down to the present moment for reference, and then go into his future as far as your imagination leads you. But if you have no faith in your personal courage and confidence in your arsenal, don't try it. It's a risky pleasure" (*DTOR*, 187).

Hurston's presentation of the assertive woman poses numerous questions for the reader. How is the assertive woman's dual skill of talking and fighting demonstrated in Hurston's art? In what type of dramatic scene does Hurston place the assertive woman in order to illustrate the conjunctive workings of her verbal and physical might? What initiates the need for a woman to draw upon words and weapons to demonstrate her self-worth? Is she to convey her positive sense of self primarily in repeated verbal squabbles within her marriage? Why does she have to square off with an opponent, often fiercely with a man, just to exist, simply to exercise her right to talk, to affirm herself and her moral values, to gain respect as a person? How can an equally gifted assertive woman stand alongside her man in home and community without arousing hostility or competition? With such talent, how is she perceived by him: as a threat or as an equal participant in all forms of the talk ritual in home and community?

The road to total verbal freedom and equality for the assertive woman is not an easy route to travel, even in a predominantly Black oral community. It is one of conflict and defiance in a majority of experiences. Her chief rival in dialogue is the Black man who vies for authority through verbal control, thus levelling his own brand of verbal oppression on her, just as the dominant race aimed to do. (But, by historical accounts, she defied both when she was told to hush.) Her voice, by his plan, is to be silenced, thus making her the non-verbal mule of the world. He regards himself as the Supreme Big Voice, Big Talker, and Word Bearer in both public talk rituals, and in private domestic squabbles; he attempts to reduce his female counterpart to the status of silence. Talking puts him at the center of the action, at the core of community praise and commendation, and he will get to the extreme of "boxing her jaws" (*TEWWG*, 98) if she verbally defies or dethrones him in the talking game. The truth is not what he desires to hear, even if it is articulated by a perceptive voice. For the protection of his own status and big image, she is to be seen and not heard—as we see expressed in the attitude of men like Sykes Jones, Ned Crittenden, Logan Killicks, Joe Starks, Spunk Banks and John Pearson. Each man expects his mate to establish a dependent relationship with him, to follow his values in marriage, church and community—something Janie initially does while sitting on Jody's high chair of silence and doing nothing. Jody tells Janie on one occasion that she is not a person, meaning she cannot think, and that "all you got to do is mind me" (*TEWWG,*110). Janie is not to become "too moufy" (*TEWWG,* 65), too participatory in mule talk; if she does, she is repeatedly told to hush in very much the same fashion that Ned tells Amy to hush, or John Pearson orders Lucy to stop her "yowin' and jawin'" (*J'sGV,* 203) about his sins. When a woman does talk and defy her mate, as Janie and Lucy eventually do, she risks a severe beating, but remains determined to assert herself.

The ideal woman for the verbally powerful male in Hurston's art is one who abandons her verbal culture and folk traditions. She is not to engage in public rituals of talk, as Jody aptly points out when he prevents Janie from speaking out at the street lighting ceremonies: "Mah wife don't know nothin' bout no speech making. Ah never married her for nothin' lak dat. She's uh woman and her place is in de home" (*TEWWG,*39). Eventually, Jody's verbal restraints on Janie cause friction in the marriage to a point where Janie rebels. She finally asserts herself by presenting a verbal defense based on insults directed against Jody's manliness. Only with the use of the dozens as a defensive weapon does she gain verbal superiority over Jody. But her verbal feat is accomplished at a great cost—the dissolution of the marriage.

Observing the potential for male verbal domination in Black folk culture, Hurston defies the norm, stressing in her literary landscape that a woman will not yield to verbal oppression, to humiliation and belittlement in either Black or white culture. Neither will she be a wife without a talking tongue, denying herself the privilege of exercising those oral qualities instilled in her as a child. She will not be the silent hard working mule of the world, but a woman of temperament and will who possesses, as a folk saying suggests, "ninety nine rows uh jaw teeth and git her good and mad, she'll wade through solid rock up to her hip pockets" (*TEWWG*, 122). Neither materialism nor the color-struck phenomenon of the mulatto experience will be a drawback to the articulation of her self-identity. When it comes to speaking up for her rights, she is sustained by simple word power and dramatic flair.

Hurston's dramatic technique for presenting this exceptional woman is delivered through dialogue. It is commonplace, almost customary, to find the assertive woman in crucial scenes of verbal confrontation battling with an adversary. This verbal platform is the escape valve allowing her the opportunity to establish who she is and to break the chain of verbal oppression binding her. Hopefully, she and her spouse can become one in a relationship strengthened by oral cohesiveness. Hurston appears concerned, secondarily, about the image the assertive woman creates for herself in the community through storytelling and lying sessions. This area of recognition is explored exclusively in Hurston's folklore with a concentration on such female personalities as Big Sweet, Armetta Jones, Mathilda Moses, Bunch, Willie Mae Clarke, Johnnie Mae, Antie Hoyt and Leafy Lee.

Only random occurrences of a fight for communal status as Big Talker appear in the fiction. It is primarily in the fiction and drama (the recording of the personalized intra-familial relationship between man and woman) where Hurston's priorities proliferated. There is specific concern about the making of the assertive woman in a courtship or marriage situation and the length to which she might go to verbally establish her self image. In the process of accomplishing this, she is also, as Robert Hemenway suggests about Hurston's assertive woman, "establishing herself in something other than a dependent relationshp with a man."[5] Equality for her in a relationship is established first and foremost through the communication process. Love and marital harmony must sprout from the oral seeds of life emanating from within the marriage bond. If there is no verbal union and expression of love, then there is marital disharmony and violence, as is the case in the deteriorating marriage of Delia and Sykes, or of Janie and her first two husbands, Killicks and Starks. When there are love, understanding, and cooperation in a relationship founded on joint participation in all levels of verbal ritual, a marriage prospers, as with Missie May and Joe, Big Sweet and Lonnie, Leafy Lee and My Honey, and Janie and Tea Cake.

In whatever marriage situation she's in, the assertive woman enters into a verbal dialogue in order to convey a positive image of herself and to maintain a level of respect from her mate. When she speaks, there is

a deep undercurrent of individualism coursing in her oral disposition.
She can be sweet and loving or mean and awesome as she takes her
place in the verbal arena. The technique by which she orally maneuvers
for space to show her worth is a process of "negotiating respect." This
term has been placed in clearer perspective in recent years by urban
folklorist Roger Abrahams. In the following passage, Abrahams
expounds on the intricate workings of the woman's temperament as she
enters the negotiation process and bargains through her talking
expertise:

> The essence of the negotiation involved in asserting one's role
> lies in a woman being both *sweet* and *tough* depending upon her
> capacity to define and manipulate the situation. Ideally she has the
> ability to *talk sweet* with her infants and peers but talk *smart* or
> *cold* with anyone who might threaten her *self-image.* She expects
> both good behavior and bad at all times and has routines prepared
> for handling and capitalizing on both. Acting and being regarded
> as respectable is not a static condition in any way; quite the
> contrary, the ladies most respected are those who maintained
> themselves at the center of action.[6]

Skill in the talking process is the way Hurston's assertive woman
maintains respect. Such women as Janie, Big Sweet, Delia, Laura Lee,
and Lucy can all be observed engaging in the negotiation process as
they establish their self identity through a mean or sweet disposition.
Robert Hemenway's provocative essay, "Are You a Flying Lark or a
Setting Dove," examines the negotiating process for Hurston's assertive
woman primarily from the perspective of the old-time Negro courtship
ritual. Here, the man and woman are amicable and equal verbal partners
engaging in the friendly dialogue of courtship talk. They challenge each
other as the marriage proposal, often initiated by the male suitor, "Are
you a flying lark or a setting dove?" is introduced. The woman's sweet
disposition, symbolized in her witty talk and verbal ingenuity, becomes
evident as she addresses herself to the man's flattery and exaggerated
speech of love and affection. Her talk and mood establish whether she
wants to remain a flying lark (unmarried) or to become a setting dove (a
married woman).

Hemenway refers to just this one example of dialogue or verbal
love-making between man and woman to point out the significance of
the concept of negotiating respect in Hurston's art. He explains it in

this context: "The courtship scene illustrates a common characteristic of Hurston's fiction, the most dramatic episodes arise from men and women squaring off for a verbal duel, a situation best understood as part of the process whereby a black woman negotiates respect, seizing the opportunity to affirm herself as a woman."[7] In contrast to the woman's assertion of self in the courting scene, the process of negotiating respect and maintaining self respect is far more crucial in scenes of hostile confrontation, as is evident in the episodes of verbal duelling between Janie and Jody, Lucy and John or Big Sweet and Texas Red. It is perhaps in the violent arguments, and not necessarily in the courting conversations, that the assertive woman's negotiating skills are more revealing of the various dimensions of her character and positive survival virtues. In a true-to-life discordant situation where her sense of being is at stake, she talks for her dear life, and, in the process, she spiritually triumphs while verbally disarming her adversary. By the end of the battle, she firmly establishes herself as a person to be reckoned with, as a person who surely has the law in her mouth. Hurston's purpose here seems to be to show that an adversarial relationship provides a wider platform for understanding the dynamics of the assertive woman's personality than does the narrow scope of courtship talk. More is ascertained about Lucy's character in verbal conflict with John than in their courtship play talk. Such is also true of Big Sweet, Janie, Delia and a host of other assertive women whose prominent direct speech actions are dramatically projected in both playful and serious conversation.

Chapter 2

The Other Woman in Hurston's Art: The Literary Foil to the Assertive Woman

All assertive women share in common a reliance on verbal fluency, although their personal challenges and social experiences are different. Big Sweet, Lucy, Janie, Leafy Lee and Amy, for example, all talk for respect, but under totally different circumstances. Their reliance on word power, direct folk speech, in tense dramatic interchanges at home or in community experiences is a common element they all employ to achieve and overcome oppression in various manifestations. Each in her own individual talking style must draw upon folk speech and its various forms to suit her social circumstances. Each must also be amply prepared to back up words with direct action.

This mutual creative verbal talent exhibited by Hurston's assertive women is also shared by many other Southern Black women and should be acknowledged more by scholars and placed alongside the Black woman's other artistic talents such as those cited by Alice Walker in the highly acclaimed essay on Black women's creativity, "In Search of Our Mothers' Gardens: The Creativity of Black Women in the South."[1]

The Southern Black woman's gift with the word has sustained the Black family inner structure and the community and race at large. It has often been said by Blacks of the Deep South that the Black assertive woman is such a flexible and diverse being that she can talk or negotiate with anybody—white, red, or Black. She is strong-minded and is perceived by many as being verbally intrepid.

One need only think here of the influence of the assertive tongue of Hurston herself, not to mention other such notable, defiant and courageously strong Black women talkers as Sojourner Truth, Harriet Tubman, Fannie Lou Hamer, Ida B. Wells, Christine Bolden, Rosa Parks, Shirley Chisholm, Barbara Jordan, Pearl Bailey, Florence

Kennedy and Patricia Roberts Harris. They all speak in their individual way for respect of self and also of community and race, and usually excel when they encounter the verbal challenges of their lives. The impact of their verbal defiance and outspokenness is forever present in the Black community, as is the case of Rosa Parks whose verbal defiance of a white bus driver on a Jim Crow bus ignited the Civil Rights protest of the fifties and sixties in the American South. Hurston's assertive women bear resemblance to these women of verbal merit and they serve, in the printed, recorded forms of Hurston's fiction, folklore and drama, as one of the few tangible telescopic pictures of Black women in oral discourse. They are firmly rooted in the language of their oral cultural heritage.

There is a long list of representative assertive women of words and direct action in Hurston's varied art, as well as those who are not so assertive or verbally fluent. In the short fiction, for example, appear such assertive women talkers as young Isie, Delia, Missie May, Pinkie, Laura Lee, Aunt Judy, and the nameless Harlem domestic. In the folklore and drama exist Big Sweet, Leafy Lee, Matildha, Dicey, Bunch, Mother Catherine, and the mambo of Haiti, the matriarch of hoodoo. In the longer novels are present Amy, Lucy, Sally, Janie, Zipporah, and Nanny. A white woman, Arvay Henson, is also included here, but only after her separation from Jim, her husband, and her subsequent growth to maturity through her verbal metamorphosis into a real, assertive, and loving wife to her husband, rather than a verbal weakling.

Influenced by her assertive female ancestors in Eatonville and also by her own research and personal interaction with Black folk women of the Southern United States and also of the Caribbean, Hurston also wisely illustrates that every woman in her art is not to be considered a verbal saint. There are women who have verbal flaws, sometimes self-inflicted, and who suffer severely for them. This type is presented as having a negative personality, and is inadequate in fighting demeanor and in overall verbal performance. She is often a misfit and symbolizes the negative side of Black womanhood as embodied in her devious ways. Acknowledging these two opposing types of women, Hurston counterbalances the positive image of the assertive woman and verbal truth bearer with that of the less articulate and individualistic woman who has no positive virtues and submits willingly to male domination. The latter is often the embodiment of evil and enjoys causing conflict with the more popular and verbally astute assertive woman. She creates disorder but is incapable of resolving it through talking or fighting skill.

For the most part, the non-assertive woman is a puny, detestable figure who ends up in misery and defeat because of her own self-inflicted deficiency and blindness. Her devious demeanor prevents her from articulating a palatable system of social values in a world where positive word power is the standard norm of self-evaluation. She is dependent on others, possessing no favorable sense of self and lacking any optimistic attitude toward life. Her Machiavellian disposition is further evident in her efforts to defeat and pull down the respectable and admirable woman bearer of the word. Her talk becomes a destructive weapon of little real substance, something like gossip and backbiting of the kind used by those talkers who aimed to pull John Pearson, Janie, Big Sweet or Lucy down to dishonorable stature. John Pearson comments perceptively about this behavioral type: "You know our people is jus' lak uh passle uh crabs in uh basket. De minute dey see one climbin' up too high, de rest of 'em reach up and grab 'em and pull 'im back. Dey ain't gonna let nobody git nowhere if dey kin he'p it" (*J'sGV*, 263).

Examples of this non-assertive and evil type of woman are just as varied and complex as the assertive women are in Hurston's works. There is Lena in "Spunk," (1925) for example. A careless woman who disregards her marital vows and all notions of marriage fidelity, trust and love, Lena remains mealy-mouth about the affair she's having with Spunk Banks, an audacious man with the raw nerve, or spunk, to boldly challenge an adversary. As a result of Lena's immoral actions rather than strong words of assertion in the tale of Spunk Banks and Joe Kanty, two men are killed. The talk of others about her controls her fate, as she makes no attempt to assert herself and end the hostility and rivalry existing between Joe Kanty and Spunks Banks. Throughout the story, she remains a quiet woman whose mere presence amongst the storeporch talkers of the village evokes conversations on characteristic themes inherent in Hurston's short stories: justice, conflict, hypocrisy, good and evil, superstition, and violence.

The most fully developed woman of the non-assertive type in Hurston's works appears in the folklore, longer fiction and drama. Examples are Hattie Tyson, fictional foil to Lucy and Sally Lovelace in *Jonah's Gourd Vine* and Dicey, Lucy (not to be confused with Lucy Pearson in *Jonah's Gourd Vine*) and Ella Wall, rivals to Big Sweet in *Mules and Men and Polk County*. Another malevolent type, Hattie, a "strumpet who ain't never done nothin' but run up and down de road from one sawmill camp tuh de other" (*J'sGV*, 138), lacks high moral values, does not have courage and is incapable of verbally asserting herself with skill. Her goals—usually of a wicked, conspiratorial nature—are never achieved, as she is verbally deficient and cannot employ words to convey her thoughts, thus resorting to trickery and devious means. In this instance, her recourse is the evil workings of hoodoo as she secures or buys the magical powers of An' Dangie and War Pete. With evil rather than good intentions, she braids her hair with a John-de-conquer root and confidently gloats that John and his good men cannot overpower her evil magic: "Dey can't move me—not wid de help Ah got" (*J'sGV*, 139).

Black magic, designed for evil purposes, Hattie believes, has the power to win John over to her side. She has faith that An' Dangie's magic portions will cause much fussing and fighting between John and Lucy. As a result, Hattie reasons that John can then be controlled to her liking in very much the way her assertive nemesis, Lucy, brings about a positive influence in John's social rise and prominence as mayor and renowned preacher of Eatonville. Surprisingly, hoodoo cannot replace a woman's word power and ability to have the authority of "the law in her mouth." Hattie, the non-assertive reliant on hoodoo and the mischievous actions of Hambo and Harris to do her evil bidding, fails miserably to maintain a sound verbal union with John, once she claims him as her husband after Lucy's death. She remarks to a co-conspirator against John, Deacon Harris, who desires to "chop down dis Jonah's gourd vine," (*J'sGV*, 154) about her lack of empowerment over John: "Ah feels lak uh cat in hell wid no claws"(*J'sGV*, 153). Hattie's evil ploys to control John with the evil and magical powers of hoodoo are unearthed (in chapter twenty-two of *J'sGV*, 161–163) and John hastily unties the false knot of love that supposedly unites them. He severely beats her[2] and verbally castigates her and wholeheartedly agrees to a divorce when she files for one.

Hattie's character as evil woman and ineffective talker is like another kind of female verbal weakling who appears frequently in the hoodoo chapters of the folklore collection, *Mules and Men*, (251–304). Here can be found a clinging-vine type who turns to the evil spirits of hoodoo doctors or hoodoo dancers as a substitute for her incompetence in generating self-made power through talk. When verbalism fails her in a woman-to-woman or even man-to-man verbal conflict in which she is a prime participant, she clings for dear life to hoodoo as a supporting rod. She believes that her opponent is eventually overwhelmed and mesmerized into immobility by the evil workings of hoodoo.

The clinging vine's method of overcoming a rival is to make a verbal request to a hoodoo doctor (or to a dancer of evil spirits like Ella or Dicey in the play, *Polk County)* who in turn employs his or her spiritual power to conjure paraphernalia in such a way that the language request is transformed into action (i.e., made into reality). It should be stressed that this is a consequence achieved with the aid of hoodoo power purchased with money instead of by the individual's own assertive voice of interaction or conversation with a friendly or evil foe. A woman resorting to this indirect method of self-expression is such a petty, pitiful figure when placed alongside of the assertive woman of natural and direct verbal power who survives on native wit in direct verbal confrontation. The latter talks to bring about action and change directly; she does not need the devious mediation of hoodoo magic to accomplish her goals. We cannot imagine a Big Sweet, Janie or Lucy soliciting the aid of a hoodoo practitioner to do evil or to win control of a man or fight a battle with a woman adversary. The drama of word power is the assertive woman's potent weapon of self defense.

In *Mules and Men,* Hurston provides several examples of the clinging-vine type of non-assertive woman in a series of scenarios representing dialogue between a verbally weak patient and a hoodoo doctor of great power. Because the patient is verbally unable to carry out her wishes against a rival or lover, she pays the doctor to accomplish it with the workings of a Black magic formula designed to "fix" the so-named party. In the first vignette (*M&M,* 251), the reader meets Dr. Turner and a woman patient who requests something be done to keep her husband true. Turner gives her a string knot that had been "treated" at the altar and instructs her how to accomplish such a wish through the workings of a prescribed Black magic ritual: "Measure the man where I tell you. But he must never know. Measure him in his sleep then fetch back the string to me" (*M&M,* 251). When she returns for advice, Turner performs another ceremonial ritual to ensure the fulfillment of her wish that her husband love her and forget others. She goes away confident that the ritual of Black magic will work (*M&M,* 252).

In another case, Turner provides service for a cheating wife who hates her husband's brother and wants something done to silence him. The cheating wife's flat and undynamic testimony for help is provided in the following doctor-patient conversation:

Patient: My husband's brother. He hate me and make all the
trouble he can. He must leave this town or die. Yes, it is much
better if he is dead. Yeah, he should be dead long time ago.
Long before he spy upon me, before he tell lies, lies, lies. I
should be very happy for his funeral.

Doctor: Oh I can feel the great hate around you. It follow you
everywhere, but I kill nobody, I send him away if you want so
he never come back. I put guards along the road in the spirit
world, and these he cannot pass, no. When he go, never will
he come back to New Orleans. You see him no more. He will
be forgotten and all his works.

Patient: Then I am satisfied, yes. When will you send him off?

Doctor: I ask the spirit, you will know (*M&M,* 252).

The Frizzly Rooster, or Father Watson, is widely known in New
Orleans because he "could curse anybody he wished—and make the
curse stick. He could remove curses, no matter who laid them on
whom. He could 'read' anyone, no matter how far away, if he were
given their height and color. He begged to be challenged" (*M&M,* 265).
He greets a patient, Sister Murchison, a weakish woman, who wants to
run a woman out of her house. She lacks the verbal fluency to do the
job herself and requests help.

Doctor: Tell us how you want to be helped, Sister Murchison.

Patient: Too many women in my house. My husband's mother is
there and she hates me and always puttin' my husband to fight
me. Look like I can't get her out of my house no ways I try.
So I done come to you.

Doctor: We can fix that up in no time, dear one. Now go take a flat
onion. . . . Core the onion out, and write her name five
times on paper and stuff it into the hole in the onion and
close it back with the cut-out piece of onion. Now you watch
when she leaves the house and then you roll the onion behind
her before anybody else crosses the door-sill. And you make a
wish at the same time for her to leave your house. She won't
be there two weeks more (*M&M,* 271).

The Frizzly Rooster meets another dependent type who is envious
and jealous at the rise of a popular man and displays her crab-like
mentality, as well, when she voices a desire to pull him down: "He's

getting too rich and big. I want something done to keep him down. They tell me he's bout to get to be a bishop. I sho' would hate for that to happen. I got forty dollars in my pocket right now for the work!" (*M&M*, 272). Faith and confidence are placed in the doctor's power, as the evil woman shuns the more immediate route of direct verbal interaction with a foe.

Such is also the case with Dr. Duke who is introduced to a working woman, Rachel Roe, who bears a similarity to Delia in "Sweat" in that she is beaten and economically exploited by a man who uses her money, "her sweat and blood," to support another woman. Rachel is tired of him and wants to send him away; verbally, she has been powerless in driving this message home to him. Therefore, she seeks the aid of Dr. Duke to "fix" him into leaving her home:

> Rachel: He won't work and make support for me, and he won't git on out the way and leave somebody else do it. He spend up all my money playing coon-can and kotch and then expect me to buy him a suit of clothes, and then he all the time fighting me about my wages.
>
> Dr. Duke: You sure you don't want him no more? You know women get mad and say things they take back over night.
>
> Rachel: Lawd knows I mean this. I don't want to meet him riding nor walking (*M&M*, 280).

The last client for study consults Kitty Brown, a practitioner who makes marriages and puts lovers together. Minnie Foster, like Arvay, constantly doubts her husband's faithfulness and wants to keep him under control. She is rather fanatical in striving to rule the man she loves and consults Kitty periodically to ask that something be done for every little flaw he has.

> Kitty: You must be skeered of yourself with that man of yours.
>
> Minnie: No, Ma'am, I aint. But I love him and I just want to make sure. Jus you give me something to make his love more stronger.
>
> Kitty: Alright, Minnie, I'll do it, but you ain't got no reason to be so unsettled with me behind you. Do like I say and you'll be alright (*M&M*, 302).

But, Minnie still doubts Kitty's total power and returns on several occasions for more work to be done:

> Kitty: Ain't you got dat man to your wishes, yet, Minnie?
> Minnie: He love me, I b'lieve, but he gone off to Mobile with a construction gang and I got skeered he might not come back. Something might delay him on his trip.
> Kitty: Oh, alright Minnie, go do like I say and he'll sure be back . . . (*M & M*, 302).

The personal and social survival of these and other women clients described by Hurston is embedded in the mysterious workings of hoodoo and not necessarily in the power of influence that might be gained from effective talking—the natural gift of word power. This idea of non-assertiveness and faith in the power of hoodoo or black folk magic is also conveyed in the character of two other non-assertive and dependent women represented in the fiction and drama. In "John Redding Goes to Sea" (1921), Mattie Redding, known for her weeping spasms of fear and self-pity, may also be perceived as a verbal misfit and an overly-protective mother. Her nagging, unproductive talk is inspired by what she interprets as the evil workings of hoodoo on her because of her marriage to Alfred Redding. She is obsessed with the belief that she and her first born child, John, have been "fixed" with travel dust sprinkled around her home by Witch Judy Davis, who wanted Alfred Redding to marry her daughter, Edna.

Mattie is so myopic that she cannot see her son's own natural and youthful inclination as being the catalyst behind his fervent desire to explore and see the world—to dream of people and far away places and to go beyond the sea to view what exists on other shores beyond his birthplace. Preoccupation with superstition prevents Mattie from engaging in a true-to-life dialogue with John and Alfred about John's dreams to jump at the sun. Because of Mattie's incessant weeping and preoccupation with the power of hoodoo as the evil force in controlling John's ambitious thirst, her communication with both family members suffers. She is so narrow-minded and provincial that her influence through the spoken word is very limited in making effective change. Without her verbal blessings of encouragement, her son, John, does make the attempt to go see the wide world at last. Tragically, though, his quest to go to sea ends in death on the St. John's River at the hands of a fierce rainstorm during the construction of a bridge which may symbolically represent his efforts to connect his ambitious thirst to travel and fulfill spirited dreams with the conflicting forces of darkness and instability represented by his mother and wife. He fails in the attempt to bridge his spiritual motivations with the verbal inhibitions of Mattie Reading. Alfred Redding, a pragmatist and sound verbal voice, laments his son's fate and unfilled dreams when he instructs that John's body be allowed to continue floating out to sea: "Mah po' boy, his dreams never come true. . . . You all stop! Leave my boy go on. Doan stop 'im. Doan' bring 'im back for dat ole tree to grin at. Leave him gowan. He wants tuh go. Ah'm happy 'cause dis mawnin' mah boy is goin' tuh sea, he's goin' tuh sea."[3]

Dicey in *Polk County* also delves in hoodoo as an element of survival; however, she is not as personally obsessed with hoodoo as Mattie Redding is. Dicey is a more extensive version of the envious Lucy in *Mules and Men,* Big Sweet's main adversary. She is a foil to both Big Sweet and Leafy Lee, a beautiful mulatto girl who is steeped in the Black cultural heritage of song and talk and who eventually marries Dicey's intended lover, My Honey, a popular Blues singer and guitar player of the jook. A dark-skinned unattractive woman, Dicey is also ineffective in expressing genuine, natural love to a man and is preoccupied with her own blackness and its supposed drawbacks. Because she is color struck, low self-esteem haunts Dicey throughout the play and she can only grasp strength to cope with them by calling upon the evil workings of a hoodoo dance to console her in efforts to overcome her arch rivals. Jealousy of a lighter skinned and far more attractive woman, Leafy Lee, and the fear of an assertive and physically agile woman the likes of Big Sweet lead to Dicey's further disenchantment with life and to her eventual downfall.

Self-hatred causes her to lash out at Big Sweet and Leafy Lee in devious ways—from false letters claiming infidelity by Big Sweet against Lonnie, to the ritualistic performance of an evil hoodoo dance to bring death or injury to Big Sweet, Leafy Lee and the entire Polk County clan. By this evil trickery (and possibly through murder, if she is given the chance by a weak opponent), Dicey aims to develop a strong sense of self and to make a reputation for herself. She cannot accomplish this merely through dialogue, a word for word battle with Big Sweet or Leafy Lee; she is not a skillful talker who is prepared to back up her words with direct action as an effective fist fighter would. Lacking these skills in her rivalry with Big Sweet and Leafy Lee for the affection of My Honey, Dicey fails in the end. She is jailed by the

Quarters Boss for disrupting the peace, while Big Sweet triumphs as
Queen and Lawmaker of Polk County.

Dicey's self-hate and the projection of a low opinion of her dark-
skinned complexion through evil deeds perpetrated to others constitute
her mortal flaw. This is also true of a host of other characters in
Hurston's art who are color struck because of their dislike of their own
blackness and because of their obsessive jealousy of the fair-skinned
Black person.[4] Emmaline in the play, *Color Struck* (1926), is a case in
point. A self-pitying and self-deprecating sense of racial inferiority, one
similar to Emma Lou's in Wallace Thurman's *The Blacker the Berry*
(1929), is at the heart of Emmaline's inability either to love herself or
to articulate any love to John, a fair-skinned Black man. Even though
John dearly loves dark-skinned Emma as a person and is unconcerned
about the hue of her skin, Emma's vision of her Black-skinned self is
mired in a demeaning self-concept and fanatical jealousy of any person
with "yaller"[5] skin. She is so color struck and prejudiced against her
blackness that she does not dance the cakewalk with John because of
light-skinned Effie's presence. Her greatest tragedy is that she is blinded
by hate and cannot love her self or anyone else. John states it best when
he describes her in this manner: "So this is the woman I've been
wearing over my own heart like a rose for twenty years! She so despises
her own skin that she can't believe any one else could love it! Twenty
years! Twenty years of adoration, of hunger, of worship."[6] Emmaline, a
clinging-vine woman obsessed with the dynamics of intra-racial color
prejudice, causes the death of her extremely ill mulatto child, fathered
by John, based on the blind belief that John is attracted to his girl child,
Lou Lillian, merely because of her light skin and other Caucasian
features. Emma's obsessive jealousy of the fair skinned African
American woman, even when it is her own daughter, is most telling
when she causes the child's death by refusing to search for a doctor for
fear of leaving the child in the protective care of her father. Tragically,
Emmaline's color struck mentality causes the personal tragedy that
unfolds in this play. She lacks spunk and is mired in prejudice and self-
hate which prevented her from expressing any positive sense of
assertive individualism.

Miriam in *Moses, Man of the Mountain*,[7] and Mrs. Turner in
Their Eyes Were Watching God, are characters similar to Emma and
Dicey in their diminished stature and positive self concept. The color
struck phenomenon is the root cause of their evil disposition and verbal
ineffectiveness. Miriam detests light-skinned pretty women with class

like Zipporah, Moses' wife (in reality, though, she is Miriam's sister-in-law), and the influence she might exert over the other women. Throughout her life, Miriam quests for leadership of the Hebrew women and feels threatened when her territory is usurped by a rival. Her verbal demeanor is antagonistic as she begins to castigate the beautifully attired Zipporah, a woman of glitter, elegance, and glamour. With "rough clothing and work-twisted feet and hands"(*MMM*, 273), Miriam spits at Zipporah and boils with anger and snarls when she observes her developing influence over the other rag-tag women who are rather awestruck at her finery and beauty: "Look at the hussy! Look what is getting down off the camal, will you! Somebody to come queen it over us poor people and rob us. Look at her trying to look like Mrs. Pharaoh! That Moses and his tricks. Fooling me and Aaron to do all the hard work for him down in Egypt and telling us all he meant to do for us as soon as he got to Sinai. Then soon as he got here, before he can talk to God, he got to send for that woman to put her over me! I'll show him. I'll show her too. I didn't aim to be robbed out of my labor like that. Just look at her—the way she walks" (*MMM*, 270). Miriam's hateful talk is powerless to alter the growing admiration of the women for Moses' wife, or to curtail Moses' own leadership command and strength. The talk rather shows the limitations and drawbacks of Miriam's own evil nature. Evil women never become great assertors of identity in Hurston's art. They fail. As Moses discerns, Miriam does not possess the positive talent necessary for leadership, for she is "too spiteful and bitter" (*MMM*, 268).[8] And, in the end, she suffers dearly for it, banished as a leper who yearns for death at Moses' powerful hand.

Mrs. Turner, Janie's fair-skinned fictional foil, is like the rest of the envious women or clinging vines who never succeed in Hurston's art. Mrs. Turner, too, is pre-occupied with the phenomenon of intra-racial skin prejudice. She is totally disenchanted with the darker hued members of the Black race. In contrast, though, to those dark-skinned color-struck women who dislike light skin and the advantage it gives women of that hue, Mrs. Turner loves light skin, is snobbish in her preference for it, and feels that it should set her and her kind in a class above the dark-skinned members of her race. Her sentiments are voiced to Janie as she attempts to secure into a class of their own the friendship of the lighter-complexioned Janie:

Ah ain't useter 'ssociatin' wid black folks. Mah son claims dey draws lightnin' . . . Ah can't stand black niggers. Ah don't blame de white folks from hatin' 'em cause Ah can't stand 'em mahself. 'Nother thing, Ah hates tuh see folks lak me and you mixed up wid 'em. Us oughta class off . . . And dey makes me tired. Always laughin'! Dey laughs too much and dey laughs too loud. Always singin' ol' nigger songs! Always cuttin' de monkey for white folks. If it wuzn't for so many black folks it wouldn't be no race problem. De white folks would take us in wid dem. De black ones is holdin' us back (*TEWWG*, 116–117).

Arvay Henson of *Seraph on the Suwanee* [9] is another member of this group with a far more complicated character than her other counterparts. Such factors as her lack of self-confidence, inferiority complex, Cracker mentality, prejudice toward non-white people, her fake epileptic seizures and her retreat to missionary work are dependent support structures that contribute to her flawed character. As a result, her marriage to Jim Meserve is affected, for a number of years, preventing her from finding her true self identity in marital union. Here, she displays an ill-fated condition of not being able to "see and know" (*SOS*, 231) things. She clings to inner drawbacks, thus revealing the fact that she lives by feelings and not by conscious reasoning. She does not know how to assert herself to her husband, how to talk and show her love. For years a verbal union of love and understanding is absent even though Jim makes every effort to prove himself as a husband and provider. Finally, Jim Meserve—an assertive man who wants his wife to be an equal talking partner in the marriage—voices his displeasure about Arvay's inexpressiveness in the love relationship. He calls it false love, unpure love, a non-showing, inactive love: "I feel and believe that you do love me, Arvay, but I don't want that stand-still, hap-hazard kind of love. I'm just as hungry as a dog for a knowing and doing love. You love like a coward. Don't take no steps at all. Just stand around and hope for things to happen out right. Unthankful and unknowing like a hog under a acorn tree. Eating and grunting with your ears hanging over your eyes, and never even looking up to see where the acorns are coming from. What satisfaction can I get out of that kind of love, Arvay? Ain't you never stopped to consider it all?" (*SOS*, 230) Jim had made every effort possible to demonstrate his love—through romantic speech, and from the heroic snake feat, purchase of the family home, compassion for the disfigured Earl, to the education of the other two children—but Arvay remains unyielding in expressive love as she clings to her inner fears and self-inflicted drawbacks. As a result, Jim announces that he aims to separate from her after fifteen years of existence in an unhappy marriage with a non-assertive wife:

> Your kind of love, Arvay, don't seem to be the right thing to me. My feelings inside is just how I look outside. Naw, Arvay, I done got my mind made up. I'm leaving you in the morning . . . Becaue I'm sick and tired of hauling and dragging you because you don't understand. I'm tired of waiting for you to meet me on some high place and locking arms with me and going my way. I'm tired of hunting you, and trying to free your soul, I'm tired. . . . If I ever see any signs of you coming to be the woman I married you for, why then I'll be only too glad and willing to try it again. Our bonds have never been consecrated. Two people ain't never married until they come to some point of view. That we don't seem to be able to do, so I'm moving over to the coast tomorrow for good (*SOS,* 233–234).

Only when self-realization comes to Arvay, after her forced separation from Jim and after a renewed understanding of her own past in a pilgrimage back to her hometown and family estate, does she purify herself of her life-long mental stumbling blocks. Once coming to grips with the drawbacks of her past—as symbolized in such experiences as the burial of her mother (the last restraining link in her upbringing), the relinquishing of ties with sister Lorraine and Rev. Carl Middleton, and in the burning of the crude rudiments of their decrepit and rat-infested home—Arvay finds her voice, a "fullness of mind" (*SOS,* 310) and a renewed intellectual vision which enable her to understand and assert herself fully as wife.

A new Arvay is verbally transformed into an assertive wife who no longer clings to her smalltown Cracker mentality as refuge from the reality of marital life. She "wanted to fully express herself in words and let Jim know how she had improved and changed" (*SOS,* 308). At the end of the novel, Arvay's growth and change are most apparent. She is now a middle-aged woman with grown children who is just in the process of learning to express, through her speech and actions, her love for her husband. Resembling a newlywed bride, she stands in spiritual and verbal union with Jim as he launches his new shrimping business. In such a scene, Arvay, after having overcome her dependency, symbolizes Hurston's belief that there is hope and possible rehabilitation for a woman of this disposition, provided that she has not committed irreparable harm or caused unnecessary violence and evil against her mate or other adversaries. Of all of Hurston's non-assertive and clinging vine type women, Arvay, a Southern white woman, overcomes her personally inflicted drawbacks and develops into a strong and courageous assertive woman, comparable to formidable Black women characters the likes of Big Sweet, Lucy and Janie. Assertive individualism, Hurston seems to be suggesting in her last novel and depiction of a white woman character who must also master the art of folk expression in her own all-white culture, has no class or racial limitations. A woman must be an individualist and assertor of her identity no matter what her racial or class distinction might be.

Chapter 3

The Assertive Woman in Conversation and Combat: Dimensions of the Talking and Fighting Phenomenon

As the course and pattern of growth toward asserting individuality and negotiating respect are virtually similar in the verbal transformation of all of Hurston's assertive female characters, an analysis of several major female characters from a few selected works will be undertaken. Each chosen assertive woman embodies a positive image of courage and spunk as she utilizes the verbal techniques of oral culture to survive. The assertive woman in Hurston's art may be of varied types, but the common thread that unifies the assertive woman in Hurston's art is her engagement in what one critic has described as "a series of linguistic moments representing the folk life of the black South."[1] The assertive woman may conform to any one of the following descriptions which reveal the diversity and range of her image in Hurston's fiction, folklore and drama:

- an unmarried woman wittingly and skillfully engaging in a play acting drama of courtship talk with a male suitor.
- an abused housewife engaged in serious real talk that culminates in the dozens and a physical altercation with a spouse. She is prepared to say as much as her back can stand in any confrontation.
- a domestic, a Southerner relocated in the Northern environment of pimps (or sweetbacks as they are called by Ralph Ellison[2]) and streetcorner slang. In street-corner conversation (in the form of the urban "hipped" version of the old time courtship talk of the folk), she is a fierce competitor in the language game. She

perceptively decodes a man's verbal flattery of exaggerated talk which is designed to financially exploit her.

- a faithful house servant and retainer of old master-servant loyalty who defends her employer's property with skill in talking and fighting.
- an unattractive jook woman (a total misfit in society at large) noted for her talk, song, dance, careless love and artistry in weapon usage.
- the faithful wife and loving mother burdened by her husband's adultery and child neglect.
- an overworked washerman and Christian church-goer turned into the "mule of the world," so to speak, as she carries the heavy financial burden of an unhappy marriage of economic inequality. Refuge in religion cannot save her as the marriage escalates into violence and domestic abuse. Driven from the experience of love, she grows to assert her disgust for a brutal husband. Eventually she develops a hateful resistance to her spouse and resorts to the verbal survival strategy of the dozens. She momentarily conquers him, only to discover to her horror that he engineers a murderous trap for her. A shrewd thinker and woman of spunk, she dispenses Old Testament justice of an eye for an eye when her husband is not warned of impending danger as he enters their home. Without her aid and assertive tongue of caution and direction, he is caught in the web of his own evil trap and is destroyed by the very trap with which he intends to kill her.
- the mulatto woman steadfastly retaining Black speech rituals, even though she could freely alienate herself from Black culture by passing the white world of class and privilege if she so desires. Surprisingly, she proves herself to be more assertive and musically talented in Black rituals than her dark-skinned counterpart
- a rival who is burdened with being "color struck" because of her dark skin and prejudice against the fair-skinned woman.

Whoever she is on the social plateau of the folk community, the assertive woman is a stoic individual determined to live life fully with talk and laughter, or to overcome tragedy and hardship by speaking her mind equally with her male counterpart, be he verbally congenial or verbally oppressive. Her mouth and the folk language it expounds become her bodyguard or guardian to ward off danger. Like Alice

Walker's Shug Avery, she is a talking fighter who on occasion might be physically "weak as a kitten, but her mouth just pack with claws."[3] In a long- or short-lived marriage or courtship relationship, she will endure to capture her dreams from the distant ships on the horizon and, in the process, she will spiritually grow from the natural seeds of Black speech power. A woman of the South where individual and land are closely linked, she is as close to nature as she is to the roots of her oral tradition. In both, she observes the beginning and ending of life. Articulating her growth from innocence to maturity and awareness is her point of achievement in Black folk culture. The spoken word, not the written medium, becomes her gift and expression of life. Her talent and resilience prove her to be an able, capable woman who is strong enough to talk her way through hardship, to analyze the conflicts of her life and arrive at verbal solutions to them. She does not have to break the traditional chain of the Black woman's oral creative talent in coming to terms with her struggles, as Walker's Celie feels compelled to do with pen and ink. Unlike her Southern female ancestors, Celie is indeed an oddity who uses the written medium in the form of letters to God as her means of coping with the unpleasant aspects of her oppressive life in Mister's home. Interestingly, she endures hardship and exploitation at the hands of men because she does not assert herself—vocalize those problems in conversation—and, as a result, she proves herself to be a dependent woman who reaches for support from an almost non-existent voice. She does not initially assert her rights, and appears to be far removed from the admirable voices that pervade Hurston's art and symbolically represent standard models of Black womanhood in Black folk culture at large.

The group which exemplifies the most positive representation of the assertive woman in Hurston's art consists of the following eight women: Big Sweet, Laura Lee, Delia, Missie May, the nameless Harlem domestic, Daisy, Lucy and Janie. Each woman is strong, loyal and faithful—magnificent in verbal disposition, astute at sounding out her experiences in the drama of talking and fighting. Each woman is wise of word and seems in her own unique individual character to possess, like Uncle Monday, "the diamond of all diamonds, the mouth or singing stone."[4] The stone, taken from the mouth of a serpent, according to Black myth and legend, is the greatest charm, the most powerful hand in the world which serves as a pilot that warns of danger and which enables its bearer to know everything without being told. When each woman is captured in the drama of talk in a marriage or courtship experience, her mouth stone or diamond of conversation is her valuable guiding light in conversation. Her words or mouth stones are her greatest charm and they indicate her brillance and powerful rigidity in overcoming danger.

Each assertive woman in Hurston's art has a "singing" or verbal diamond in her mouth which enables her to negotiate respect for herself and to articulate an understanding of the life experiences through dramatic dialogue, as Lucy and Delia do in conversation with their husbands, as Janie does in recounting her oral history to Phoeby in woman-to-woman dialogue, and as Big Sweet and Leafy Lee do in their girlish or "kissing friends" type dialogue about their varied upbringings.

The following analyses provide a study of each of these women, pointing out those positive assertive qualities each employs in crucial scenes of verbal confrontation with a man or with a malevolent female rival. Beyond doubt, each woman proves herself to be an effective talker who can confidently and truthfully declare, "Ah got the law in my mouth" (*MM*, 162). The truth and power of verbal authority she exerts in the home or public arena bear this out.

Chapter 4

Big Sweet, Polk County's Queen of Talk and Song

In the folklore anthology, *Mules and Men,* Big Sweet stands out as the major assertive female voice. Her personality is manifested in verbal interaction with other characters, be it during the storytelling sessions when she asserts herself in an all-male social environment, or during the night-life experience of jooking, dancing, singing, card-playing and fighting, or during her few encounters with white people who restrain their racial prejudice and dominance when faced with her assertive individualism. Wherever her verbal disposition is evident—in work, fun, or hostile confrontational settings—Big Sweet's character traits are firmly rooted in her speech demeanor. Through the talk experience, she creates an image of herself as a big and sweet woman. She is sweet in the sense that she possesses such good and admirable Christian virtues as love, loyalty, kindness, courage and leadership.

Big Sweet is a woman of words who believes in right over wrong, order over disorder, and friendship instead of violence. There is in her value system little hesitation about forthrightly lashing out at evil, wrongdoing or exploitation by the powerful over the weak and downtrodden. In her sweetness, she is also a loving and protective woman to her man, Joe Willard. In a community based on suitoring (*i.e.,* a woman laying claim to a man even though they are not legally married) and careless love—instead of the traditional value of marriage—her performance in the jook as a good blues singer, and in the home as caring lover to Joe merits her the positive reputation of a good jook woman who fulfills her duty to her mate. Though physically unattractive in the white sense of the word, with her stoutness, manly features, loud voice and such poor habits as dipping snuff, and wearing paper bags on her nappy head, she is a beautiful woman in the jook sense of the word. Verbally and musically, she is Queen of the jook in that she can "jook, has a good belly wobble, and has broad hips that shake like jelly all over,"[1] when she talks or sings in the vernacular of the jook.

In addition to her accomplishments as mistress of the jook, Big Sweet also excels as a fighter. Her physical strength is used to her advantage particularly when she is an active participant in the more violent aspects of jook life, *i.e.,* maiming and killing. She proves herself to be a big, powerful woman—Hurston describes her as being "large and portly, but light on her feet" (*MM,* 190)—who can physically defend herself, and fight to negotiate respect or establish order. Her sweetness and strength are merged into her talking and fighting superiority. With such authoritative qualities, she has the law and the voice of truth and authority in her mouth and hands, as we observe her in various scenes of life in the quarters and jook.

Big Sweet's voice stands out conspicuously from the discordant ones in a world of violent social misfits and fugitives from justice who establish reputations for themselves through sometimes cowardly deeds of murder. Her life on the job, a locale of turpentine and lumber camps during the day, and the blues and careless love of the jooks at night, necessitates that she not only be a woman of words, of oral ritual indigenous to the working-folk experience, but also a woman of direct action. As Polk County folk can react unpredictably, she has to be capable of backing up her talk with fists or weapons of cold steel, provided she does not exceed the murder quota in the Quarters. Words, weapons, and physical strength therefore comprise her image as the Big Sweet woman of Polk County. At one moment, during the lying session or courtship talk ritual, she can be sweet and pleasant in manner while maintaining respect and keeping order or preventing a killing. At the next, she can turn big and mean, erupting into the hostile language of the dozens, signifying or putting her foot on an opponent's doorstep. Whites may also come under her verbal fire and physical might as she is not bound by the racial stereotypes of verbal docility. She asserts herself as a person, not as a Black woman in the white notion of the word. As individual of word and direct action, Big Sweet may further be described as a woman "quick to sunshine and quick to anger" (*DTOR,* 178).

Big Sweet's overall reputation and influence on the job make her appear to be a complex woman of words and direct action, but then again, when viewed in the eyes of her peers, she represents simplicity in the talking and fighting game. For instance, an acquaintance of Big Sweet's, Mrs. Bertha, addresses herself, in conversation with Hurston, the newcomer to the Quarters, to the conflicting image that Big Sweet's dual qualities of might and sweetness present for some observers: "Taint a man, woman nor child on this job going to tackle Big Sweet. If God send her a pistol she'll send him a man. She can handle a knife with anybody. She'll join hands and cut a duel. Dat Cracker Boss wears two pistols round his waist and goes for bad, but he won't break a breath with Big Sweet lessen he got his pistol in his hand. Cause if he start anything with her, he won't never get a chance to draw it. She ain't mean. She don't bother nobody. She just don't stand for no foolishness, dat's all" (*DTOR*, 187–188). And, in the play, *Polk County*, Do Dirty and Lonnie express similar observations about Big Sweet's character: "If folks leave her alone, she'll leave them alone. She just don't like to see nobody bulldozing the place and running the hog over other folks. She'll cold crawl you for that" (*ACT I, Scene 1*, 21). And: "Taint nothing bad about Big Sweet at all. She got plenty friending in her if you let her be" (*ACT II, Scene 3*, 17). An examination of the Polk County chapters of *Mules and Men* (85–178) reveals that Big Sweet's image as a big and sweet woman is evident in her verbal demeanor in each oral ritual in which she asserts herself. She is a woman knowledgeable about Black speech styles and their appropriateness or function in a given social milieu, and she confidently situates herself at the center of the verbal action in such talk rituals as storytelling, woofing and courtship banter, verbal chatter accompanying the tense games of card play in the jook, along with the dozens, signifying and bulldozia (intimidation) speech styles that occur in interpersonal conflict. Throughout the verbal experience, she skillfully asserts herself as she negotiates respect and recognition of herself as individual, as mistress of talk and verbal law-enforcer in lying contests, as sole lover of Joe Willard, as expert card player, and as the real boss of the wayward Polk County clan.

When the talk experience exceeds the bounds of play and when fantasy impinges on reality, thus causing individual conflict and violence to erupt between two adversaries, Big Sweet is prepared to fight, to use her full physical might, if need be, to maintain order. This is precisely what happens in the Polk County sections of the book, particularly during the oral rituals of storytelling and jooking. Initially talk is of a playful nature, where Big Sweet asserts herself creatively and imaginatively; but, as the talk experience intensifies, it transforms itself into real, often intimidating, talk between two opponents. Big Sweet then re-adapts her talk to a more aggressive and formidable style. She is prepared to personally challenge an opponent with the idea that she will say no more than her back can stand. In this way, the talk experience becomes a part of social interaction. Individual warfare thus takes shape when playful language expands into a true-to-life dimension.

The dynamics of Big Sweet's two-fold capacity, as playful and then serious assertive voice, are evident during the swamp gang's lying and woofing sessions (*MM*, 107–178). Initially, in the playful lying contest, Big Sweet asserts herself as an able talk participant—a Big Liar like Mathilda Moseley of Eatonville—as she holds her rightful verbal place alongside the men. (Big Sweet, Hurston and Lucy are the only women present during the storytelling ritual.) Crayon enlargements of life in figurative language, far distant from the reality of life and interpersonal conflicts that she and the men are so familiar with, are in the making as a wide assortment of folktales are articulated on the spot to idle away time while they hike through the woods en route to the fishing hole.

For a moment, Big Sweet is engrossed in the storytelling as she laughs with her mouth wide open and then tells two "why" folk stories, one about the mocking bird's absence from the woods on Fridays (*MM*, 128) and the other about Brer Rabbit's cunning triumph over Brer Gator (*MM*, 141–142). But as the storytelling continues, there is a change in the language and story format of some of the tales. Speech techniques (such as the dozens, signifying, and sounding) that often elicit emotional responses from listeners are incorporated, consequently developing into friction among the talkers. When this takes place (*MM*, 141, 161), a new side of Big Sweet's assertive individualism emerges. Her verbal mannerisms show her to be both aggressive and defensive, a genius of verbal technique for self-preservation. Her unique style of verbally negotiating for respect from men commences in a truly functional way.

Understanding the delicate nature of her presence among men who often are inclined to employ hyperbolic loose talk in a style called signifying, wherein they exploit and indirectly scorn or humiliate a woman in their midst, Big Sweet is ever on verbal guard for such an infraction. This is one reason why friction develops at times during the storytelling between her and Sam, Joe Willard, Jim Allen and Arthur. In one instance, Big Sweet aims not to be exploited or disrespected by

Sam as she establishes her verbal territory about Brer Rabbit. She warns that other talkers are not to steal her ideas, and she grows angry when she senses that Sam intends to do so anyway. Her boldness is apparent when she stops the tale and draws the conversation back to reality with the use of emphatic figurative language addressed to Sam: "When Ah'm shellin' my corn, you keep out yo' nubbins, Sam," (*MM,* 141).

In another case, Big Sweet's spunkiness and bold tongue are obvious when she adapts another speech style to her personal advantage during the storytelling. She redirects talk about animals and personal ownership back to the reality of her relationship with Joe Willard, just as Sack Daddy feels obliged to do in recounting his personal experiences about a cat he once owned (*MM,* 161). As the Polk County folk are bent on suitoring—women claiming ownership of working men in the camp as their mate—Big Sweet senses an opportune moment to assert her claim on Joe in the presence of the entire male community at a time when they are not distracted by work and other real problems of the job. Talk is drawn into the boundary of reality and Big Sweet employs the verbal technique of specifying (a way of stating a true fact about a person in his presence in an indirect metaphorical manner) as a means of publicly cautioning Joe about his moonlighting with Ella Wall, the Queen of Sex among men on the job. By way of this public broadcasting technique of indirect signifying, Big Sweet asserts her authority as Joe's woman, voicing both her dissatisfaction with him and the possibility of impending retribution: "And speakin' 'bout hams (cut in Big Sweet meaningly) if Joe Willard don't stay out of dat bunk he was in last night, Ah'm gointer sprinkle some salt down his back and sugar-cure his hams" (*MM,* 161).

Coupled with her verbal assertions, Big Sweet uses body language for total effect by "standing sidewise looking at Joe most pointedly" (*MM,* 161) as she awaits his acceptance or rejection of her challenge. She is prepared for action. Joe also realizes the seriousness of the matter and escapes her wrath through a shrewd evasion, accusing Big Sweet of trying to signify (this time meaning that she is trying to show off): "Aw, woman, quit trying to signify" (*MM,* 161). But Big Sweet is a woman of truth, and she pursues the matter further by fully asserting her right to talk: "Ah kin signify all Ah please, Mr. Nappy-chin, so long as Ah know what Ah'm talkin' about" (*MM,* 161). Feeling bold in her talk, Big Sweet even cunningly insults Joe with her name-calling of him as a "Mr. Nappy-chin." Here she is serious as she pokes fun at the nappy or kinky hair comprising the beard covering his chin. She knows well that it's not good etiquette to make fun of a Black person's "bad" or coarse textured hair where ever it appears on the body. Big Sweet's indirect insult exhibits a close affinity to the dozens, the verbal ritual of ridicule of an individual or of female members of his family, most notably the mother.

The tension between the challenging words by Big Sweet and the evasiveness by Joe subsequently draw in the crowd as Joe talks in a broad and general manner about the ways of women: "See dat? We git a day off and figger we kin ketch some fish and enjoy ourselves, but naw, some wimmens got to drag behind us, even to the lake" (*MM*, 162). Big Sweet is not to be outdone in the talking game of indirect insult; she asserts herself further by announcing that she is surely the possessor and guardian of her man, despite Joe's antics of denial. Unlike other Polk County women of careless temporary love, she feels a permanent attachment to Joe and she employs the technique of specifying (stating explicitly a point of view) to explain to him the basis of her claim: "You didn't figger Ah was draggin' behind you when you was bringin' dat Sears and Roebuck catalogue over to my house and beggin' me to choose my ruthers. Lemme tell *you* something, *any* time Ah shack up wid any man Ah gives myself de privilege to go where ever he might be, night or day. Ah got de law in my mouth" (*MM*, 162). This bold possessiveness is Big Sweet's way of establishing respectable recognition for herself in the male community as Joe's rightful partner in love. Her verbal technique in directly establishing ownership of Joe is so well executed that it merits praise from Wiley, who remarks, "Lawd, ain't she specifying'!" (*MM*, 162).

The most dramatic scene of the storytelling ritual occurs when Big Sweet adeptly decodes the various expressive speech styles of the men talkers. As they talk, their topics move away from pure animal tales to people-oriented stories that are closely linked to immediate life situations. As she listens, Big Sweet suspects one of the talkers is using the technique of signifying in a most negative fashion so as to insult and ridicule her under the cover of a plain folktale. In this context, signifying is defined as a way of indirectly insulting or shaming a person by speaking about him to others through the protective cover of coded speech. If the listener is unaware of this style of talk, she is belittled in good fashion as the two levels of language co-exist at her expense. In this case, however, Big Sweet is on the alert and rather quick-tempered when the lying contest borders on intentionally insulting talk. She is too wise to let insults go unchallenged once a talker willfully exceeds the limits of play.

Old Man Allen's signifying is a case in point when he joins Joe Willard in general talk about the habits of women. Still angry about Big Sweet's boldly laying claim to him before the gathering of men who know of his illicit affairs, Willard protests bitterly yet discreetly. On safe verbal ground, he signifies at Big Sweet, but unlike Old Man Allen, he does it subtly by making a broad philosophical observation about the speech habits of Black people: "Lawd, my people, my people, as de monkey said. You fool wid Aunt Hagar's chillun and they'll sho distriminate you and put yo' name in de streets" (*MM*, 162). Old Man Allen, representative perhaps of the old school of thought about the Black woman and the fact that she is only to be seen and spoken of, but not heard, is less restrained in his talk about man's fate at the hands of two similar creatures, a woman or a cow: "Well, you know what they say —a man can cackerlate his life till he git mixed up wid a woman or git straddle of a cow" (*MM*, 162).

Detecting more than literal surface meaning, Big Sweet is angered and addresses herself to the hidden implications in Old Man Allen's signifying. She interprets his saying as being close to an insult with the magnitude of the dozens, a blow to her respectability as woman and person, and a further slur to her mother for birthing a cow rather than a daughter. Big Sweet turns viciously upon the old man—without due respect for his age—for shrewdly playing the dozens interfaced with the technique of signifying, brandishing her own style of namecalling and challenging his choice of words: "Who you callin' a cow, fool? Ah know you ain't namin' my mama's daughter no cow" (*MM*, 162).

Big Sweet is now ready for a battle of word and fist as she awaits an explanation for Allen's blatant show of disrespect. Allen's reply is a defensive, almost pleading one of self-preservation, as he overlooks Big Sweet's depiction of him as a fool and defuses her rage by explaining the linguistic context from which he takes the reference, "cow": "Now all y'all heard what Ah said. Ah ain't called nobody no cow. Dat's just an old time by-word 'bout no man kin tell what's gointer happen when he gits mixed up wid a woman or set straddle of a cow. I done heard my gran' paw say dem very words many and many a time. There's a whole heap of them kinda by-words. . . . They all got a hidden meanin', jus' like de Bible. Everybody can't understand what they mean. Most people is thin-brained. They's born wid they feet under de moon. Some folks is born wid they feet on de sun and they kin seek out de inside meaning of words" (*MM*, 163). Allen engages in successful plea-bargaining, so to speak, in order to protect his own neck in a manner similar to the wise-talking Uncle July whose diversionary tale about Cock Robin's death on Beale Street causes him to lose verbal ground with A'nt Dooby when she politely listens to the evasive designed tale and then demands his week's wages. Perhaps guilty of the violation of name-calling against Big Sweet, Allen wisely becomes a practitioner of the old-time deceptive ritual of laughing and talking to keep danger at arm's length. He cleverly ends his misunderstanding with Big Sweet by returning to the safe confines of the storytelling ritual with a man sitting straddle a cow (*MM*, 163). The point to be addressed here is not so much the fact that Big Sweet may be at fault in misinterpreting Allen's possibly innocent talk, but rather the commendable way she defends her integrity by combating the potential insult. In the process of negotiating and maintaining respect, a woman must never allow a male talker to verbally dominate or insult her, even within the confines of play ritual talk. She is ever on the defensive when language borders on reality and insult. This is important because once a weakness in her verbal stature is unravelled, a male talker will continuously exploit it, as happens with such weak women talkers as Dicey, Mrs. Tony, Lucy (of Polk County) and Good Bread. In the folklore, Good Bread is exemplary (*MM*, 205–206). She is the opposite of Big Sweet in combating the insults of signifying talk. Like Matt Bonner's old mule, she is a constant target of derision, proving herself to be inadequate in the ability to decode the insulting language of the dozens.

In the storytelling episode between Mack, Christopher Jenkins, Mah Honey and Hurston, Good Bread is ineffective in countering the barrage of insults to her womanhood. The male talkers know that she is not assertive or overly outspoken, so they antagonize her when Mack starts the verbal round by signfying at her in an indirect way with the question of why both the little slim women and the big fat women were put on earth (*MM*, 205). Mack's answer seems to be an intended slur or crack at Good Bread's obvious rotund size. She is the only big woman there, so it is obvious to all that he is boldly alluding to her when he provides Hurston with an answer as to why fat women were put on earth: "To show dese slim girls how far they kin stretch without bustin'" (*MM*, 205). All of the talkers laugh, indicating that his point is well-taken, even though Good Bread, feeling offended by Mack's sly way of ridiculing her size, turns angry.

An unskilled talker, Good Bread falters miserably as she attempts to establish a plausible verbal defense and negotiate respect for herself. A barrage of unflattering insults about her looks and body shape (the most poignant way to verbally scorn an opponent in Hurston's art) are levelled by the gang of men once she starts a weak challenge to Mack— a challenge that they all know she is incapable of backing up with effective words or weapons. Consider, for example, Mack's and Mah Honey's attack as the talk moves from the confines of the initial process of indirect signifying to open criticism and real hostility against her:

> Mack: Jus' cause you done set round and growed ruffles around yo' hips nobody can't mention fat 'thout you makin' out they talkin' bout you. Ah wuzn't personatin' yuh, but if de cap fit yuh, wear it.
> Good Bread: G'wan Mack, you knows dat a very little uh yo' sugar sweetens mah tea. Don't git me started.
> Mack: Gwan start something if dats de way yuh feel. You kin be stopped. Now you tryin' to make somebody believe you so bad till you have tuh tote uh pistol tuh bed tuh keep from gettin' in uh fight wid yo self! You got mo' poison in yuh than dat snake dat wuz so poison tell he bit de railroad track and killed de train, hunh (*MM*, 205–206)?

Mah Honey joins the verbal attack with laughing scorn and insults of the dozens directed at Good Bread's womahood: "Tain't nothin' tuh her. She know she ugly. She look lak de deveil ground up in pieces. . . . Hey, lady, you got all you' bust in de back" (*MM*, 206)!

Unlike the weak Good Bread, Big Sweet surely would handle such signifying insults differently, as it is in her nature not to be verbally overpowered by any combatant in the talking game. Even as the episode of the lying ritual with the swamp gang ends, she is at the center of the talk as she maintains a level of respectability in the male community. She culminates the storytelling experience with her own brand of specifying (meaning here to state directly an idea as opposed to indirectly hinting or implying it through signifying) when she is advised by the men not to fight Joe, their leader. She states rather explicitly in graphic and crisp words the range of her power and might if Joe proves himself unfaithful again: "Well, if Joe Willard try to take dese few fish he done caught where he shacked up last night, Ah'm gointer take my Tampa switch-blade knife, and Ah'm goin' 'round de hambone lookin' for meat . . . Ah been baptized, papa, and Ah wouldn't mislead you" (*MM,* 178).

Big Sweet speaks here with the law of authority in her mouth regarding her claim to Joe and she is prepared to back up her word power with a fist fight, as all the men well know. To avoid the possibility of a fight between the two lovers if Joe challenges her, Gene Oliver tactfully changes the subject and, with Joe Wiley, forecasts another and different approaching confrontation for Big Sweet. They specify about the impending big showdown between Big Sweet and Ella Wall over possession or ownership of Joe:

> Gene: Hey, hey! Big Moose done come down from de mountain. Ah'm gointer be at dat jook tonight to see what Big Sweet and Ella Wall gointer talk about.
> Joe Wiley: Me too. De time is done come where big britches gointer fit lil'l Willie (meaning things have come to critical pass).
> Larkins: Oh, wese all gointer be there. Say Big Sweet, don't let de 'gator beat you to de pond (meaning don't be out-done, or don't be too slow), do he'll give you mo' trouble than de day is long (*MM,* 178).

Chapter 5

Big Sweet and the Talk Experience in the Jook

In the jook scenes of *Mules and Men* (185–201 and 220–229), several additional aspects of Big Sweet's assertive individualism come to light. Amidst all of the dramatic action of the jook—the singing, dancing, card playing, and throbbing piano music—Big Sweet's character prevails in a natural way. She is not bent on making herself a heroine, or becoming a woman with a bad reputation for killing, like many other lesser known jook women; but rather she desires to be her simple self while having fun. She proves herself to be a damned sweet woman, a good love, who can jook, sing the blues, and dance to the crowd's satisfaction. As well, she is variously friend or foe to other jook women as the reader of *Mules and Men* obtains a first glimpse of her in communication with fellow jookers. She can decipher the antagonistic verbal language of intimidation (bulldozin' as it is locally called in the lexicon of the jook world, *MM*, 194) and name calling engaged in by rivals, Lucy and Ella, who have established a name for themselves as being "bad." With these foes, Big Sweet's skill at talking and fighting is captured in dramatic encounters of woman-to-woman violence never before recorded to my knowledge in Black folklore.

Among her fluent abilities is her mastery of the winning techniques of talk that accompany card playing. The card game is accompanied by dynamic language and hand movements by players. It is a little drama in itself within the jook and functions as one of the liveliest and most spirited activities in Big Sweet engages. In the Florida skin game, she assertively holds her own and has no misgivings about loudly voicing her displeasure with a male member of the jook, as she does when she feels offended by the loud nasal tones of Texas Red. When he stands behind her and inadvertently sings in her ear while watching the game, Big Sweet boldly sounds off in a condescending and threatening voice: "Did somebody hit yuh tuh start yuh? 'Cause if dey did Ah'm goin' ter hit yuh to stop yuh" (*MM*, 187). Waiting for Texas Red to call her bold bluff, Big Sweet is ready for action. In her moment of victory, she and Texas Red engage in non-verbal communication, a use of body language that is locally called "eyeballing" (*MM*, 187) as Texas Red backs away: "His eyes fell lower. Her knife was already open, so he strolled on off" (*MM*, 187).

Big Sweet also asserts her individualism as a skilled card player when she takes her place in the game—a game usually played strictly by strong, fighting men of the jook. She actively participates in the call/response pattern of verbal exchange between the dealer and other players (*MM*, 185–187). Observe, for instance, Big Sweet's verbal exchange with the dealer as the game begins:

> Dealer: You want a card, Big Sweet?
> Big Sweet: Yeah, Ah wanta scoop one in de rough.
> Dealer: Aw right, yo' card is gointer cost you a dollar. Put yo'
>   money on de wood and make de bet go good and then again,
>   put yo' money in sight and save a fight (*MM*, 187–188).

Big Sweet draws a card from the deck and puts it face up beside her, with a dollar bill. The play continues as the dealer deals cards from the deck and converses in a sing-song style with Hardy and Larkins. The singing of Jenkins accompanies the play as the dealer takes verbal command and charge of the card play. As the dealer sings, he arranges the cards so he can deal winning cards to himself and losing cards to others. His singing power helps to capture his competitors and avert early detection of his cheating:

> Let de deal go down, boys.
> Let de deal go down.
> When yo' card gits lucky, oh padner:
> You ought to be in a rollin' game.
> (Each of the lines is punctuated by "hah!" and a falling card) (*MM*, 188).

As the game intensifies with the singing and exchange of cards between the dealer and players, Big Sweet gets a turn. She appears to be a wise, confident player, bent on winning. She asserts herself in a brazen and intimidating manner as she beckons the players to make sizable bets. Observe her rapport with the dealer and players in the following interchanges during card play:

> Big Sweet: De four (card she holds) says a dollar mo.
>
> Dealer: Oh hell and brothers! Ah'm strictly a two-bit man.
>
> Big Sweet: (Arrogantly) You full of dat ole ism blood. Fat covered yo' heart. Youse skeered to bet. Gamblin' wid yo' stuff out de window.
>
> Dealer: Dollar mo!
>
> Hardy: Hell broke loose in Georgy!
>
> Big Sweet: Ah mean to carry y'all to Palatka and bring yuh back by de way of Winter Park.
>
> Hardy: Big Sweet, Ah don't b'lieve Ah'll see yo' raise.
>
> Big Sweet: Oh G'wan and bet. You got mo' sense than me. Look at dem damn kidneys all over yo' head. (Now singing)
> Ain't had no trouble, Lawd padner
> Till Ah stop by here.
>
> Dealer: Take it and cry, children. (His card falls.) Dey sent me out by de way of Sandusky. Lemme see kin Ah find me a clean card.
>
> Big Sweet: Ah caught you guilty lyin'! Make a bet and tell a lie about it.
>
> Hardy: He done cocked a face card. Look out we don't ketch you guilty.
>
> Big Sweet: He got de cards in his hand.
>
> Hardy: Dat's me. Ah thought dat card was in Bee-luther-hatches.
>
> Dealer: Tell de truth and stay in de church! Ah'm from down in Ginny-Gall where they eat cow-belly, skin and all. Big Sweet, everybody fell but you. You must be setting on roots.
>
> Big Sweet: Nope, Ah got my Joe Moore in my hair (*MM*, 189–190).

At this point of the card game, Big Sweet becomes more assertive and formidable as she suspects cheating by the dealer. Her demeanor in the following dialogue indicates she's ready to reprimand him when he brags of his power with the cards:

> Dealer: Well, Ah got de cards. I can cheat if I want to and beat you anyway.

> Big Sweet: You mess wid dem cards and see if Ah do't fill you full
> of looky-deres.
> Hardy: Whut a looky-dere?
> Big Sweet: A knot on yo' head so big till when you go don de
> street everybody will point at it and say 'Looky-dere'.
> Dealer: (His card falls.) Ah'm hot as seven hells.
> Big Sweet: Ah played de last card. Ah don't tell lies all de time.
> Now, you rich son of a bitch, pay off.
> Larkins: God! She must be sittin' on roots! Luck is a fortune (*MM*,
> 190).

Big Sweet's persuasive talk and teasing of the dealer and other players
set the stage for her eventual winning of the game. The men respect her
card playing repertoire and know not to try and cheat her. She always
wins on all counts and in the process of reigning supreme even in the
traditionally male dominated card playing games, she proves herself to
be the mistress of talk even in the oral ritual of card game play, a feat
many of her female acquaintances could not accomplish. She, indeed,
has the law of authority in her mouth when she speaks the language of
card play with the men.

   Another illustration of Big Sweet's assertive individualism in the
jook occurs in her confrontation with two women rivals of the jook,
Ella Wall and Lucy, the first time violence is depicted between women
in the jook, or Black fun house which Hurston calls the capital of
Negro theatre in America. Violence between women in rivalry over a
man is a common occurrence in the jook, and the showdown over
ownership of Joe Willard dramatizes this point. Each party must prove
herself before the crowd of onlookers; her reputation and personal sense
of self-respect depend on this performance. When Ella Wall and Lucy
enter the jook, for example, they aim to build a reputation for
themselves by shaming or "scoring on" Big Sweet, the recognized
queen of the jook and declared mistress of Joe Willard. Ella Wall and
Lucy appear ill-equipped for winning the battle, however, as they utilize
devious verbal techniques of signifying, loudtalking, whispering and
bulldozia (a form of intimidating talk to arouse Big Sweet's temper
although they do not speak her name or address themselves directly to
her).

   Unskilled talkers and fighters, as they later prove themselves to be,
Ella Wall and Lucy are verbal cowards, lacking a sufficiently aggressive
speech demeanor and the bold courage and spunk to put their feet upon

Big Sweet's doorstep. Rather, in the strategy they display on entering the jook to lay claim to Joe Willard, they employ indirect speech styles as a protective shield against the wrath of their opponent, so that like the shrewd talkers, Old Man Allen and Mack, they can claim they were not speaking about Big Sweet. Such a tactic is risky with Big Sweet, however, as they prove themselves unprepared to freely talk their mind. As one of the jookers suggests, they are merely filled with "plenty of propaganda" (*MM*, 190) as they hide for a while under the protective cover of signifying with its dual meanings and indirect tones. Big Sweet is such a genius of speech styles in the jook that she eventually unravels their deceptive speech and prepares herself for a talking and fighting showdown with them. She is a realist and pragmatist in her talk, applying it to negotiate social respect from her enemies and to maintain ownership of her man.

In the first encounter with Ella and Lucy (*MM*, 224–227), Big Sweet draws on her expertise with fists and weapons. The initial verbal confrontation reveals Big Sweet responding in kind to Ella's malevolent talk and body mannerisms as Ella later enters the jook and makes a "show" for attention with loudtalking and signifying. Ella becomes the center of attention, revealing her disrespect for Big Sweet by indirectly ridiculing and (under the guise of signifying talk) hurling slurs at Big Sweet in front of onlookers. Hurston (the participant and scientist-observer) senses imminent trouble erupting as she describes the change in the mood of the once lively and friendly jook to one of tense silence as Ella Wall and Lucy stroll in by creating an attention-getting ruckus:

> Ella Wall flung a loud laugh back over her shoulder as she flourished in. Everybody looked at her, then they looked at Big Sweet. Big Sweet looked at Ella, but she seemed not to mind. The air was as tight as a fiddle string. Ella wrung her hips to the Florida-flip game. Big Sweet stayed on at the skin game but didn't play. Joe Willard, knowing the imminence of forthright action, suddenly got deep into the crap game. Lucy came in the door with a bright gloat in her eyes and went straight to Ella. So far as speaking was concerned she didn't see Big Sweet, but she did flirt past the skin game once, overcome with merriment (*MM*, 190–191).

Big Sweet is wise about the motives behind the showy signifying technique and remains in control of the situation as she analyzes for

Hurston the exact meaning of the behavior of her rivals, voicing in a
direct statement of fact her remedy for combatting it:

> Dat li'l narrer contracted piece uh meatskin gointer make me
> stomp her right now! De two-faced heifer! Been hangin' 'round me
> so she kin tote news to Ella. If she don't look out she'll have on
> her last clean dress befo' de crack of day. She mad 'cause Ah dared
> her to jump you. She don't lak Slim always playing JOHN HENRY
> for you. She would have done cut you to death if Ah hadn't of took
> and told her. . . . She know Ah backs yo' fallin'. She know if
> she scratch yo' skin Ah'll kill her so dead till she can't fall.
> They'll have to push her over. Ella Wall look lak she tryin' to
> make me kill her too, flourishin' dat ole knife 'round. But she
> oughter know de man date made one, made two. She better not
> vary, do Ah'll be all over her jus' lak gravy over rice (*MM*,191).

A loyal friend to Hurston and a foe to Lucy and Ella, Big Sweet
does not intend to let their boasting go unchallenged, proving her point
by saying that she doesn't mind dying or killing. As her cronies well
know, it is characteristic of Big Sweet's assertive nature to confront the
two signifiers at any moment she chooses. Being a fair opponent in the
talking and fighting game, however, she allows her antagonists a
chance to stop the dangerous play. She therefore observes and listens,
not taking immediate action. But as the signifying intensifies with
more blatant stabs at her integrity, her temper reaches its limits. This is
the case when Ella and Lucy begin eyeballing Big Sweet and "shoo-
shooing" (*MM*,191) or whispering and laughing loudly. The drama
escalates as Ella is encouraged in her devious play by someone singing
a jook or blues tribute to her:

> Go to Ella Wall
> Oh, go to Ella wall
> If you want good boody (sex)
> Oh, go to Ella Wall
> Oh, she's long and tall
> Oh, she's long and tall
> And she rocks her rider
> From uh wall to wall
> Oh, go to Ella Wall
> Take yo' trunk and all—(*MM*, 192).

Ella Wall then brags and loud talks about her popularity with the men—another way of downplaying Big Sweet's status in the jook and influence over Joe. Ella further snaps her finger, revolves her hips and reports: "Tell 'em 'bout me! I'm raggedy, but right; patchy but tight; stringy, but I will hang on" (*MM,* 192). Big Sweet understands the intent of Ella's technique of implying a slur against her and explains in clear words the meaning of it to Hurston: "Look at her puttin' out her brags. Loud-talkin' de place. But countin' from yo' little finger back to the thumb; if she start anything Ah got her some" (*MM,* 192). Big Sweet is prepared for a direct altercation if Ella signifies again. The spring blade knife is not yet open as Ella mocks Big Sweet's size, directly disrespecting Big Sweet by engaging in insulting name-calling: "Hey, bigger-than-me!" (*MM,* 193). Angered, Big Sweet in turn demeans Ella to Hurston: "Didn't dat storm-buzzard throw a slam at me?" (*MM,* 193). But Hurston lies to maintain peace. Ella, on the other hand, though, is not satisfied without a reply from Big Sweet, returning to the technique of loudtalking to slyly challenge Big Sweet's might as a fighter. This time Ella boastfully refers to Big Sweet as "nothin" (*MM,* 193) when she remarks in a supposedly indirect fashion: "'Taint nothin' to her. She ain't hit me yet" (*MM,* 193). Big Sweet prepares for action. Ella is not to besmirch her reputation in full view of the crowd. At Ella's next verbal thrust, Big Sweet will counter with direct action.

A direct exchange between the two begins when Ella disregards Big Sweet's power of authority over Joe and lays public claim to him herself. Hurston recounts the drama of this confrontation as Ella's loudtalk and sly dozens' insults arouse Big Sweet's rage:

> Ella crowded her luck. She yelled out, "Lucy, tell Mr. Lots-of-Papa Joe Willard Ah say come here. Jus' tell 'im his weakness want 'im. He know who dat is." Lucy started across. Ella stood up akimbo, but everybody knew she was prepared to back up her brag with cold steel in some form, or she wouldn't have been there talking like she was. A click beside me and I knew that the spring blade knife that Big Sweet carried was open (*MM,* 193).

Big Sweet is about to reestablish the fact that she is Joe's woman. In response to Ella's specifying emphatically that Joe, her Mr. Lots-of-Papa, is her property, Big Sweet spurts out her own verbal fireworks as she orders Lucy to halt and keep her distance from Joe: "Stop right

where you is, Lucy, lessen you want to see yo' Jesus" (*MM,* 193).
Angry, Big Sweet adeptly turns Ella's specifying language against her:
"Maybe Ah ain't nothin'. What you sendin' her for? Why don't you go
yo' self? Dere she is." Ella meets the challenge with bold talk, once
again: "Well, Ah kin go, now"(*MM,* 193–194). Big Sweet steps
forward right in Ella's path, assuming a formidable stance and taunting
her to fight: "Ah can't hear what you say for yo' damn teeth rattlin'.
Come on!" (*MM,* 194). Ella is saved from meeting certain death at Big
Sweet's hands when the Quarters Boss with his .45 on his hip and
another gun in his hand mediates the dispute.

Big Sweet's response to the Quarters Boss's intervention further
supports the point that Big Sweet is a totally assertive woman not
bound by the politics of skin color or white power. She maintains her
assertive individuality even when conversing with whites who have
historically used their oppressive power to keep Blacks in their verbal
place. Blacks were not to assert themselves before whites; rather, they
were simply to follow commands. Big Sweet does not submit to verbal
obedience and docility when the Quarters Boss, or white Law Enforcer,
appears. Dialogue with him shows her true unchanging verbal
disposition and her continuation of the process of negotiating respect
from a verbal opponent—who happens now to be white.

In upholding her humanity, she is as characteristically Big Sweet
here as she is when speaking to the swamp gang or to Ella Wall, who,
on the other hand, is a weak verbal voice in conversation with the
Quarters Boss. Here, Ella's verbal disposition with white presence
reveals an obvious change from her boastful talk with rival, Big Sweet.
Ella no longer draws on the bold talk of signifying or bulldozia to
express her views. She retreats from this posture to a typical Jim Crow
style where she mumbles to the Quarters Boss, while Big Sweet
maintains the stature of skillful, loud talker with the law in her mouth.
Big Sweet appears to be more a symbol of authoritarian power than the
Quarters Boss once conversation commences. Observe, for example, the
following interchange between Big Sweet, Ella and the Quarters Boss,
as he intercedes in the on-going feud between the women:

> Quarters Boss: What's the matter here, y'all? Big Sweet, what you
>   mean tuh do wid that knife?
> Big Sweet: Ahm jus' 'bout tuh send God two niggers. Come in here
>   bulldozin' me.

> Quarters Boss: (Pointing at Ella) What the hell you doin' in here wid weapons? You don't belong on this job nohow. Git the hell outa here and that quick. This place is for people that works on this job. Git! Somebody'll be in Barton jail in twenty minutes.
>
> Big Sweet: You don't need tuh run her off, Cap'n. Ah can git her tuh go. Jus' you stand back and gimme lief. She done stepped on mah starter and Ahm rearin' tuh go. If God'll send me uh pistol Ah'll send 'im uh man!
>
> Quarters Boss: You ain't gonna kill nobody right under mah nose. Gimme that knife you got dere, Big Sweet (*MM*, 193–194).

Unlike the silent Ella, Big Sweet stands her verbal ground and refuses the Quarters Boss's request, as it violates her personal principle of demonstrating authority by using a weapon. As talking and fighting go hand in hand in her scheme of survival, she will not relinquish her knife to anyone, not even the white boss or law enforcer. She tells the Quarters Boss in a stern voice: "Naw suh! Nobody gits *mah* knife. Ah bought it for dat storm-buzzard over dere and Ah means tuh use it on her, too. As long as uh mule go bareheaded, she better not part her lips tuh me. Do Ah'll kill her, law or no law. Don't you touch me, white folks" (*MM*, 194)! Ella's response to Big Sweet's specifying about the purpose for keeping her knife is not as firm or dramatic, "Aw she ain't so bad! (Ella sneered as she wrung her lips toward the door.) She didn't kill Jesse James" (*MM*, 194), at which point the Quarters Boss takes the opportunity to scold her severely and order her off the job: "Git on 'way from here! Lessen yuh wanna make time in Barton jail. Git off these premises and that quick! Gimme that knife!" He took the knife and gave Ella a shove. She moved sullenly behind the crowd away from the door, mumbling threats (*MM*, 194–195).

By contrast, the Quarters Boss appears reserved and more cautious in his words of instruction to the awesome Big Sweet. He does not confront her in face-to-face talk; instead he speaks to her from a distance with the remark: "Now you behave yo' self, Big Sweet. Ah don't wanna hafta jail yuh" (*MM*, 195). Certainly, another verbal round with her would have ensued had he not been so circumspect. He thus acknowledges and respects her talking and fighting superiority as do the jookers like Joe Willard and Presley who praise her eminence in standing up to the white man:

Joe: You wuz noble! You wuz uh whole woman and half uh man.
You made dat Cracker stand offa you.
Presley: Who wouldn't? She got loaded muscles. You notice he
don't tackle Big Sweet lak he do de rest round here. Dat's
cause she ain't got uh bit better sense then tuh make 'im kill
her (*MM*, 195).

The Quarters Boss is absent from the jook when the second and
final confrontation develops between Lucy and Big Sweet (*MM*, 224–
227). Appropriately, it occurs on pay night, a time which means either
a killing or two or a big fight. It is an occasion when the jookers
celebrate the experience of having money to lavish. Men usually lay
claim to women with money. Women also aim to improve their
popularity by voicing possession of a man, or by killing a rival so as
to establish a reputation as a killer. Such is Lucy's purpose as she tries
to gain fame by attacking Hurston, Big Sweet's friend who has
penetrated the male community in search of folklore material.

The pay night in the jook culminates with Big Sweet's exhibition
of her fighting prowess as she battles Lucy, particularly when Lucy
resists Big Sweet's verbal technique of "putting her foot on Lucy's
doorstep." With a powerful tongue in a bold conversation with Lucy,
Big Sweet warns her not to "steal" or jump Hurston from behind; if she
does, Big Sweet aims to kill her. Big Sweet does not want her friend,
Hurston, to be a scapegoat for Lucy to build her image upon. Big
Sweet is a better target.

As the events unfold, Lucy begins her plan to attack Hurston when
Big Sweet appears to be absent from the jook. She is momentarily the
center of attention as she takes verbal command of the jook with the
yelled order: "Stop dat music. Don't vip another vop till Ah say so! Ah
means tuh turn dis place out right now. Ah got de law in mah mouf"
(*MM*, 227). She thinks herself the voice of power, now ready to back
up her words with a switchblade as she eyes her prey and walks hippily
toward Hurston prepared for the kill. But Big Sweet, the trickster that
she is in this scene, appears from her darkened hiding place in the jook
and challenges Lucy's threats. She beckons Lucy on to fight her as the
battle heats up. Big Sweet proves herself to be a mighty warrior as she
battles Lucy with her knife, thus turning the jook from the drama of a
pleasure house into a violent battlefield. In the following passage,
Hurston graphically describes the unfolding chain of events as Big
Sweet resorts to direct action:

A flash from the corner around ten feet off and Lucy had something else to think about besides me. Big Sweet was flying at her with an open blade and now it was Lucy's time to make it to the door. Big Sweet kicked her somewhere about the knees and she fell. A double back razor flew thru the air very close to Big Sweet's head. Crip, the new skitter man, had hurled it. It whizzed past Big Sweet and stuck in the wall; then Joe Willard went for Crip. Jim Presley punched me violently and said, "Run you chile! Run and Ride! Dis is gointer be uh nasty ditch. Lucy had been feedin' Crip under rations tuh git him tuh help her. Run clear off dis job! Some uh dese folks goin' tuh judgment and some goin' tuh jail. Come on, less run!" Slim stuck out the guitar to keep two struggling men from blocking my way. Lucy was screaming. Crip had hold of big Sweet's clothes in the back and Joe was slugging him loose. Curses, oaths, cries and the whole place was in motion. Blood was on the floor (*MM*, 227).

So concludes the jook section of *Mules and Men* with plenty of dramatic action which Hurston describes as an essential element of Black life in the essay, "Characteristics of Negro Expression." The dramatic qualities of the jook life are revealed largely through the character of Big Sweet in her formidable image as assertive voice and skillful fighter. Her talking and fighting skills amplify her assertive individualism.

Chapter 6

Big Sweet in *Polk County*

In the play, *Polk County*,[1] Hurston maintains Big Sweet's assertive individualism, but shows her using it in a more structured and less violent manner. Big Sweet guides the Polk County folk into a well-ordered society of people unified in a series of marriage relationships. There is no longer the divisiveness or temporary careless love identifiable with the Polk County folk as represented in the folklore anthology. Where *Mules and Men* ends with Big Sweet embroiled in a violent demonstration of her assertive individualism, *Polk County* closes with a peaceful illustration of her character. There is peace between her and the folk as they unite as neighbors and friends, celebrating love and communal spirit in a marriage ceremony. She appears far more of a peacemaker, a creator of the Rainbow of life and brotherhood, than a violent enforcer of law and order.

An examination of the play (which Hurston wrote in collaboration with Dorothy Waring in 1944, nine years after the publication of *Mules and Men*) will further illustrate Hurston's extensive representation of Big Sweet's character in dramatic form. Big Sweet's talent as assertive voice grows to positive fruition as she speaks with constructive persuasion as community leader and organizer of the folk. She so restructures individual and community values that, by the end of the play, her renewed Polk County can almost be likened to Hurston's own hometown of Eatonville. Her strong qualities of leadership enable her to demonstrate the more positive ramifications of an assertive female voice in the Black community—a community long dominated by male voices of authority. Big Sweet's leadership is most apparent in the representation of her multi-faceted character in each of the three acts of the play. The play centers on a devious plot by three troublemakers—

Nunkie, Dicey and Ella Wall—who conspire to overthrow Big Sweet, thereby neutralizing her power as the strong voice in the Quarters. Each feels victimized by Big Sweet for some reason and seeks revenge through ploys ranging from the writing of a bogus letter about her unfaithfulness to Lonnie, gossiping to the Quarters Boss about her troublemaking on the job, to procuring a hoodoo dance and evil spell to "fix" her into submission before them as a weakling they can overpower and eventually kill. But in a strong display of her talking and fighting experience, coupled with a show of unified help from her comrades and other folk on the job, Big Sweet prevails, while the troublemakers are finally banished for good at gunpoint by the Quarters Boss. The message of the play (a far contrast to that of the Polk County action in *Mules and Men*) seems to be that the forces of communal and domestic good will remain intact once evil and wrongdoing are eliminated.

The play operates around several inter-related themes, all of which focus on Hurston's dramatic representation of Big Sweet's image as skillful talker and effective fighter, although the latter quality so prominent in *Mules and Men* is minimized here. We see her fighting in just one major encounter with Nunkie in Act 1, Scene 1. Hurston primarily concentrates on the constructive merits of Big Sweet's leadership efforts as big voice, as protector and friend of the homeless and downtrodden, as spokeswoman for women on the "job," and as the true heartbeat and law enforcer or the real Quarters Boss of her community. To maintain order and respect for herself, she is prepared only as a last resort to kick heads and behinds. All of these qualities are revealed by Hurston through comedy and the dynamics of music (especially the blues expressive form). Big Sweet is viewed in scenes of song and dance and of high comedy balanced against intensely realistic scenes. Think here of her opening confrontation with Nunkie; it borders both on the hilarious and the serious as she beats him severely for misdeeds and insulting talk. For the most part, though, love, song and talk permeate Big Sweet's behavior as she fulfills her verbal allegiance to self and community, while simultaneously maintaining love ties with Lonnie. Only the evil acts of others cause her mean face to project itself through physical violence.

One of the main themes of the play centers on the question of the assertive woman's place as leader in the Black community. With her verbal power and accompanying leadership capabilities, the folk community can initiate a self-governing environment with little need for a white Quarters Boss or overseer. Big Sweet is capable of creating cohesiveness, harmony and brotherhood in the community at large, while fostering moral values in the home through the institution of marriage and family. If men work on "the job" in unity, they should also be capable of maintaining that oneness with their women folk in the home life world of the Quarters, Big Sweet believes. She aims to displace the ephemeral love relationshps on "the job" with marriage ceremonies symbolizing permanent love and meaningful attachments. Men will ask women for their "hand in marriage" instead of the usual "can you" request for temporary careless love. Abolished will be the old public announcements in song that men make about women and how easily they secure them at will: "Let every town furnish its own. It's a damn poor town that can't furnish its own. Take no woman anywhere."[2]

The relationship of Big Sweet and Lonnie (a man of ideas who dreams of peace and friendship as opposed to the roughness and violent disturbance so intrinsically a part of Polk County lifestyle) is the embodiment of the moral values and strong love Big Sweet envisions for all the men and women of Polk County. If the folk pattern their relationships after these two role models, the Quarters will be a loving and harmonious place to live and work. As well, My Honey and Leafy Lee, lovers united in music, feeling, and spirit, are also examples of the new marriage relationship Big Sweet encourages.

A second major theme of the play (set in juxtaposition to Big Sweet's positive personal and moral values) is that of jealousy, self-hate and vindictiveness. These traits are treated from within the context of women and intraracial color prejudice. Hurston has ingeniously dealt with an aspect of color prejudice amongst Black women that is generated not by light-skinned women but instead by a dark-skinned one who hates her self and feels victimized by society at large, and particularly by her main competitor, the attractive bright-skinned woman. Dicey Long is the embodiment of such destructive characteristics and is her own worst enemy. She thinks her ability to hold on to a man is limited because of her color and because of the behavior of light-skinned mulatto women; but in fact her problems are the result of her own malign personality and inferiority complex.

Out of jealousy and hate of light-skinned Leafy Lee, Dicey seeks revenge for the loss of My Honey's affections. She is determined to cause trouble and enlists the aid of her evil companions, Nunkie and Ella Wall. The ploys originated by Dicey subsequently draw her into conflict with Big Sweet—a conflict which might best be described as a battle between the attractive and unattractive woman, and between the light and dark opposing forces of Black womanhood. Throughout the play, antagonism between Dicey and Big Sweet (who is also fair-skinned and attractive, despite her huge size) results from Dicey's claim of ownership of a handsome man like My Honey, a close friend of Big Sweet who is drawn to the attractive Leafy Lee and asks for her hand in marriage. The three acts, as they unfold, reveal the growing tension existing between the dark-skinned Dicey and the fair-skinned Big Sweet and Leafy Lee.

The verbal power and strong moralistic values of the light-skinned women eventually prevail while the dark-skinned women with their evil and hateful qualities succumb to crushing defeat and silence. They become the least effective talkers of substance and merit in the play, not because their associates are downright prejudiced toward them and their dark skin, but because of their own inabilities to come to terms with their Blackness in the midst of their own people where individuals are basically judged by character and not by looks or skin color. The opposing forces of dark and light, and evil and good, thus permeate the play as we observe Big Sweet and Dicey in ever-revolving conflict— one whose major force of opposition can be attributed to the color phenomenon and its varied meanings among Black women and their male counterparts. As the play opens, the reader learns of the positive qualities of two characters who represent the good qualities fostered in fair-skinned people, not because of their complexion but because of their basic good nature and resolve to defend themselves when wronged by an evil-natured person who happens to be dark skinned. Hurston's mulatto folk represented in the play are a far contrast to Mrs. Turner in *Their Eyes Were Watching God.* They do not show intraracial color prejudice toward their darker fellow man or woman. They are concerned, rather, with the business of living in their natural Blackness of speech, song and dance.

Act I, Scene 1 sets forth the character of Big Sweet and Lonnie juxtaposed with that of their rivals, Dicey and Nunkie. As the scene begins, we observe Lonnie using his singing skills (just one dimension of his leadership role among the men workers) in his work-related function as Shack Rouser—a watchman who patrols the shack community during the early morning hours and wakes the men, by way of loud wake-up songs, to prevent them from over sleeping after a night of fun at the jook. They are a unified group and they do not want to be separated as a result of tardiness on the job.

As the men congregate, more is learned about Lonnie's character. Although he expects goodness and fairness from his fellow man, Lonnie has been cheated out of a week's pay by an unscrupulous gambler, Nunkie. A dreamer, Lonnie is a non-violent man who envisions a Quarters free of violence and trouble, a place of peace and sunshine where he can happily sing of his day-dream like presence in it: "I ride the rainbow. Trouble will be over. Amen" (*Act I, Scene I,* 6). Lonnie is soft-spoken, the opposite of the outspoken Big Sweet who promptly corrects a moral wrong when she observes it. She speaks and acts with authority when she puts Lonnie's dreams of peace in motion. To get peace, she first eradicates evil by verbal or physical confrontation. Together, she and Lonnie are as united in their determination to establish a peaceful life in Polk County as they are in their love for each other. Big Sweet appears in this scene as Lonnie's protector, and when she discovers Nunkie's unfair exploitation of him in card playing, she goes on the offensive (*Act 1, Scene 1,* 12). Her talking and fighting skill immediately comes into play as she battles Nunkie.

Like all Polk County women, she is unconcerned about her outer appearance. She wears a man's felt hat set rakishly on her head; she smokes, and she cocks her legs up on a step in an un-ladylike posture while waiting to attack Nunkie. She is in an angry mood as she demands Lonnie's money be returned to her: "You know I don't allow none of you low-life-ted gamblers to hook Lonnie out of his money. Give it to me!" (*Act 1, Scene 1,* 13). When a sullen and sly Nunkie refuses her verbal orders, Big Sweet seizes him by the lapels of his coat and shows sternly that she's boss with a technique of dominance in the Black community called "buttoning one's opponent up." She has full control over him even to the point of figuratively dressing him up in her preferred style as a mother might take command of authority over an uncooperative child. Big Sweet is soundly at the helm as she admonishes Nunkie of his misdeeds. She treads on his private space by boldly taking authority over him, his private property, and his clothing or dress attire.

In complete command, Big Sweet shakes Nunkie violently and lands a terrific blow to his stomach as he attempts to secure a pocket knife and talk biggity. Bringing her fighting skills to bear, she kicks him hard and threatens to kill him if the money is not handed over (*Act*

I, Scene I, 479). But Nunkie demonstrates a survival plan of his own. He fakes injury at Big Sweet's hands and calls for help from onlookers. Well aware of his plan, however, Big Sweet goes into a frenzy and scolds him about play-acting death at her hands: "Dont you lay there all curled up like that! (Puts her foot on top of him and presses down to make him straighten up) Straighten up and die right! See? That's how so many lies gits out on me. They twist themselves all up and dies ugly, and then folks swear I kilt 'em like that. (Kicks Nunkie) You aint going to die a lie on me like that! Straighten up!" (*I, I,* 16) Big Sweet follows up her talk with a more deadly threat as the seriousness and humor of the scene are intermingled in characteristic Hurston style: "And I am going to kill him too. Old trashy breath and britches aint got no business beating folks out of money they worked hard for. Run get me my gun, Bunch! If God send me a pistol, I'll send him a man!" (*I, I,* 16). Terrified at Big Sweet's threat, Nunkie throws the money at Big Sweet's feet and jumps to his knees, but Big Sweet considers this a disrespectful act and knocks him down again, while drawing on more forceful talk: "Pick it up! You didn't get it off the ground did you? You got it out of Lonnie's hands. Pick it up! You aint going to discount me like that. Git up from there and place it in my hand" (*I, I,* 17). Nunkie finally hands over the money but not before Big Sweet does a bit of signifying about him, wherein she relegates him to the demeaning status of a broom whose sole purpose is to sweep away dirt: "I ought to beat you till your ears hang down like a Georgy mule for putting me to all this trouble. You aint no good for what you live, no how. Just like your no-count brother, Charlie. Git! Sweep clean! Broom!" (*I, I,* 17).

As in *Mules and Men*, the white Quarters Boss intervenes with gun in hand just at the crucial moment when Big Sweet's power is most imminent. It is his job to prevent the male work force from being killed off by the women, and he grows alarmed at Nunkie's ruffled condition. Nunkie (with the white man as his protector) lies that Big Sweet jumped and robbed him and the Quarters Boss chastises her for her meanness. At the same time that Big Sweet is prepared to either verbally challenge or even physically battle the Quarters Boss to get him to listen to the true facts of the situation with Nunkie, the crowd grows unified as it defends her by identifying Nunkie as an outsider who is not supposed to be on the job in the first place.

This announcement renders Nunkie virtually helpless at the hands of the Quarters Boss—a plight similar to his fate in Big Sweet's hands. But while he arrogantly shows disrespect for Big Sweet on the basis of color, he is humble and appears virtually helpless with the Quarters Boss. The Quarters Boss, a symbol of white authority that Nunkie fears, is at liberty to demean him more thoroughly than Big Sweet. A case in point occurs when the Quarters Boss handles him roughly as he discovers greasy cards and weapons in Nunkie's possession. Nunkie stands by helplessly as his money is taken and as he is threatened with jail for his misdeeds on the job. He subsequently pleads in the traditional Uncle Tom fashion of survival—a style of talk he does not address to Big Sweet: "Please, Cap'n. Lemme go this one time" (*I, I*,17). As the Quarters Boss instructs him to "Git," Nunkie survives the ordeal with a humble "Yassuh!" (*I, I*,17).

Although he escapes from both Big Sweet and the Quarters Boss without any real physical harm, he is personally weakened by the experience, his manhood "shamed" before the community. Somehow this poor image must be rectified if he is to retain a meaningful degree of respect in the Quarters community. Through further evil acts, he plans to re-establish credibility. To improve his image on the job, he steers clear of the Quarters Boss (a power he cannot overthrow with impunity) while at the same time he plots a revengeful act against Big Sweet, discovering in Dicey a willing partner. They hope to eliminate her from the community while at the same time elevating their reputation as bad, powerful people to be revered.

As two evil forces united solely by their dislike of Big Sweet and her combative style and assertive individualism on the job, Nunkie and Dicey are naturally attracted to each other. They are drawn to each other during Nunkie's first melee with Big Sweet during which Nunkie overhears sympathetic words from Dicey. She opposes everything Big Sweet does and engages in her own style of loudtalking, defending Nunkie when she comments: "Poor Nunkie hasn't done a thing" (*I, I*,20). Dicey does not dare accuse Big Sweet of wrongdoing in a direct or open fashion, so she mutters by signifying out loud: "Some folks thinks they is lord-god sitting by-god. They just love to 'buke and boss'" (*I, I,* 20). Big Sweet senses the indirect criticism and challenge to her authority and answers in kind to Dicey's smart talk and evil demeanor. She is ready to challenge Dicey to a fight, saying bluntly: "Who you personating, Dicey? You must of woke up with the Black-ass this morning" (*I, I,* 20). Do Dirty intervenes with an interpretation of Dicey's evil nature—scorning her in a manner similar to Mack's harsh criticism of Good Bread, a weak but overly pompous talker in *Mules and Men*—thus preventing Big Sweet from pursuing the matter further. A fist fight, challenging Dicey to back up her talk with physical action, certainly would have occurred had not Do Dirty taken the helm to alleviate potential violence initiated by Big Sweet who was prepared to back up her words with a fist fight.

Act I, Scene I is also important because it not only captures Big Sweet asserting her identity through various forms of talk with her Black rivals, but it also reveals her in crucial conversation with the gun-toting Quarters Boss, her main white rival for power over the folk. Unlike the verbally ineffective Nunkie, Big Sweet stands up boldly to the Boss and justifies the reason for her heavy-handedness with wrongdoers in the Quarters. In the following verbal interchange, Big Sweet is bold and direct with the Quarters Boss. In her characteristic fashion as aggressive talker and combative fighter, she is ready for battle as the Quarters Boss cautions her about her meanness and physical harm of some members of the male work force:

> Quarters Boss: Not that I fault you for what you done this morning, but I been laying off to caution you for some time.
> Big Sweet: Caution me? Caution me about what?
> Quarters Boss: Now, I aint after no fuss. I gets paid to keep order in these here quarters, and I tries my level best to do it.
> Big Sweet: Well, who told you not to? I know it wasnt me.
> Quarters Boss: You been lamming folks a mighty heap round here
> (*I, I,* 20).

The Quarters Boss's demeanor is a compromising and friendly one, very unlike his rough, unfriendly attitude toward Nunkie. To eradicate possible confrontation between the quick-tempered Big Sweet who shows no verbal restraint and the gun-equipped Quarters Boss, Sop-the-Bottom and the other workers come to Big Sweet's aid with persuasive talk to convince the Boss of her real innocence and good intentions to reform the social environment (even if it means killing a few of the evil troublemakers who themselves are prone to violence to settle disputes). But the Quarters Boss arouses Big Sweet's ire when he delves into her private love life and accuses her of beating up Lonnie, a good man and hard worker, on every pay day. She responds forthrightly to this accusation of abuse against the man she loves, especially when it comes from an outsider—a white man: "I dont aim to let *nobody* tell me that I mistreat Lonnie. It's my life time pleasure to do what I know he wants done. Lonnie, he's different. He dont like all this old rough doings and fighting, so I make 'em live better cause what Lonnie says is right. (Tenderly) Lonnie is just a baby, in a way of speaking. He thinks everybody will just naturally do right, but I knows different! So I gets around to see to it that they do" (*I, I,* 22).

The Quarters Boss is finally convinced of Big Sweet's innocence and sincerity. The talk employed by her and her comrades suggests they have all mastered the white man at the verbal game in a way similar to the historical verbal technique employed by Blacks to survive in the Jim Crow South. They are well aware of their accomplishment of "putting on ole massa" because, when the Quarters Boss leaves, they all dance and caper boisterously. They know just what to say to win him over to their side, thus alleviating violence.

Another view of Big Sweet's assertiveness is also represented in *Act I, Scene 1,* in her relationship with Dicey. Although Big Sweet tries to befriend the weak and downtrodden woman, Dicey is so mean-spirited that she refuses Big Sweet's friendship. Dicey is color-struck about her blackness and has developed a low-down case of the Black Ass, as Hurston, in very unsympathetic terms, describes her in the introductory descriptions of the characters in the play: ". . . . a homely, narrow-contracted little black woman, who has been slighted by nature and feels "evil" about it. Suffers from the "black ass." Her strongest emotion is envy. What she passes off as deep love is merely the determination not to be outdone by handsomer women. She yearns to gain a reputation as "bad" (the fame of a sawmill camp) to compensate for her lack of success with men. She is extremely jealous of Big Sweet. Being short, scrawny and black, a pretty yellow girl arouses violent envy in her" (Play Character Description).

Dicey is bent on maintaining her short-lived love affair with My Honey, a popular blues singer and friend of Big Sweet and Lonnie. When My Honey publicly announces his disassociation from her (a way of shaming her) with the assertion, "I done told you I don't want no parts of you" (*I, 1,* 28), Dicey is furious. She attempts to lay ownership of him by boldly attacking him with a knife, announcing, "I want stand a quit. I mean to cut you as long as I can see you. I mean to kill you and go to jail for you. You ain't going to quit me like I was some old dog" (*I, 1,* 28–29). Other men come to My Honey's assistance as they condemn Dicey in a boastful game of woofing. Big Sweet (once angry at Dicey for her evil ways and inflammatory talk) now sympathizes with Dicey, a woman rejected and scorned in public view by a man she boastfully has laid claim to and dared other women to touch, and understands her heartache. She offers Dicey words of advice as kindly and gently as a mother might give to a daughter, or as she might give to a close woman friend in a "kissing friends" relationship: "Dicey, on the average, I am for the women folks, because the mens take so much undercurrents of us. But, Dicey, My Honey's case done come up in court. He aint fooled you and mistreated you. All he ever done was joke with you a time or two. He done told you he dont want you. I wouldnt want no man that dont want *me*. Pulling after a man that dont want you, is just like peeping in a jug with one eye. You cant see a thing but darkness. Take a fool's advice and leave the man alone, like Lonnie says" (*I, 1,* 29).

Dicey rejects Big Sweet's talk and initiates a verbal feud between the two arising from her belief that Big Sweet has taken My Honey away from her. Dicey now feels she has to kill, to "make a graveyard of her own" (*I, 1,* 32), to be respected by the community. Her first victim will be Big Sweet as she threatens to put Ella Wall (the popular Queen of the jook for her prowess with men) on Big Sweet for taking her man. The dialogue between Dicey and Big Sweet grows tense as Big Sweet (turning angry now at a person she's tried to console only to be insulted and threatened) responds in kind by playing the dozens: "Ella Wall aint my Mama. I aint a bit more scared of her than I is of you. And then again, what I got to be scared about? Ella Wall aint no big hen's biddy, if she do lay gobbler's eggs" (*I, 1,* 34).

Dicey in turn signifies at Big Sweet by suggesting that Big Sweet is unfaithful to Lonnie: "You'll find out. You done more than Lonnie think you done to git My Honey away from me, and keep him tied round your house like a yard dog" (*I, 1,* 34). Big Sweet flings a challenge to Dicey to fight as she demeans her by calling her a liar: "That's a lie! I called you a *liar*. You don't like it, dont you take it. Here's my collar, come and shake it!" (*I, 1,* 34). The atmosphere becomes tense as the onlookers expect Dicey to accept the verbal challenge to take direct action, but Dicey, coward that she is, backs off cringing and muttering a warning: "Your time now, be mine after while" (*I, 1,* 34). Prepared for whatever unfolds in her life, Big Sweet confidently replies, "So be it in the grand lodge" (*I, 1,* 34). The conflict between Dicey and Big Sweet has ended with what appears to be Dicey's final retreat.

As *Act 1, Scene 1* ends, Big Sweet has changed from Dicey's friend advisor to being her foe, a move prompted by Dicey's own insulting talk and mean temperament and not because of her dark-skinned color or unattractiveness. Detesting Big Sweet's overpowering of Nunkie as well as her friendship with My Honey (the man Dicey claims as her lover), Dicey plans to retaliate with some malicious act, for she cannot count on ever mastering Big Sweet verbally or physically. Big Sweet is too daring a combatant in both the talking and fighting game.

Act I, Scene 2 is significant because it reveals a contrasting side of Big Sweet's personality—her assertive behavior and good nature in the company of a trusted friend as opposed to Scene one's show of her character in conflict with Nunkie, Dicey and the Quarters Boss. Here, she extends friendship and a loyal helping hand to Leafy Lee, a young urban outsider who wants to be taken into the Quarters community so she can learn to sing the blues. A fictional foil to the dark-skinned and unattractive Dicey, Leafy Lee is a mulatto who is not color struck about her light skin and long "nearer-my-God-to-thee-hair." Neither does she act snobbish or request special treatment because she is a high "yaller" (I, 2, 8). On the contrary, she makes an effort to express her Black identity and cultural heritage through talk and song. As the play progresses, she makes oral ritual as superbly as Big Sweet and reveals herself to indeed be definitely Black in spirit, voice, and thought despite her light skin and conspicuous Caucasian characteristics. Her personality, speech habits, respectable mannerisms, and total innocence, and not her looks, attract Big Sweet's fancy and eventual acceptance in a community which is normally hostile to all outsiders. It seems Big Sweet is friendly in sisterhood to any woman such as Leafy Lee whose actions prove her to be of sound and genuine character. Big Sweet does not discriminate against Leafy becaue of her external appearance, but judges her by her assertive posture from within the context of the Black folk spirit. How well and genuinely she expresses herself through various Black speech styles is Big Sweet's measuring rod.

It should be noted, however, that Leafy Lee's acceptance is not an automatic one when she is first observed in the play. She has to pass Big Sweet's verbal scrutiny and "feather bed resistance" (MM, "Introduction") in order to be legitimately accepted. Her initial entry into the Quarters arouses the suspicion of all the women because of her color and what it connotes among the folk. Judging her solely on appearance, they believe she looks too white and as a result, she must be snobbish and sophisticated, certainly not one of their kind to live on the job. They also conclude she may even be a law officer (disguised) and in search of fugitives from justice, or a woman who is simply there to steal their men on pay day. But her natural friendliness and down-to-earth behavior with the children as she joins them in the play dance dispel some of the tension and misconception that her presence stirs. When the dance with the children ends, though, she has to gain acceptance and verbal unity with the women folk before she is fully accepted as one with them.

As she communicates with the women (who do not in the least appear friendly or sympathetic to her), she is well scrutinized, especially when she specifically asks for Bunch by referring to her as *Miss* Bunch (*1, 2,* 4), a show of her respect for an elder (an act which Black folk regard highly, a thing Hurston calls in the essay, "The Pet Negro System" a way of showing manners and knowing one's place among elders). Leafy also establishes an immediate identification of her Blackness by her speech and behavioral mannerism. Language as a defensive mechanism comes into play here for both Leafy and the women. Leafy defends her individual territory while the women go on the defensive to protect their community against an outsider, a symbol of the unknown.

The women in particular become evasive and protective of Bunch, who is a member of their clan. They loud talk and rely on coded language to indirectly signify to Bunch that she is being sought by a suspicious-looking outsider. Bunch, tuned in to the evasive ploy, stands in the crowd and does not identify herself as she listens to Laura B's public query of Leafy Lee. Leafy Lee's survival and social inclusion therefore depend on her verbal rapport, *i.e.,* her ability to amicably converse with Laura B. In other words, she is measured by how well she asserts herself in a convincing and believable style. All of the other women scrutinize her performance with great care as Laura B boldly sounds her out in the talking game. The dynamics of assertive individualism are apparent as both women hold their own in the verbal interchange:

> Laura B: (Raising her voice so that Bunch can hear) You say, you looking for Bunch? Is you some kin to her?
> Leafy: Oh, no. I never seen her in my life. The man at the office just *give* her name on this piece of paper and said she might let me have a room to stay if she had one to spare.
> Laura B: Bunch aint around home right now. Seems like I seen her going to the Commissary awhile back. You say you aim to stay here? You going to teach the school? You sort of looks like a school teacher.

Leafy: Ma'am. I'm not a school teacher at all. I just come to stay around a while.

Laura B: Is you married?

Leafy: Oh, no ma'am. I haven't got no husband at all. All by myself.

Laura B: Oh, I see, you got a man friend here, and you come to live with him.

Leafy: (Shocked) Oh, no ma'am. I haven't got nobody like that at all. I don't know a soul here so far (*I, 1,* 4–5).

Leafy is convincingly respectful as the other women give each other significant glances about her answers to Laura B's questions. But the evil-thinking Dicey halts Leafy's chance for full acceptance here when she cautions the women that Leafy is not to be trusted and that she is a "fan foot, a regular old strumpet making pay-days to steal men. Color struck, too. Crazy about that little color she got in her face, and that little old hair on her head" (*I, 2,* 8). Intervention by Big Sweet in another test of Leafy's worthiness for entry into the Polk County community will resolve the matter. Leafy represents goodness and genuineness to the women in her verbal rapport (despite her fair skin), while she symbolizes evil and mistrust in Dicey's color struck vision of people.

Big Sweet's encounter with Leafy is one of the most dramatic and tense moments of the play, as Big Sweet prepares to verbally sound out the newcomer and to battle her if necessary. Spirited by Dicey's negative assessment of Leafy, Big Sweet draws on the verbal technique of playing the dozens and "putting her foot on her enemy's doorstep," positioning herself appropriately for the commencement of the technique with her left foot on the steps and her left elbow on her left thigh ready for war. She's of the mind that Leafy has no place on the job and it is her duty to order her to leave. All of the women expect a fierce confrontation, first verbal and then physical, but Leafy stands her verbal ground, turning the encounter into peace, love, and unity. She is a naturally assertive Black voice like Big Sweet and the two merge into verbal cohesiveness and eventually establish a "kissing friends" kinship comparable to the Phoeby/Janie friendship in *Their Eyes Were Watching God.*

Hurston describes the mood of their first encounter as it shifts from one of open hostility and mean eyeballing (on Big Sweet's part) to one of friendship and warm acceptance of Leafy by all of the women, except

Dicey. Of the nonverbal communication that evolves in the first Big Sweet/Leafy Lee encounter, Hurston writes: "Big Sweet looks Leafy over from head to foot slowly and deliberately, and back again. There is either hostility or cold indifference in the faces of every woman about her, as Leafy stands there on the porch and takes in the circle. Finally she meets Big Sweet dead in the eye. They eyeball each other well, then Leafy breaks into a grin" (*I, 2,* 10). Leafy's natural humor saves the day as she and Big Sweet converse in friendly talk:

> Big Sweet: (Tries to hold her solemn pose, but she also begins to grin. Finally Big Sweet gives in, takes her foot down, stands akimbo and with an attempt to conceal her admiration under rough good humor and says) You crazy thing!
>
> Leafy: (Laughing, imitating Big Sweet's stance) Crazy your ownself.
>
> Big Sweet: Youse all right, *Little Bits.* Taint nothin wrong with you. I been told you was *stuck up and color struck,* but youse all right. You grins natural. If you was stuck up you would try to smile (*I, 2,* 10).

Once Big Sweet displays laughing acceptance of a genuine friend in their midst, even Bunch ends her deception and with a convincing display of big lies, she identifies herself as the person Leafy wants to see: "Did you say Bunch? Here I is. I thought all the time you was asking for Lena Branch. But you said Bunch, didn't you? You can git your suitsatchel and come on cross the way right now. I got a good room you can use" (*I, 2,* 12). But Big Sweet turns away Bunch's offer and, acting like a mother to an orphaned and homeless child, shows her Christian charity and welcomes Leafy to her home (a one room shack).

All seems well in verbal harmony and friendship between Leafy, Big Sweet and the other women, but Dicey becomes disturbed by this union because she now considers both Big Sweet and Leafy a threat to her plan to dominate My Honey as her own lover. As the play unfolds, the tension and animosity existing between these two factions of women—the good and the evil—will grow more pronounced. Dicey will be no match for the two assertive women who will eventually rank at the top level of the Polk County verbal hierarchy. They symbolize good which eventually conquers evil in all of its manifestations.

Act I, Scene 3 furnishes a further illustration of the comradeship and verbal harmony existing between Big Sweet and Leafy. Though different in many ways, their assertive individualism and love of talk and song bind them. Leafy proves herself to be a voice of folk wisdom like Big Sweet as they delve into their family history and philosophy of life. Their coming together in mutual oral friendship highlights the woman-to-woman dialogue and exchange of ideas that Hurston cherishes in Black women, for "women folks dont stand with one another like men friends do. Not on the average they dont" (*I, 4,* 11). An assertive woman not only talks serious talk to a foe but she also shares her articulate voice with a close woman associate in sisterhood, be it her mother or Nanny (as with Janie and Nanny), or with a close, bosom friend, a kissing girl-friend companion, as with Janie and Pheoby or with Big Sweet and Leafy (*I, 3,* 1–4).

An assertive woman also remains loyal and trustworthy to her best friend as illustrated in *Act I, Scene 4.* Big Sweet stays committed to Leafy in her efforts to learn to sing the blues like Ethel Waters, ensuring that Leafy is taught decent blues songs and preventing the men from using slack talk (or vulgar language) about sex in her presence. Here, Hurston seems to be suggesting that Black women also, beyond the marriage or love relationship with men, need a verbal relationship and social union to strengthen their friendship ties with other women and to ward off malevolence from adversaries. There can be unity and strong kinship and assertive individualism exhibited in woman-to-woman friendship. This is exactly what Big Sweet and Leafy require to counter Dicey in *Act 2.* Words bound in mutual friendship and social cohesiveness help them to overcome the evil talk and actions of Dicey and others.

Act 2 uncovers the evil ways of Dicey and her two initial plots to overthrow Big Sweet, thus causing disharmony in the Quarters. Much of the action thus focuses on Dicey, the evil and ineffective talker. *Act 2, Scene 1* takes place in the jook as Dicey again voices claim to My Honey and signifies about Big Sweet's approaching downfall. Optimistic about the adverse effect of the bogus letter she wrote to Lonnie announcing Big Sweet's affair with Three Card Charlie, Dicey anticipates the results of her devious action: "Before the night is far spent, I'll be having my proper amount of fun. (Mysteriously) Some that goes for a great big stew will be simmered down to a low gravy. (Laughs) Then I'm going to show 'em my ugly laugh" (*II, 1,* 3). This type of signifying in the jook, a place of fun, merits Dicey criticism and scorn from the men; they grin at her as she is again disowned by My Honey (*II, 1,* 4–6), for his affection is directed at the newcomer,

Leafy. But Dicey is not totally disheartened; she is enlivened when she sees the impact of her devious letter on Lonnie's forlorn heart. Remarks an unhappy Lonnie to Dicey's delight: "Somebody done wrote me a letter. And I'm so out done, till I just opened my mouth and laughed" (*II, 1*, 10). At this, Dicey laughs loudly; in fact, she gloatingly falls all over herself as she signifies further: "Aye, Lord! A heep sees, but few knows. God dont love ugly" (*II, 1*, 10). Unable to do harm more directly to Big Sweet through verbal or physical methods, Dicey (a striking symbol of the clinging-vine and verbally ineffective woman in Hurston's art, as has been previously illustrated in Hurston's fiction and folklore) relies on the bogus letter to do her dirty work for her. It does temporarily alter the merry atmosphere of the jook as Lonnie grows sad over what he has read and assumed to be true.

Big Sweet's and Leafy's entrance to the jook changes the downcast mood to one of happiness, but only after Dicey signifies one more time that she knows the motive for Lonnie's anger at Big Sweet: "Some folks better sweep around they own door before they go trying to clean around mine. They got plenty to worry about they ownself." (She throws Lonnie a triumphant look and then purses her mouth in a knowing way. All look at Lonnie to see if that is the answer to his strange behavior.) (*II, 1*, 22). Against the backdrop of Dicey's raucous laughter and indirect talk, the disharmony between Big Sweet and Lonnie is resolved as they unite in love.

The letter, a written correspondence which Dicey originates because she cannot verbally accomplish her evil feat, is proven to be a hoax and Dicey's first ploy fails, as does her brief malicious merriment at having defeated Big Sweet. The men scorn Dicey for her evil ways and then they humiliate her even more when they turn admirably upon Leafy for a round of old time courtship talk. Unlike the evil Dicey, Leafy is a symbol of goodness and proves herself to be as verbally astute in her Blackness as Big Sweet when she engages in the oral ritual of courtship conversation with Sop and Box Car. Leafy's verbal engagement in this talk further enhances her acceptance by the male community:

> Box Car: Miss Leafy, which would you ruther be, a lark a'flying or
>   a dove a' setting?
> Sop: He mean would you ruther be a married or a single?
> Leafy: (Bridling) Oh, you done asked me a hard question, Box Car.
>   It all depends.
> Box Car: Depends on what?

Leafy: (With an under-eye at My Honey) It depends on whether I was in love or not. If I was in love, I would want to be a dove a'setting like Big Sweet. If I wasnt in love, I would choose to be a lark a'flying like I been doing.

Box Car: Now, we gitting deep. Is you see anybody around here up to now that you figger you could nest with?

Leafy: (Sits thoughtful) Well, and then again, I cant say. But I did have a dream last night. No, it wasnt true. It was just a dream. He came right into my room last night. He pressed me there on my bed. But it was just a dream. A shadow thrown by moonlight (*II, 1, 36*).

Act II, Scene 2 concerns Dicey's second attempt to rid the Quarters of both Big Sweet and Leafy Lee. The impetus for her second action springs from the announcement that Leafy and My Honey plan to marry and the fact that they are encouraged to do so by their close friends and main leaders of the Quarters community, Big Sweet and Lonnie. Dicey's indirect ploy for combatting this joyous occasion is to inform the Quarters Boss that Big Sweet (far from the actual fact) is a troublemaker on the job. The Quarters Boss is convinced that such is really the case, for Big Sweet has in fact beaten or killed a large number of his workers.

In a superior mood to start a fight with Big Sweet, the Quarters Boss in an arrogant and ruthless show of force throws open the door of Big Sweet's shack (this is what Blacks would call a white man rather presumptuously "putting his foot on your doorstep," preparing for verbal and physical battle like Blacks generally do to an adversary) and talks to her sternly about her actions. When Big Sweet is warned about beating Vergible Woods, she is verbally as cocky as ever. "They told you right," (*II, 2, 7*) she remarks, and admits, too that she killed three other men for a valid reason: "I kilt 'em my ownself didn't I? and not one of them minks died a day too soon, neither. They was low and mean and bulldozing and had done kilt folks they ownselves. They wouldn't do for theyselves, they wouldn't do for nobody's else. They ought to been dead ten thousand years, the no-count things" (*II, 2, 7*).

As the Quarters Boss scolds her more intensely, Big Sweet remains undisturbed until he orders her to leave the job. At this instruction, she is shocked and at her weakest, most helpless state in the play. Such a pending loss she cannot bear. The job, or Quarters neighborhood, is home for her, the place where she feels like somebody despite its drab appearance to an outsider. Poignantly yet assertively she soliloquizes about her fate and the hurt such a forced departure would cause herself, Lonnie, and the folk of the job: "But how can I leave here? I wont have no home no more. Be like I was before. Just on the road somewhere (Overcome). No! No! I just cant leave. I'm somebody now. Folks need me. I cant go off feeling like nothing no more. And everybody here will feel like nothing again—just like sawdust. Some more sawdust piled up like that behind the mill with the rain and storm beating on it. Poor Lonnie! He's going to follow me off and he ain't never going to be satisfied no more" (*II, 2,* 8). Saddened, Big Sweet prepares to meet Lonnie at the jook, putting on a laughing face to keep from crying. A strong role model for the folk, she would dance and sing rather than tell them bad news for fear of their retaliation against the Quarters Boss.

Act II, Scene 3 is set in the jook. Big Sweet appears to be her old self, very sociable with the jook crowd and caring to Leafy. But when Ella and Dicey strut in with an air of triumph, well aware that the Quarters Boss has issued an ultimatum, Big Sweet becomes her mean and aggressive self again, although still as friendly as ever to her comrades. Although Ella's aim is to shame or score on Big Sweet before the jook crowd, Big Sweet holds her own by uttering in turn a few slurs and insults. Consider the following dialogue as Ella attempts to be sarcastic in what is supposedly a friendly chat with Big Sweet:

> Ella: (Looking at Big Sweet up and down in a sneering way) Hello, there, Big Sweet. Look like you got changing clothes, now.
>
> Big Sweet: It do look like it, don't it?
>
> Ella: You sure done improved up from what you used to be. I knowed you when you was just as naked as a jay-bird whistling time. (Laughs excessively and Dicey joins her in the slur by laughing)
>
> Big Sweet: (quietly) You sure telling the truth Ella. (Cruelly) But that was before I *got* the man that you was trying to *git*. Lonnie dont let me want for nothing. Every day I sits on my porch and rock and say, Here come Lonnie and them.
>
> Ella: Them? What them?
>
> Big Sweet: (Arrograntly) Them dollars! You hear me. You aint blind.
>
> Ella: Lonnie! I just let you have him because I seen you was in need. I can git any man I wants (*II, 3,* 9).

In a unified show of support behind Big Sweet's words, Lonnie and Sop-the-Bottom come to her verbal assistance as they also aim to shame and demean Ella. Lonnie scorns Ella's claim of being able to possess him: "Excepting me. Not since I came to know Big Sweet, anyhow" (*II, 3,* 9). And Sop further insults her with these signifying words: "Pay Lonnie no mind, Ella. What you care about him when you can git me? If you handles the money you used to handle about 10 years back and let me spend it like I please, I'm yours anytime" (*II, 3,* 10). Sop's talk prompts a big laugh as Ella is insulted to the point of laughing ridicule, her prestige as Queen of Love at an all-time low.

To make matters worse in such a climate, Big Sweet, not in the least weakened by the Quarters Boss's threat, continues to verbally strike out at Ella. Now she signifies at Dicey, too, and lands such a severe blow that the men (jokingly) coach Dicey on how to defend herself against the insult, knowing full well she is an ineffective talker and fighter against Big Sweet. She is vulnerable to a severe beating or to a killing for even attempting to tangle with Big Sweet on the talking or fighting turf. The men therefore slyly set the bait for Dicey's defeat as they entice her to challenge Big Sweet to a game of the dozens in the following interchange:

> Big Sweet: (With a catty smile to Ella) I see you got something too, Ella, that you didn't use to have.
> Ella: What is it? I always had jewelry and things.
> Big Sweet: You got you a yard dog (Indicating Dicey) to do your barking for you.
> Box Car: (Pretending sympathy for Dicey) Aw, aw! Big Sweet, what make you play so rough? Dicey, I wouldn't take that if I was you.
> Stew Beef: (Egging the fight on) Now, what you want to try to start something, for, Box? You know Dicey aint going to get on Big Sweet not unlessen she's braver than I figure her out to be (*II, 3,* 10).

A frightened Dicey does not accept the challenge to repay Big Sweet for the dog insult. Rather, she avoids the issue entirely by landing an indirect verbal blow through signifying at Big Sweet's plight at the Quarters Boss's hands: "I dont have to be fighting and carrying on. Some folks thats around here thinking they got the world by the tail aint going to be here long. Then everything will be nice" (*II, 3,* 11).

Dicey's talk draws the verbal fire of Leafy who joins the conversation.
Words of praise for her talking performance against Dicey are interjected
by Laura B after Leafy takes a turn at verbally shaming and outwitting
the evil Dicey:

> Leafy: (To Dicey) If you're talking about me, I'm in the *be* class—
> be here while you're here, and be here when you're gone.
> Laura B: (Proudly) Listen at little crowing!
> Leafy: Yeah, I'm getting married to My Honey, and it wont be
> long, either, and it aint no help for it. I got more right here
> than you have. I got a *husband* on this job (*II, 3,* 11).

Angered as a result of the public humiliation, the hateful Dicey
draws her fighting weapon, but Big Sweet is amply prepared to deter
her. She dares Dicey to use it, and in a humorous, but then again, rather
serious voice, orders Dicey and Ella to vacate the jook. Their only
means of fighting back at the powerful talking and fighting Big Sweet
is through the cowardly act of signifying. Observe, for example, the
character of each in the following interchange. Big Sweet is bold and
direct in her speech, while the two evildoers employ indirect talk of a
prophetic nature to combat her:

> Big Sweet: Dont you pull no knife in here. I dare you to even take
> it out! And Ella Wall, you dont belong on this place at all.
> The Bossman said *particular* he didnt want no stragglers on
> the premises. Git on out here and take your yard dog along
> with you. Git!
> Ella: (Showing resentment and realizing no possible help from the
> crowd) I'm going, but I'll be back. Your time now, but it will
> be mine after while. Come on, Dicey.
> Dicey: Hanh! Big Sweet wont be here long. (Laughs gloatingly)
> Nobody didnt tell me, but I heard. Then other folks (pointedly
> at Leafy) can be straightened out.
> Lonnie: Big Sweet can stay here just as long as she please, and go
> when she gits ready.
> Dicey: That aint what the Quarters Boss say. (She and Ella exit
> laughing triumphantly as a profound silence settles over the
> place.) (*II, 3,* 11–12)

Dicey's signifying affords Big Sweet the opportune moment to report the Quarters Boss' instructions to the crowd to the effect that she leave the job on payday. A deep gloom comes over the jook as the jookers unite in spirited resolve to find the source of the malicious lies given to the Quarters Boss against Big Sweet (*II, 3,* 16–18). At the end of the scene, they lament in talk and song-chant the loss of Big Sweet.

In providing a perceptive analysis of their condition in an environment of sun and sawdust in the wild and primitive backwoods of Florida that is compared to a "cage-like existence similar to a mule-lot down in a swamp," (*II, 3,* 18), Lonnie acts like a preacher expounding the Biblical word to a responsive congregation in the call/response pattern of Black religious expression. They are pushed to emotional frenzy as they consider what their oppressive work-situation at the job would be without the powerful leadership of Big Sweet to add joy and a sense of moral and purpose to their existence.

The third and final act of the play illustrates the folly of the evil ploys directed by Dicey and co-conspirators, Ella and Nunkie, at Big Sweet. Happiness and good fortune prevail for Big Sweet and the Quarters community as the three plotters are entrapped in their own mean scheme. *Act III, Scene 1* provides an in-depth study of Dicey's evil ways, spirited largely by her own self-hate and pity. Her obsessive dislike of Blackness often causes her to mourn over her fate as a dark-skinned woman: "How come I got to look like I do? Why couldnt I have that long—straight hair like—like—Big Sweet got, and that Leafy? They own looks like horses' mane, and mine looks like drops of rain. And these mens is so crazy! They aint got no sense. Always pulling after hair and looks. and these womens that got it so grasping, and griping, and mean. They wants EVERYTHING—and they gits it too. Look like they would be satisfied with *some.* Naw, they wants it all. Takes pleasure in making other folks feel bad" (*III, 1,* 2–4). Clearly, Dicey abhors light-skinned women whom she feels receive all of the love and affection from men, while she herself feels as though she's treated like a mule by the men on the job: "I aint a woman in a way where men have anything to say of love, and tenderness, and such. I'm just another kind of mule—a bad exception to a rule. So what I feel dont seem to matter much" (*II, 1,* 3).

Act III, Scene 2 reveals Dicey's plans to overcome Big Sweet and Leafy. Nunkie and Ella Wall come to her aid as they resort to yet another ploy—this time they resort to the Black magic of a hoodoo dance to cast an evil spell on their rivals. To their shock, however, the magic doesn't work in immbolizing Big Sweet and the Polk County clan as they congregate for Leafy and My Honey's wedding (*III, 3,* 6–11). With knives in hand, they flee from the scene, while Big Sweet and her cronies follow their own clever plan to have them exposed to the Quarters Boss as the real troublemakers plotting to murder Big Sweet and Leafy. Observing first-hand the actions of Dicey and her gang, the Quarters Boss intervenes and consigns them to lengthy prison terms.

With peace thus restored to the Quarters, Big Sweet is united with Lonnie and friends in a climate of harmony and communal spirit. Absent, though, is a sense of pity for Dicey, the maker of her own evil ways, for, as Big Sweet believes in her folk wisdom: "She couldn't see no further than from the handle of a tea cup round the rim" (*III, 3,* 8). Such narrowmindedness is the origin of Dicey's troubles, and not the prejudice of the Quarters' menfolk toward her dark complexion. For them, being a woman is not measured by one's external features, but rather by one's inner character, speech behavior, and actions. Dicey's self-inflicted condemnation of her individuality thus contributed to her unhappiness and fueled her desire to project that feeling in evil acts against others.

As a whole unit, then, the play ends on a happy note with Big Sweet's powerful image as talker, fighter, community leader and peace maker among the folk still intact. Under her guidance and power of the word, there is a spirit of kinship and community as the folk symbolically celebrate their coming together as a more cohesive body in a marriage ceremony between My Honey and Leafy. As these two join hands in the union of marriage and harmony, so does the community peacefully and idyllically bond itself. Minds are no longer quick to action and trouble; rather they are drawn to sunshine and an appreciation of life as the folk all partake of the beautiful "rainbow of life" (*III, 3,* 11), representing, as Lonnie, the dreamer, says, "Love, Baby, with the sun and the moon thrown in. That's right. EVERYTHING! with the sun and the moon thrown in" (*III, 3,* 11).

Thanks to Big Sweet, the assertive woman of words prone to direct action, Polk County, a hard-working and vital American community, stands out in Hurston's fictional landscape as a place of familial and social unity just as Hurston's beloved Eatonville does. Big Sweet remains in the minds of Hurston readers as a powerful force in the establishment of stability in the folk environment. Without her fluent tongue and inclination for direct action in crucial times of conflict, the

Black community and family structure would be severely weakened. Big Sweet's presence in the play has clearly established this point. It is through the ultimately positive thrust of her words and desire for order that Polk County thrives; it is not the result of capricious authority represented by the white Quarters Boss. Her word power, in its various modes as demonstrated in serious or playful confrontations, functions as the essential path to order and civility in the community. Indeed, Big Sweet has the law in her mouth.

Chapter 7

Laura Lee in "The Conscience of the Court"[1]

The humble, unlettered and common-clad Laura Lee Kimble is another interesting representation of Hurston's assertive woman as she speaks with a voice of authority and truth in the domain of a white home and courtroom. Well over two-thirds of the story consists of her talking voice as it is asserted exclusively in an all-white middle-class setting, far removed from the poor white Cracker environment of which Hurston acknowledges her dissatisfaction in such works as *Seraph on the Suwanee*, "The Pet Negro System" and "I Saw Negro Votes Peddled." In this setting with good-minded white folks, Laura Lee's technique of verbalizing her innocence to refute the complaints made by a white plaintiff becomes her medium for negotiating respect, freedom, and justice. Her unschooled, yet honest voice challenges the conscience of both judge and jury when she mounts the witness stand. Like a preacher delivering a sermon to an attentive congregation, she conveys a powerful message that enlivens her listeners who in making their judgment do not question or debate the truthfulness of her story of innocence and self-defense.

Laura Lee bears semblance to Big Sweet in personal disposition as she employs talking and fighting skills to demonstrate her character and system of moral values. She shows herself to be a friendly woman of good yet occasionally mean temperament. Like many of her domestic sisters employed in Southern white homes, she seems determined to say no more than her back can physically stand.[2] She will talk her mind, no matter what. Her words know no color barrier. In appearance, she is an attractive mulatto woman of large build like Big Sweet.

Laura Lee is "an odd Negro type. Gray-green eyes, large and striking, looking out of a chestnut-brown face. A great abundance of almost straight hair only partially hidden by the high-knotted colored kerchief about her head" (*"Conscience,"* 23). Physically, she is tall and strong, "a man-killing bear of a woman," (23) fierce enough to have beaten a man within an inch of his life. When angered, she is, indeed, "a two-legged she-devil no less" (23). But when happy and among her family and employer, she is sweet and kind, perhaps too loyal and too kind, too faithful a servant, for as her dead husband, Tom, often said of her, "the world had no use for the love and friendship she was ever trying to give" (23). She was usually the victim, often suffering for her complete loyalty to employers and for giving too much of herself to others. A faithful servant and loyal companion to her white employer, Miz' Celestine Clairborne, Laura Lee is so overly concerned about serving her employer that she overlooks her own welfare and happiness. Her husband, Tom, often likened her to a wishbone in the sense that Laura "always placed other folks' cares in front of my own, and more especially Miz' Celestine. Said that I made out of myself a wishbone shining in the sun. Just something for folks to come along and get their wishes and good luck on. Never looked out for nothing for my ownself" (116). So loyal is Laura to her employer that she risks her life to defend and uphold her employer's home and property. For the maintenance of this trust, Laura pays the consequences as the story unfolds the legal and personal penalty she suffers for her avowed faithfulness—a faithfulness maintained by her two most individualistic and self-defensive assets: her talking and fighting skills.

Like Big Sweet, Laura Lee maintains her assertive individualism throughout the story and in spite of her occupation as a domestic servant (or faithful watchdog) and lifelong family friend to her white employer. She talks and fights as quickly in the presence of white folk as she does before her own Black kinfolk. She maintains her sense of worth where ever she is, the Jim Crow South posing no limitations on her tongue. Rather, it affords her freedom to speak under its unwritten code of ethics within the pet Negro system of racial relations.[3] And, in this oddly privileged tradition of the Negro maid's place in the middle-class white family structure of the South, Laura Lee takes full charge of the home as if it were her own, feeling verbally free to speak her mind to her employer and other family members and to any white intruder or canvasser appearing at the door where she has the authority to refuse or accept a caller.

"The Conscience of the Court" concerns Laura Lee's protection of the owner's property and the upholding of her own humanity in a verbal encounter with an insurance collector, Clement Beasley, who tries to gain forceful entry in order to repossess furniture for an allegedly overdue loan. Laura Lee disregards his threats and stands by her principle of trust, even if it means beating and nearly killing a white man, and then going to jail for it. It is up to the white court to determine her innocence in resorting to physical violence to uphold that trust. Justice prevails as it is Laura's assertive individualism which wins her freedom and admiration from the judge, in particular.

As the story begins, a trial is in process. After three weeks in jail, Laura Lee in a shabby housedress stands before the court to be judged and sentenced for her actions against Beasley, her victim, who appears on a hospital cot, swaddled in bandages. Laura Lee is disheartened that her employer, whose property she protected in the fracas with Beasley, has not come to aid her. Laura questions if she is in fact just a wishbone for her employer's use. In keeping with Hurston's assertive woman's capacity to nobly endure hardship, Laura Lee stoically faces the crisis before her as she bears the hostility of the white faces peering at her. She looks straight ahead in a proud, erect way with the inner knowledge that although unpleasant consequences lay ahead, "she was ready for this moment. She had come to the place where she could turn her face to the wall and feel neither fear nor anguish. So this here so-called trial was nothing to her but a form and a fashion and an outside show to the world. She could stand apart and look on calmly" (23).

A proud unlettered woman, Laura Lee is not in the least disturbed by white perceptions of her actions, as when the clerk crisply describes in formal legal language the charges filed against her: "Charged with felonious and aggravated assault. Mayhem. Premediated attempted murder on the person of one Clement Beasley. Obscene and abusive language" (23). Neither does she falter when the clerk tersely requests her plea as if she were a notorious criminal; instead she feels rather spunky and at ease when the judge's friendly rapport strikes her fancy, for, in Black perceptions of the ways of white folks,[4] he is a man with manners and principles who knows how to talk his way to the hearts of folk. A white man (or Cap'n) with manners and class is to be respected.[5]

Rightfully, then, Laura Lee immediately reciprocates with a friendly and respectful voice toward the judge. She refers to him as "His Honor" as she strikes amicable verbal ground. She is not the fierce bear-cut of a woman the judge assumes her to be as the tone of her response to his question of her plea bears out: "Oh I didn't know. Didn't even know if he was talking to me or not. Much obliged to you, sir. (Sends His Honor a shy smile) Deed I don't know if I'm guilty or not. I hit the man after he hit me, to be sure, Mister Judge, but if I'm guilty I don't know for sure. All them big words and all" (23). Her refusal of a lawyer in her amiable voice to the judge also alters his image of her as a "two-legged she-devil" (23). "Naw sir, I thank you, Mister Judge. Not to turn you no short answer, but I don't reckon it would do me a bit of good. I'm mighty much obliged to you just the same" (23).

Laura's unlettered polite easiness has an impact on the judge's conscience, her innocent manner penetrating his own thoughts about fairness, human rights and justice for all individuals—Black Laura included. In effect, her verbal style challenges the judge to do right, to treat her fairly as the court proceedings unfold. He is well aware of the prosecutor's brisk cynicism toward the sincere defendant as he argues the plantiff's case and appraises Beasley's condition as a result of Laura's fighting power: "Left arm broken above the elbow, compound fracture of the forearm, two ribs cracked, concussion of the brain and various internal injuries" (23). He then allows Beasley a chance to tell his side of the story—a testimony delivered in a glib manner and without sufficient tangible proof to substantiate his charge against Laura Lee who claims that he was trespassing on her employer's property. And, in fairness to Laura and the principles of democratic law, the judge demands that the note of the loan be brought in evidence. Such a request in favor of justice un-nerves the prosecutor and Beasley, for they are of the belief that the judge, because of his race, will favor them. But the judge proves himself to be impartial as he turns to hear Laura Lee's defense—the truthful telling of her side of the story in an assertive and humble manner in the style of her own Black folk speech. Here again, it must be noted that the judge's verbal rapport with Laura Lee is crucial because it is his friendly, almost paternal, interaction with her which sets her testimony in motion and leads to her eventual freedom. Laura Lee had initially decided to remain silent. Somehow her assertive and honest voice aroused the conscience of the judge and his early training about fairness and justice in the American judicial system for all people.

In the absence of her white employer's influential voice, Laura Lee believes that she will be automatically found guilty on the basis of Beasley's lies, knowing a Black person's word can't count for too much against the legal manipulations and intimidating terminology of a white court. But there is hope and justice for her after all in the voice and proper actions of the responsive and kindly judge. As she is without a lawyer, he duly counsels her about her right to be sworn in and her obligation to tell the truth to the jury: "Tell them anything that might help you so long as you tell the truth to the jury" (112). In a coaxing and somewhat paternal tone of voice, he coaches her on how to talk, while reminding her of the importance of giving full testimony: "Believe it or not, Laura Lee, this is a court of law. It is needful to hear both sides of every question before the court can reach a conclusion and know what to do. Now, you don't strike me as a person that is unobliging at all. I believe if you knew you would be helping me out a great deal by telling your side of the story, you would do it" (112).

Like a cooperative and well-disciplined child, Laura Lee responds meekly to the judge's authority: "Yes, sir, Mister Judge. If I can be of some help to you, I sure will. And I thank you for asking me" (112). Her humble folk speech thus reveals her sincere character and intent to the judge and jury. In a style that might be compared to story-telling or preaching, Laura Lee tells why she beat Beasley. Refuting his version of the encounter, she tells how he came to her employer's home with a moving van and forcibly tried to gain entry so as to collect valuable antiques. As she delves into detail, Laura Lee respects her audience's authority by repeatedly referring to the jurors as Jury-gentlemans. This repetitive refrain is a clever way of preparing them to accept the more energetic language which subtly demeans her accuser. They grow engrossed in her talk as she vividly recreates the scene with Beasley in what may be termed the verbal process of making "crayon enlargements of life."[6] The conflict is recounted with an increasingly assertive flair as she addresses herself to the all-white jury: "You jury-gentlemans, I told him in the nicest way that Miz Celestine was off from home and she had left me there as a kind of guardeen to look after her house and things, and I sure couldn't so handly leave nobody touch a thing in Mrs. Clairborne's house unlessen she was there and said so" (114).

As her story narrative continues, Laura Lee is particularly convincing when she idiomatically describes her angry verbal and physical responses when Beasley disrespects her with the dozens insult: "He just looked at me like I was something that the buzzards laid and the sun hatched out, and told me to move out of his way so he could come on in and get his property. I propped myself and braced one arm across the doorway to bar him out, reckoning he would have manners enough to go off. But, no! He flew just as hot as Tucker when the mule kicked his mammy and begun to cuss and double-cuss me, and call me

I could be wrong for staying all them years and making Miz' Celestine's cares my own. You gentlemens is got more book-learning than me, so you would know more than I do. So far as this fracas is concerned, yeah, I hurted this plaintive, but with him acting the way he was, it just couldn't be helped. And tain't nary one of you gentlemens but what wouldn't of done the same" (120, 122). The manner and tone of Laura's speech has a profound influence on the once hostile-appearing jury. Laura is so effective and sincere in her argument that even the prosecutor does not dare cross-examine her. Rather, the judge takes the verbal helm and confirms her innocence from another angle—the legal side. He discloses that the due date of Mis' Celestine's note with Beasley is more than three months away, and, as a result, Beasley had no legal justification whatsoever for being on the premises (122). Gasps and mumbles follow this revelation as it is clear to all that Laura's actions now appear even more justifiable.

The fairness and goodness of white people in the carriage of justice for this Black woman is obviously clear in the judge's final legally-worded comments. He praises Laura's innocence and faithfulness to her employer, while he utters contempt for Beasley and his maligned attempt at knowingly exploiting the law against the rights of a seemingly helpless domestic. In effective contrast to Laura's common language, the judge comfortably draws on his own educated style of talk to condemn Beasley: "This is the most insulting instance in the memory of the court of an attempt to prostitute the very machinery of justice for an individual's own nefarious ends. The plantiff first attempts burglary, with forceful entry and violence and, when thoroughly beaten for his pains, brazenly calls upon the law to punish the faithful watch-dog who bit him while he was attempting to trespass. Further, it seems apparent that he has taken steps to prevent any word from the defendant reaching Mrs. Clairborne, who certainly would have moved heaven and earth in the defendant's behalf, and rightfully so" (122).

Praising Laura Lee, the judge speaks of her courage, loyalty and goodness of heart—all qualities which speak powerfully for acquittal: "The defendant did more than resist the plantiff's attempted burglary. Valuable assets of her employer were trusted in her care, and she placed her very life in jeopardy in defending that trust, setting an example which no decent citizen need blush to follow. The jury is directed to find for the defendant" (122). As the story ends, it becomes clear that Laura Lee wins her freedom largely because of her well modulated fluency in describing her effective talking and fighting skills. Most definitely, she is a woman of both words and direct action who successfully defends her individual integrity in the entirely white world of her employer's home and in the public courtroom.

Big Sweet and Laura Lee are two of the most publicly assertive women in Hurston's art, primarily asserting themselves in public settings like the jook and the courtroom. The other assertive women to be discussed are individuals who assert themselves in more private interpersonal situations, in close verbal communication with their men in marriage or in common-law or courtship relationships. Some relationships may border on marital harmony and happiness as expressed through the oral ritual of playful imaginative talk, while others may verge on marital discord demonstrated through heated quarrels and a play of the insulting dozens. Examples of women who fall in the category of negotiating respect for themselves in harmonious verbal relationships are Missie May, Daisy and the nameless domestic in "Story in Harlem Slang." Their relationships are similar in the sense that they are all involved in some kind of money entanglement with their male counterpart. Women who exist in unhappy love relationships of verbal discord are Delia, Emmaline and Lena. More complex versions of these personality types in relationships with Black men are to be found in the extended stories of Lucy and Janie in the two major novels, *Jonah's Gourd Vine* and *Their Eyes Were Watching God*.

Chapter 8

Missie May in "The Gilded Six Bits"[1]

Missie May is a happily married woman who cherishes her role as dedicated wife to her hard-working provider and husband, Joe. Their marriage is a loving and joyful one where "everything was right" (213). Each is a willing and equal contributor to the overall stability of the marriage relationship. The work ethic and its influence on a marriage relationship is a key theme in this story, just as it is in Hurston's "Sweat." In this story, however, love is at the center of the marriage's economic health, while in "Sweat," hate and domestic abuse against Delia, a washerwoman, are at the story's core. How each marriage revolves around the verbal and econmic well-being of the married couple is Hurston's main focus. Materialism, like any other marital vice, can take its toll on a marriage relationship in different ways as these stories bear out. The verbal relationship of each couple in their selected economic environment is the telescopic lens through which Hurston depicts each marital relationship and the assertive woman's place in it.

 In "The Gilded Six Bits," verbal freedom is equally shared by Missie and Joe to express their love, sometimes in mock courtship talk. As a result of this cohesive bond, they share an abundance of happiness and beauty. Missie is a woman in love and she joyfully performs the wifely duties of cooking, washing, ironing, cleaning and serving with a smile; most certainly, it appears that she has the keys to the "kingdom of Black life" (*MM*, 51–54). Joe dutifully labors at the G & G Fertilizer to support his wife. Going home to her with his paycheck in his pocket is the highlight of his work-week. He knows that a beautiful and loving wife—who holds the keys to the bedroom, kitchen and generations[2]— awaits his arrival. He is the spiritual and economic backbone of his castle. Her loving reception of him is his inspiration for maintaining his status as the man and economic bread winner of his home. Missie equally holds her end of the bargain as mistress of her beautiful and orderly house. Both have made their marriage virtually perfect. They are indeed happy in marital union. The marriage is not one of work and drudgery. It is one of play, of total participation in the love experience. Happiness is expressed for this couple through an oral ritual of playful verbal mocking and make-believe physical battle, behavior which symbolizes their love and affection for each other. This ritual is the fabric of their marital union— a union that is consummated every Saturday pay day in a verbal play ceremony and mock courtship battle initiated when Joe hands over his weekly wages to Missie. It is here that the true nature of love and affection in their marriage becomes evident. It is also here that Missie asserts herself and maintains self-respect as woman and wife. She is clean and pure in body, mind and spirit as she partakes of this union of the word with her husband.

The story begins on Saturday morning with Missie's preparation for the verbal and dramatic play ritual that is the lifeblood of their marriage. Joe is enroute from his night job. Laughter and banter will express their true love and affection for each other. Missie's wifely duties are fulfilled; everything at their residence is whitewashed to perfection for the marital ritual of love. The house and yard are immaculately clean for this occasion; in fact, "everything was clean from the gate to the privy house," and "there was something happy about the place" (208). Spiritually, her love for Joe is symbolized all around her. It is genuine, pure and clean, as is her dark-brown skin which "glistened under the soapsuds" (208). The other link in this purifying ritual is her actual talking and participating in the love experience, once Joe begins it by wooing her with silver dollars thrown at her feet. The silver dollars are genuine symbols of Joe's love for Missie and they will stand out throughout the story in mock contrast to the fake or deceptively attractive gilded six bits that Slemmons uses to attract Missie into marital infidelity. For a total of six gilded six bits which have the real equivalent of thirty seven and a half cents (with two bits equal to twenty-five cents in folk monetary terminology), Missie traded the real love and affection she received from her hard working husband for the false love emanating from a fly-by-night city, Chicago-slicker, Slemmons, a man of many unknown places and spots.

Missie is an energetic assertive voice, and without her the union is not possible. As she dresses, the talk play springing from their spiritual and economic attachment in marriage begins. "There came the ring of singing metal on wood. Nine times by a man grinning happily at the joyful mischief he was about to commit" (208). He hurls the money in the door and scurries to a hiding place to wait for Missie. She promptly appears in the door in mock alarm and demands in a pretending angry voice to know her suitor: "Who dat chunkin' money in mah do' way. Nobody ain't gointer be chunkin' money at me and Ah not do 'em nothin'" (209). She spies her philanthropic prey, gives chase and captures him. A rough and tumble play (comparable only to that of Tea Cake and Janie) commences: "For several minutes the two were a furious mass of male and female energy. Shouting, laughing, twisting, turning, tussling, tickling each other in the ribs; Missie May "clutching onto Joe and Joe trying, but not too hard, to get away" (209).

Next, the friendly verbal battle of words and laughter starts as in courtship talk, with Missie equally asserting herself to secure from Joe's pocket those sweet candies and goodies he has purchased to further demonstrate his total love for her. But Missie has to prove herself worthy of obtaining them. Another friendly word battle ensues as Missie pleads her case. As wife, she has to playfully talk with the law in her mouth as an authority over Joe, as a big voice bold enough to usurp his personal property as if it were her own. The following dialogue captures the spirit of this play drama of love and romance as Missie triumphs in gaining entry to Joe's pockets and securing what she thinks is rightfully hers:

> Joe: Missie May, take yo' hand out mah pocket! (He shouted out between laughs.)
>
> Missie May: Ah ain't, Joe, not lessen you gwine gimme whatever it is good you got in yo' pocket. Turn it go, Joe, do Ah'll tear yo' clothes.
>
> Joe: Go on tear 'em. You de one dat pushes de needles round heah. Move yo' hand Missie May.
>
> Missie May: Lemme git dat paper sack out yo' pocket. Ah bet its candy kisses.
>
> Joe: Taint. Move yo' hand. Woman ain't got no business in a man's clothes nohow. Go way.
>
> Missie May: (Gouges way down and gives an upward jerk and triumphs) Unhhunh! Ah got it. It 'tis so candy kisses. Ah knowed you had something for me in yo' clothes. Now Ah got

to see whut's in evey pocket you got. (She finds gum, soap
and a handkerchief.) (209).

The ritual then moves to the kitchen table which is traditionally a
place of harmony and family unity during the meals. The peaceful
sharing of a meal is also a sign of the purity and spiritual unity of the
marriage. Joe, too, must be a clean participant in the ritual; so he
washes himself in the bedroom, yet another sign of the purity and
goodness of the marital union between him and Missie. Missie
performs her wifely duty of preparing her husband's bath water and
clean clothes and cooking his food. She is proud of fulfilling this duty
and in a happy but persuasive voice tells Joe that she is indeed a "real
wife, not no dress and breath. Ah might not look lak one, but if you
burn me, you won't git a thing but wife ashes" (210).

Missie's cooking talent is also an extension of her love for Joe. It
provides warm nourishment for his Southern taste: "Big pitcher of
buttermilk beaded with pale drops of butter from the churn. Hot fried
mullet, crackling bread, ham hock atop a mound of string beans and
new potatoes, and . . . a pone of spicy potato pudding" (210). So
delicious is her potato pone that it leads to another verbal play of words
with Joe teasing Missie that she is as pretty and sweet as the pone and,
as a result, doesn't need to eat any: "Y'all pritty lil frail eels don't need
nothin' lak dis. You too sweet already. Naw, naw, Ah don't want you
to git no sweeter than whut you is already" (210).

A test of the marriage's strength and viability in the face of
adversity develops when Joe's admiration of Otis D. Slemmons, "a man
of spots and places" (210), becomes a subject of conversation. Joe
doubts his meager status against Slemmons' prosperous material looks
and wishes to emulate him. But, Missie, now proving herself a wise
assertive voice of folk wisdom, senses Joe's misdirected social values as
being in conflict with the simple lifestyle to which they are
accustomed. Now talking realistically, apart from her playful voice in
their fanciful drama of love, Missie advises Joe that he is far superior to
Slemmons and provides words of praise and admiration for him just the
natural way he is: "He don't look no better in his clothes than you do
in yourn. He got a puzzle-gut on him and he so chuckle-headed, he got
a pone behind his neck . . . Ford and Rockefeller and dis Slemmons
and all de rest kin be as many-gutted as dey please, Ah'm satisfied wid
you jes' lak you is, baby. God took pattern after a pinetree and built

you noble. Youse a pritty man, and if Ah knowed any way to make you mo' pretty still Ah'd take and do it" (211).

Missie is also assertive in her simplistic folk wisdom about distinguishing appearance from reality when it comes to measuring the essence of Slemmons. She speaks with a cautious tongue about Slemmons' possible false appearance as a rich man, asserting her wise tongue further when she alerts Joe about being deceived: "His mouf is cut cross-ways. . . . he kin lie jus' lak anybody else. . . . Ah hates to see you so dumb. Dat stray nigger jes' tell y'all anything and y'all believe it" (211–212).

Missie's folk wisdom goes unheeded as Joe is bent on emulating the rich-looking Slemmons. His obsession with Slemmon's five-dollar gold piece stick pin and a ten-dollar gold watch chain causes him to parade his beautiful wife in the ice cream parlor in full view of the lustful Slemmons. Such an act eventually leads to Missie's infidelity— a sin committed out of her love for Joe. She is so willing to obtain the material possessions that Joe desires that she sacrifices herself in an effort to make him happy. She discovers to her horror the falsity of Slemmons's materialism—a vice that briefly destroys her love ties with Joe. But because their love has been so strong, there is hope for reconciliation.

She and Joe grow to appreciate the genuineness of their attachment and in a symbolic movement from darkness to light, from uncleanliness to cleanliness, from guilt to innocence and forgiveness, and from deception to reality, they experience the rebuilding of their marriage. This growth is depicted by Hurston as beginning with the discovery of Missie's sin. Hurston plays the setting of a Saturday night (for the act of sin) against the locale of a Saturday morning (for reunification through love and a resumption of the verbal love ritual) toward the end of the story, artistically reinforcing the significance of the beautiful love relationship between Missie and Joe.

The brief disharmony in the marriage suspiciously occurs on a Saturday night (as opposed to a bright sunny morning of Joe's usual homecoming) when neither partner demonstrates the customary loving behavior. Missie is not at the door to welcome Joe who arrives at an unexpected time. Neither is she available to help in the symbolic washing of his skin before he presents himself to eat in the kitchen. As well, the kitchen, usually a place of order and warmth, is in total disarray. Joe "bumped into a pile of dishes, and something crashed to the floor" (213). The bedroom is dark, and the usually exuberant and assertive Missie gasps in fright as the light is turned on to expose her sin with Slemmons in exchange for the gold jewelry which Joe had desired.

The once mock play shared between them on his arrival home turns into mayhem as Joe reacts to the shock of marital betrayal. Remaining the man of words that he his, Joe commands Slemmons to vacate the premises: "Git into yo' damn rags, Slemmons and dat quick" (214). Slemmons is no longer the man of high esteem Joe assumed him to be. There is also a change in Joe's Missie. She is no longer the assertive woman of love words in a marriage of love and fidelity, instead she is an unhappy woman sobbing and weeping in her guilt. On this night —an atypical meeting of the two which does not allow for the play ritual and love fight that normally greet Joe's homecoming after pay day—they both realize their sins and their false perceptions of materialism and the urban outsider.

But their love and verbal amicability prevail in due time. After a troubled period of months, one daybreak finds Joe finally communicating with his wife as before, asking her to perform wifely duties of symbolic love for her husband—cooking, washing and eventual child-bearing. Her cleaning duty finds her examining for close inspection the chain Slemmons used to entice her. It is a gilded half dollar, as the daylight clearly reveals. He falsely purchased her love with fifty cents—coins which have no value when she equates them with her love of Joe and his show of affection for her on pay day. She has been misguided in her love for Joe, but now she is ever more enlightened about the true nature of their marital union. Luckily for her, she is forgiven and Joe rebuilds their ties by starting anew the love play, patterned after the old time Negro courtship conversational ritual, which is such an essential part of their marriage.

On a bright Saturday morning, he resumes his wooing of Missie like a courtship talker. He buys her candy kisses (purchased with Slemmons's gilded six bits) and, before handing over his love-gift, serenades her at the front door (as opposed to the back door where he entered and found sin) with the ring of singing metal on wood, fifteen times. In the initial ringing of metal when the marriage was free of difficulties, Joe rang nine times (208), but on this occasion, he does not take his love for granted. He truly loves Missie and strives mightily to sound out his love in momentous fashion. Missie, in turn, answers Joe's love call with her assertive but playful voice: "Joe Banks, Ah hear you chunkin' money in mah do' way. You wait till Ah got mah strength back and Ah'm gointer fix you for dat" (218). This is the beginning of their renewed love, a relationship in place where the only significant function of money is to initiate the verbal ritual through which they precipitate their outpouring of affection and love.

The story ends as it begins, on a bright Saturday morning with a verbal confirmation of the marriage union between two equally assertive individuals. Despite the diversionary setback involving the false values represented by Slemmons, the big city villain who corrupts the peace and loving relationship of Missie and Joe, the couple triumphs through the sustaining power of talk. Through the verbal banter and laughter that celebrate their love, Missie and Joe heal their wounds and carry on with the business of living, asserting their love and domestic moral values. At its best, the verbal ritual, patterned after the old courtship conversations of Black men vying for the attention and affection of womenfolk,[3] is the unifying force that binds Missie and Joe through joys and tribulations.

Chapter 9

Daisy in "Mule Bone"[1] and The Domestic in "Story in Harlem Slang"[2]

Daisy and the Harlem domestic continue the pattern of the assertive woman expressing her humanity from within the confines of the old-time courtship ritual. Here again, men employ exaggerated, hyperbolic talk with falsetto voice to buy a woman's love and win her over in romance, marriage, or for economic support. Camouflaged admist the humor, hyperbole, and exaggerated romantic language in the encounters experienced by Daisy and the domestic is the work ethic theme and how some men, vagabonds of love and song, aim to exploit Black women to survive. Hurston shows how even the most verbally gifted Black men of exaggerated talk cannot surpass the genius and wisdom of the assertive Black woman in the survival game. Words are indeed a woman's weapons of survival; men cannot overcome on mere word power alone, as the encounters of unemployed men with Daisy and the nameless domestic will illustrate.

Daisy represents the rural folk version of the courtship ritual, as Hurston perceived it, with the standard refrain "Are you a flying lark or a setting dove?" The Harlem domestic (a product of the Great Migration experience of Southern Blacks moving to the Northern urban cities during the 1920s and 1930s) illustrates the re-adapted urban version of the ritual. In hipped, urban style, two pimps in zoot suits position themselves on a streetcorner in the ghetto and rap and woof for the affection (in reality, economic support in exchange for love) of an employed woman with money in her pocket. In this case, it happens to be a domestic worker who is by nature one of the most assertive personality types we find in Hurston's fiction. A surprising turn of events occurs when she ventures into the arena of urban courtship conversation. Her wit and verbal fluency in Harlem slanguage are her saving graces as she battles on the turf of two big talkers who rely on the persuasive word to live and avoid a day's work at hard labor.

Like Missie, Daisy and the domestic excel in the varied forms of the courtship ritual they participate in; their skill is evident as the talk experience moves from a playful and exaggerated expression of superficial love by the men to a serious but realistic one of purposeful talk by the women. Unlike Missie, though, Daisy and the domestic are very aggressive and vigilant in their speech relationships. The circumstances of their conversation with men are totally different from Missie's. Daisy and the domestic are unmarried women who are not in love and who have no financial ties to men. They do not talk of love in playful, imaginative words as Missie does; they consider the love talk they hear from men to be useless woofing.

To the men, on the other hand, these women are economic bait for a life of leisure and sex. These two conflicting views are therefore represented in a transformed and protective version of the courtship relationship. Women are well aware of their vulnerability and they are ever on guard against men who survive by words alone. Least interest is in men who are woofers, the likes of those lazy unemployed bums like Jim and Dave or Sweet Back and Jelly who intend to sweet talk their way into an economic safety net that will secure them food and shelter. A sincere man of words and meaningful work, such as Missie's Joe Banks, a working individual and genuine bearer of love to a wife he supports, is the ideal suitor both women aspire to engage in imaginative courtship talk. When accosted by men the likes of Slemmons who prey on innocents like Joe's Missie, these women fight for survival and self-respect with fiery words. They assert themselves to avoid economic exploitation, not to gain cheap talk about love.

The stories of Daisy and the domestic are similar in plot and theme. There is a false love triangle in the working as the courtship talk begins. Two unemployed men, who excel in talk or song, compete amongst themselves for the favor of a woman. The talk is hilarious and believable at times, but it turns for the worse when the onus is placed on the woman to "pay for the men's verbal flattery" by taking them under her monetary wing. Love emotions are obviously absent as the woman generates a verbal tug of war focusing on the reality of work, avoiding talk about a fictitious romance. She scorns them and brands their talk worthless and totally ineffective at winning her over. The assertive woman gets on with the business of working to satisfy her immediate survival needs. Love and marriage will eventually result from a real courtship (like that of Missie and Joe, Lucy and John, or Janie and Tea Cake, perhaps), and not from an unreal one founded on exaggerated lies by woofing con-men.

In *Act III* of *Mule Bone*, two boyhood friends, Jim and Dave, verbally squabble for the affection of Daisy, long after they have gone to trial for a previous fight over her. Jim assaults Dave with a mule bone, is found guilty, and is banished from town. As he walks away along the railroad tracks, Jim meets Daisy and woofs about his love for her: "I could kiss you every day—just as regular as pit tracks" (104). But his serenade comes to an end when the two are joined by his rival, Dave. Both men compete for Daisy's affection as they simultaneously solve their differences through a lying contest. Aggression is channelled into word battle. Daisy remains neutral as the contest unfolds because she is suspicious that "neither one of y'all dont keer nothin' 'bout me" (194). But the men act more civil and Daisy pretends to be influenced by the flattery she hears:

> Jim: Cross my feet and hope to die! I'd ruther see all de other wimmen folks in de worl' dead than for you to have de toothache.
>
> Dave: If I was dead and any other woman came near my coffin de undertaker would have to do his job all over—'Cause I'd git right up and walk off. Furthermore, Miss Daisy, ma'am, also ma'am, which would you ruther be—a lark a-flying' or a dove a-settin', ma'am, also ma'am?
>
> Daisy: 'Course I'd ruther be a dove (105). Since Daisy expresses a preference for marriage (which means long-term security for the men), Jim and Dave go into a frenzy of poetic talk to win her hand. The flattery to win her over almost lapses into a fist fight when Dave assumes Jim is trying to play the dozens and lowrate him with the inflammatory reference, "nigger."
>
> Jim: Miss Daisy, ma'am, also ma'am . . . if you marry dis nigger over my head, I'm goin' to git me a green hickory club and season it over yo' head.
>
> Dave: Don't you be skeered, baby. Papa kin take keer o' you. (To Jim, suiting the action of the word) Countin' from de finger back to de thumb . . . Start anything, I got you some.
>
> Jim: Aw, I don't want no more fight wid you, Dave.

Dave: Who said anything about fighting? We just provin who love
Daisy de best. (To Daisy) Now, which one of us you think you
love de best?
Daisy: Deed I don't know, Dave (105).

As Daisy is impressed by neither, the men have to battle once
more until she declares a winner. The exaggerated talk intensifies:

Dave: Baby, I'd walk de water for you and tote a mountain on my
head while I'm walkin'.
Jim: Know whut I'd do, honey babe? If you was a thousand miles
from home and you didn't have no ready-made money and you
had to walk all de way, walkin' till yo' feet start to rollin',
just like a wheel, and I was ridin' way up in de sky, I'd sep
backwards offa dat air-plane just to walk home wid you (105).

Jim's talk wins Daisy's praise and a real marriage proposal as she
proclaims to him in her assertive voice: "When you talk to me like dat,
I just can't stand it. Let's us git married right now" (105). Jim agrees
for a moment, but is then brought back to his senses when Daisy
speaks of the real meaning of the marital relationship. She desires a
place to stay and food to eat, favoring the work ethic over false love and
Jim's guitar playing: "You can throw dat box away and work as a yard
man using a hoe and spade" (106). Such realistic talk precipitates a
change in Jim's mood and conversation. He and Dave grow closer
together based on their mutual indifference to working for white folks
and supporting a wife. They are so upset at the prospect of taking Daisy
in marriage for a life of work and love that they engage in a word battle
wherein each man now rejects her. Jim offers her to Dave who quickly
shuffles her back to Jim:

Jim: Come to think of it, Dave, she was yourn fist. You take and
handle dat spade for her.
Dave: You heard her say it is all I can do to lift up dese feets and put
'em down. Where I'm goin' to git any time to wrassle wid any
hoes and shovels? You kin git 'round better 'n me. You won
Daisy—I give in. I ain't goin' to bite no frien' of mine in de
back (106).

Daisy realizes their insincerity and prefers to let them remain bosom musical friends, voicing her rejection of both with a few fiery words of her own: "Both you niggers can git yo' hat on yo' heads and git on down de road. Neither one of y'all don't have to have me. I got a good job and plenty men beggin' for yo' chance" (106). For all three participants in the love triangle, the courtship talk is quickly forgotten once words of truth and reality are uttered by the assertive woman. She will not be exploited by any man who refuses to do a decent day's work to demonstrate personal responsibility, and love and protection of her.

In "Story in Harlem Slang," two penniless but verbally shrewd pimps, Sweet Back and Jelly, hustle on a streetcorner for an existence off female labor. The main device in their survival game is their effective use of the courtship ritual in a verbal encounter with a promising-looking female passerby.[3] If they secure the right woman through the use of convincing flattery and a display of rich non-verbal mannerisms to cockily highlight their own stylish attire, then they can carry out their plan to gain wealth by not working. Through carefully crafted slang, they can "sugar-cure a lady's feelings" (84) to a point where she is so "hungry for love" (90) that she pays for it by providing them with free meals or even room and board. If, however, they meet a woman just as astute and clever as they are in the courtship ritual, then they fail miserably. Such is the latter case when they engage an assertive woman in the verbal love game on a Harlem streetcorner. A word battle of humor and derision unfolds as the talkers delve deep into the Harlemese vernacular of streetcorner communication for their survival against real hunger.

On Wednesday afternoon (payday for the domestics in New York), Sweet Back and Jelly position themselves in lounging poses on the avenue. Their plight is desperate, for they are penniless and hungry and are confident that they can con their way to a hot meal. Having no interest in working, they are prepared to talk and love their way into a good meal. Before the encounter, the two idle their time in conversation which clearly demonstrates how verbally efficient they are at masking their poverty. Each is such a competent trickster who convincingly lays claim to the fact that he is not "cold in hand" (86) by making mock pocket gestures to indicate the presence of money. In this deceptive game, played with precision, there is a stalemate, as neither outwits the other. But when Sweet Back speaks more directly by shaming Jelly about the ugly woman, "a beat broad, a coal-scuttle blonde" (88, 89), he escorted the previous night, there is bound to be a clear winner or loser in the verbal tug of war. Sweet Back's scorn takes on the characteristics of the dozens, bringing them almost to the point of fighting when Jelly voices his anger.

> Jelly: Sweet Back, you fixing to talk out of place.
> Sweet Back: If you trying to jump salty, Jelly, that's your mammy.
> Jelly: Don't play in the family, Sweet Back. I don't play the dozens. I done told you (88, 89).

Jelly's fighting temperament is short-lived as Sweet Back wisely changes the conversation to a general discussion about the color of women they prefer. Even this talk comes to an end when they realize the urgency of breaking into lounging poses and looking rich and cocky, for the female object of their mutual survival need is approaching. Exaggerated play talk takes on a real, hidden purpose for them now. They have to create appealing words to arouse the fancy of a listener, just as the preacher does in performance before a congregation or as the storeporch talker does before a woman passing Joe Clarke's store.

Sweet Back and Jelly, expert lovers in arousing the passion of lonely women, are in performance as they put on the conquering look and begin their verbal gestures of flirtation to attract the domestic who is as urbanly hipped in language and dress as they are. As she approaches them, she is in the groove; she is "reeling and rocking her hips down the avenue" (91). They shower her with flattery as the courtship ritual begins on a Harlem streetcorner:

> Jelly: (In a loud voice) Big stars falling! It must just be before day!
> Sweetback: Yeah, man! Must be recess in Heaven—pretty angel like that out on the ground.
> Jelly: I'd walk clear to Diddy-Wah-Diddy to get a chance to speak to a pretty lil' ground-angel like that.
> Sweetback: Aw, man, you ain't willing to go very far. Me, I'd go slap to Ginny Gall, where they eat cow-rump, skin and all.
> Jelly: Baby, what's on de rail for de lizard (91)?

The girl engages the two in talk as she condescends to Jelly's question: "A Zigaboo down in Georgy, where I come from, asked a woman that one time and the judge told him ninety days" (91). Sweet

Back overlooks the uncompromising insult and tries to befriend her by striking up conversation about Georgia, her home state. But the ploy is unsuccessful as the woman is completely unresponsive. She tersely ridicules them when they deny their Southern origins and the fact they have come North to avoid hard labor: "Oh, don't try to make out youse no northerner, you! Youse from right down in 'Bam your ownself! One of them Russians, eh? Rushed up here to get away from a job of work" (91).

Both men realize that this bold and realistic talk will not lead to their main goal—a free meal. They hustle with words again. This time they eyeball the domestic with a killing look and commence to flatter her about her shape and class; she's real people, somebody important. Following this talk is an invitation to enter the cafe and grab a meal, but, again, the smart-talking girl demurs, growing "stiff like a ramrod" (91) as she pointedly asks: "You got any money? Nobody ain't pimping on me. You dig me" (91). But the two men are desperate as they continue to beg for her cooperation. "Aw, now, baby!" (91), Jelly pleads as the girl speaks more insults about their line of business as male prostitutes: "I seen you two mullet-heads before. I was uptown where Joe Brown had you all in the go-long last night. Dat cop sure hates a pimp. All he needs to see is the pimp's salute, and he'll out with high night-stick and ship your head to the red. Beat your head just as flat as a dime" (91, 92)!

Sweet Back takes a turn at countering the girl's superior scorn and laughter by offering to change the subject from the law to one of socializing and eating: "Oh, let's us don't talk about the law. Let's talk about us. You going inside with me to holler 'let one come flopping! One come grunting! Snatch one from de rear!'" (92). But, she remains resistant as she infuses her rejection of the invitation with a folk wisdom couched in harsh laughter and insulting name-calling: "Naw indeed! You skillets is trying to promote a meal on me. But it'll never happen, brother. You barking up the wrong tree. I wouldn't give you air if you was stopped up in a jug. I'm not putting out a thing. I'm just like a cemetery—I'm not putting out, I'm taking in! Dig? I'll tell you like the farmer told the potato—plant you now and dig you later" (92).

Sweet Back will not bow to defeat, for he has not eaten a good meal in two days. Making a desperate gesture to physically restrain her, Sweet Back is frightened off when the domestic threatens to loud talk the avenue and get the attention of a cop. She develops a little ingenious drama of her own when she finally emasculates Sweet Back, delineating him as a bedbug, a leech and thief, and aiming to damage his prized possession, his zoot suit, if he doesn't leave her alone. She is a mistress of the dozens as she threatens and insults him: "Trying to snatch my pocketbook, eh? (Instead of running, grabs hold of Sweet Back's draping coat-tail and makes a slashing gesture) How much split you want back here? If your feets don't hurry up and take you way from here, you'll ride away. I'll spread my lungs all over New York and call the law. Go ahead, Bedbug! Touch me! And I'll holler like a pretty white woman" (92)!

Although both Sweet Back and Jelly have momentarily fallen from the pimp's exagggerated stature at the hands of the wise and assertive domestic, their talking ritual will resume as soon as they spot another non-assertive prey who yields to their convincing love talk and deceptive rich-looking appearance. Like Slemmons and Sykes, the pimps will eventually be dethroned for good by another bold and assertive woman the likes of the assertive domestic. Hurston makes it clear in her satire of the hipped, citified talk of the urban ghettoes like Chicago and Harlem, that it is merely exaggerated play talk similar to the Eatonville storeporch courtship talk and that it is all fantasy talk, big lies, that the assertive woman clearly understands and readily challenges with positive results as is the case with the combative domestic or the initially wise Missie.

Chapter 10

Delia in "Sweat"[1]

Marital disharmony and the assertive female voice will be surveyed here with an anlaysis of the character and actions of Delia, a washer woman destined for years to work, sweat, and toil in an unhappy and oppressive marriage. Throughout "Sweat," verbal discord gradually becomes a way of life for Delia and her husband, Sykes, a wife beater who has abused her "nough tuh kill three women, let 'lone change they looks" (200). Their bedroom and kitchen (as contrasted to Missie and Joe's) are battlefields of hate, insulting talk and physical combat. There is no room for peace or love and affection. It is ripe for serpents like Sykes to nest in evil and mischief perpetrated on the sweat, blood and tears of Delia.

Although Delia, a durable Christian woman, hopes for the best and remains committed to the marriage as long as she can, she eventually realizes the futility of her efforts after living fifteen years in misery and hate. During this period, Delia, unlike Missie who learns to love totally in a harmonious marraige relationship, grows to hate vengefully as the unhappy marriage decays into a state of mutual bitterness. The animosity is most apparent in their oral relationship and in the eventual death of Sykes, which is brought about by his own wicked trap set against Delia. Quarrels encompassing the dozens and economic exploitation are common features of the marriage which find Delia bravely standing her ground as the oppressive marriage to Sykes comes to a tragic end.

Throughout the deteriorating relationship, Delia negotiates for respect and lets it be known that her fifteen years of hard work and sweat over a washtub cleaning white folks' clothes will not make her the mule of the world for Sykes' pleasure. He has brutally beaten her into a pitiful sight (likened only to Matt Bonner's old mule in *Their Eyes Were Watching God*) and she does not intend to let him cast her out of her house, her prized possession which she bought and paid for. In behavior uncharacteristic of her habitual meekness, Delia changes as she responds to the physical abuse proliferating in the marriage. For one thing, she verbally defies her husband, the perpetrator of evil "who aint fit tuh carry guts tuh a bear" (201) with a few verbal fireworks of her own. Words become her weapon of survival against the hulking Sykes who constantly preys on his frail and burdened wife with a superior voice and physical brutality. Joe Clarke, one of the storeporch talkers who comments on the marriage, likens Delia's years of oppression and domestic abuse experienced at the hands of Sykes to a work-worn piece of sugar cane:

> There's plenty men dat takes a wife lak dey do a joint uh sugar-cane. It's round, juicy an sweet when dey gits it. But dey squeeze an' grind, squeeze an' grind an' wring tell dey wring every drop uh pleasure dat's in 'em out. When dey's satisfied dat dey is wrung dry, dey treats 'em jes lak dey do a cane-chew. Dey thows 'em away. Dey knows what dey is doin' while dey is at it, an' hates theirselves fuh it but they keeps hangin' after huh tell she's empty. Den dey hates huh fuh bein' a cane-chew an' in de way (206).

This story of Delia's oppression and her eventual growth to freedom through an assertion of her identity is one of Hurston's finest pieces of writing, on a par with the great novel, *Their Eyes Were Watching God*. "Sweat" is about one of the assertive women in Hurston's art growing to hate. Delia's story is one of hate, whereby a Christian woman learns to hate with a cold, bloody rage and red fury so complete that she lets her spouse (now an enemy) die in the very trap he plants for her. Though unattractive from years of hard work and beatings that have left her "thin and frail with stooped, sagging shoulders, work-worn knees, knotty, muscled limbs, harsh knuckly hands. . . . an unhappy little ball in the middle of the big feather bed" (198, 199), Delia overcomes. Her powerful verbal performance projects the image of a strong and bold woman energetically battling her adversary. Her spirit is revitalized as her assertive strengths unveil her stoicism and resistance to marital oppression. After fifteen opressive years, she becomes verbally dominant in crucial confrontational scenes

where Sykes tries to verbally overpower and physically abuse her.
Through blood, sweat, and tears, she prevails and eventually secures the
peace and contentment she long cherishs without the presence of an evil
serpent the likes of Sykes.

The story begins on a Sunday night with a meek but mournful
Delia working and sorting white folks' soiled clothes in her bedroom.
Her toiling figure is balanced against the ruthless and abusive image of
the non-working but able-bodied Sykes. He is a despicable sight as he
enters and disturbs Delia in her work: scowling at the clothes she has
sorted, frightening her with a whip which resembles a coiled snake,
scorning her as "one aggravatin' nigger woman!" (197), and threatening
her about her objection to his meddling with the clothes. His
oppressive tone is blatantly clear as he commands her: "Dont gimme no
lip neither, else A'll throw 'em out and put mah fist up side yo' head to
boot" (198). In addition to this cruelty is Sykes' brutal plan to benefit
from Delia's labors by running her from the home and then securing it
for his sweat heart, fat Bertha.

As Sykes' verbal abuse and physical threats intensify, a new Delia
emerges to combat this menace in her home. She no longer fears him
and the big bull whip he carries. Neither does she design a plan of her
own to remove him from her home. Rather, she reasons his case with
Old Testament justice by asserting to herself, "Oh well, whatever goes
over the Devil's back, is got to come under his belly. Sometime or
ruther, Sykes, like everybody else, is gointer reap his sowing" (199).
There is an inward, spiritual change in her overall attitude toward
Sykes: ". . . she was able to build a spiritual earthworks against her
husband. His shells could no longer reach her. Amen" (199). She
possesses a "triumphant indifference to all that he was or did" (200).

Delia's new attitude is more apparent in her verbal relationship
with Sykes, the living exemplification of a snake. Verbally, frail Delia
triumphs over Sykes long before his demise, by the very plot he
attempts to carry out against Delia. He is already diminished and
dispatched in her eyes when she challenges him early on in two crucial
scenes, one occurring in the bedroom and the other in the kitchen. Her
victory is a verbal one whereby she plays the dozens and ridicules Sykes
to the point where he is virtually helpless and speechless. She
emasculates him as she methodicly strips away his once superior
voice and mighty fighting hand. His revenge for the verbal dethroning
can no longer be physical, for fear of white intervention from her
employers. So he hatches the plot which costs him his life and

foreshadows Delia's freedom, that of planting the snake in the bedroom
for Delia's death. Delia holds her own from the beginning scenes
recording their numerous verbal confrontations to the ending scenes
where she dispenses Old Testament justice on Sykes by remaining
inactive and letting him confront the serpent which he originally
intended for her. Delia's growth as assertive woman, in her marriage of
evil in the symbolic Garden of Evil which Hurston has created, is at the
center of the story's plot.

In the first confrontational scene, Delia's stoicism and assertive
skills displace her former meekness. Of this change in demeanor,
Hurston writes: "Delia's habitual meekness seemed to slip from her
shoulder like a blown scarf. She was on her feet; her poor little body,
her bare knuckly hands bravely defying the strapping hulk before her"
(198). Her new verbal aggressiveness occurs in the untidy bedroom. Its
unkempt state represents the breakdown and disorganization of the
marriage. It is an unclean place where dirty linens are sorted, where
disorder and argument occur, and where only Delia's livelihood
represents a positive economic presence. It is also a place where she has
to defend herself for her dear verbal and physical life. In the following
dialogue, a bold, assertive Delia rebukes the brutal Sykes for further
soiling the white folks' clothes which in reality form her occupation.
She speaks about the importance of the work ethic and brandishes her
own threat of physical violence with an iron skillet if Sykes attacks her
again:

> Delia: Looka heah, Sykes, you done gone too fur. Ah been married
> to you fur fifteen years, and Ah been takin' in washin' fur
> fifteen years. Sweat, sweat, sweat! Work and sweat, cry and
> sweat, pray and sweat!
> Sykes: (Brutally) What's that got to do with me?
> Delia: What's it got to do with you, Sykes? Mah tub of suds is
> filled yo' belly with vittles more times than yo' hands is
> filled it. Mah sweat is done paid for this house and Ah reckon
> Ah kin keep on sweatin' in it. (She seized the iron skillet
> from the stove and struck a defensive pose, which act
> surprised him greatly, coming from her. It cowed him and he
> did not strike her as he usually did.) Naw you won't. That ole
> snaggle-toothed black woman you runnin' with aint comin'
> heah to pile up on mah sweat and blood. You aint paid for

nothin' on this place, and Ah'm gointer stay right heah till
Ah'm toted out foot foremost.

Sykes: Well, you better quit gittin' me riled up, else they'll be
totin' you out sooner than you expect. Ah'm so tired of you
Ah dont know whut to do. Gawd! how Ah hates skinny
women! (A little awed by this new Delia, he sidled out of the
door and slammed the back gate after him) (198–199).

A new Delia—a woman of words and weapons—causes the once
omnipotent Sykes to retreat from the reality of her speech. He shows
himself to be a coward, as he can only respond covertly to her powerful,
talk later in the night while she's sleeping in bed, by abruptly
announcing his presence with threatening behavior directed at her
having earlier brandished the skillet for self defense: "Gimme some
kivah heah, an' git yo' damn foots over on yo' own side! Ah oughter
mash you in yo' mouf fuh drawing dat skillet on me" (199). Delia
remains indifferent to his antics, for she has triumphed in round one of
their on-going battle for possession of her property rights from her
years of washing and ironing white folks' clothes.

Before the second confrontational scene, Sykes and Delia fight
more frequently, with no peaceful interludes. Sykes is bent on taking
the house and bringing in a more appealing woman to replace Delia.
But Delia stands her ground and shows her backbone, even when Sykes
carries out a plan to cause her death. On this occasion, he torments
Delia by bringing a six foot snake to the home. Delia fears snakes and
works herself into a fury that grows bloodier by the hour as Sykes
places the snake in a box at the back door entrance to the home. He
refuses to move it, announcing that he has more affection for the
serpent than he does for Delia: "Ah thinks uh damn sight mo' uh him
dan you! Dat's a nice snake an' anybody doan lak 'im kin jes' hit de
grit" (203).[2]

Delia will not remain silent at Syke's devilment. She is in a
bloody rage at Sykes' actions and takes the initiative to approach him
about the snake. This act leads to the second major quarrel between
them—one that now takes place in the kitchen at the dinner table, a
place of turmoil, of total disharmony because Delia cannot eat in peace
with Sykes. The kitchen, like the bedroom, thus, becomes a second
battlefield for them as Delia asserts herself in a more hostile, aggressive
tone. She now draws on the dozens as she scorns Sykes about his looks
and her degree of hate and contempt for him. Sykes is no match for her

verbal wrath as the conversaton heats up into downright name-calling
and personal insults. It initially begins with her complaint about the
snake and ends with her description of Sykes as an abominable dog:

> Delia: Sykes, Ah wants you tuh take dat snake 'way fum heah. You
> done starved me an' Ah put up widcher, you done beat me an
> Ah took dat, but you done kilt all mah insides bringin' dat
> varmint heah.
>
> Sykes: (Pours out a saucer full of coffee and drinks it deliberately
> before answering her.) A whole lot Ah keer 'bout how you
> feels inside uh out. Dat snake aint goin' no damn wheah till
> Ah gits ready fuh 'im tuh go. So fur as beatin' is concerned,
> yuh aint took near all dat you gointer take ef yuh stay 'roun
> me.
>
> Delia: (Pushes back her plate and gets up from the table and speaks
> calmly.) Ah hates you, Sykes. Ah hates you tuh de same
> degree dat Ah useter love yuh. Ah done took an' took till mah
> belly is full up tuh mah neck. Dat's de reason Ah got mah
> letter fum de church an' moved mah membership tuh
> Woodbridge—so Ah don't haftuh take no sacrament wid yuh.
> Ah dont wantuh see yuh 'roun' me atall. Lay 'roun' wid dat
> 'oman all yuh wants tuh, but gwan 'way fum me an' mah
> house. Ah hates yuh lak uh suck-egg dog (204).

Here, Delia strikes a severe blow at Sykes' ego. She hates him
deeply enough to associate him with a kind of dog that most rural
farmers detest and will shoot instantly: one that scavenges a hen house,
raids nests of their eggs, and then lays around sucking them.[3] Such a
dog conjures up revulsion in the same manner that Sykes arouses
Delia's disgust when she sees his behavior in her home and
community. The canine reference serves Delia's purpose sufficiently, as
it whittles Sykes down to a size and status beneath hers. She scorns
him so effectively that he is dumbfounded and momentarily unable to
defend himself: "Sykes almost let the huge wad of corn bread and collard
greens he was chewing fall out of his mouth in amazement. He had a
hard time whipping himself up to the proper fury to try to answer
Delia" (204). When he does gain the strength to respond, he engages in
his own style of ridicule and a mild form of the dozens to convey his
hatred for Delia: "Well, Ah'm glad you does hate me. Ah'm sho' tiahed
uh you handlin' ontuh me. Ah don't want yuh. Look at yuh stringey

ole neck! Yo 'rawbony laigs an' arms is enough tuh cut uh man tuh death. You look jes' lak de devul's doll-baby tuh me. You cain't hate me no worse dan Ah hates you. Ah been hatin' you fuh years" (204).

Delia is the verbally superior of the two, as she responds in kind to Sykes. She engages in the dozens, too, as she denigrates Sykes even more harshly about his looks. Humor is interwined with the frankness of Delia's assertion of his ugliness. She delivers a final knock-out blow to Sykes' manhood when she levels a firm warning about the repercussions in store for him if he ever assaults her again. She speaks with no signs of fear: "Yo' ole black hide don't look lak nothin tuh me, but uh passle uh wrinkled up rubber, wid yo' big ole yeahs flappin' on each side lak uh paih uh buzzard wings. Don't think Ah'm gointuh be run 'way fum mah house neither. Ah'm goin' tuh de white folks bout you, mah young man, de very nex' time you lay yo' han's on me. Mah cup is done run ova'" (204).

Sykes is frightened by Delia's threats of white involvement and does not respond to Delia's threat. Instead, he departs the house a broken man, knowing full well he has lost the second verbal fight with frail Delia. She has, in a word, killed him off verbally, and he is no longer the man of the house. His subsequent attempt to murder her with the planted snake further verifies the fact that the marriage is ended, with Delia being the victor and rightful owner of their communal property.

Delia's triumph over Sykes is also demonstrated by her actions in the final scenes, once she discovers the snake planted in their bedroom on a Sunday night, the very time she sorts her clothes for washing early Monday morning. She is first horrified as the bedroom now becomes a place of total darkness and evil. Then, after taking refuge in religious doctrine and the adage of an eye for an eye, she develops into a cold, bloody rage as she thinks of Sykes' planned malice against her, intending to abandon him to the same fate he had designed for her. She is no longer a devoted wife willing to assist him in overcoming his misdeeds. He alone must suffer the consequences of his actions with the snake and reap what he sowed in the whole process. A cold, bloody rage overcomes Delia, and then coherent thought as she experiences a period of introspection, a space of retrospection and then a mixture of both followed by an awful calm. She reasons, as she contemplates Sykes' forthcoming doom: "Well, Ah done de bes' Ah could. If things aint right, Gawd knows taint mah fault" (208).

When Sykes unwittingly climbs into the marital bed of discord, symbolized graphically by his struggles with the snake, Delia stands beneath the bedroom window to witness the attack. Through his death, she starts a new life, symbolized by the sun's rising to start a new day in her life, free for good of the evil Sykes, the embodiment of a serpent in her life for over fifteen years. She revives herself from the terror of witnessing Sykes' death by creeping over to a flower bed of four o'clocks near the cool earth. Nature is her comfort. A firm Chinaberry tree is her rod of support as she rises to the occasion without fear, ignores Sykes' cries for help and waits for the warmness of the day to begin her life anew. The sun is her keeper; it beams as brightly on her re-birth as it does on Syke's cold death. It is the sign of hope that guides her to a stage of peaceful widowhood where she can take refuge in religion and enjoy the fruits of her blood, sweat and tears. As well, her assertive individualism, employed in the effort to break free of an unhappy marriage, has afforded her this final opportunity to secure tranquility. She symbolically killed Sykes, the evil serpent, in dialogue of the dozens long before she let Sykes sweat and die at the hands of his own evil plot.

Chapter 11

Lucy in *Jonah's Gourd Vine*[1]

Lucy and Janie are the most assertive women voices that we find in Hurston's longer fiction. For both, the experience of loving totally and speaking one's mind freely functions as a basic survival element in their development to maturity and happiness in marriage. To be one with a man means the total freedom to assert the self in a mutual union of word power, love, and respect. Through various stages of the marriage experience, each woman undergoes a verbal metamorphosis that reveals her eventual growth from youthful innocence to emotional maturity. The experiences she undergoes are all evident in the disposition of speech she demonstrates when talking love words in courtship or speaking in tones of displeasure and reprimand. She might also speak the dozens if she is angered by her spouse's behavior.

Lucy and Janie are very much alike in the sense that they both assert themselves in love relationships, but, at the same time, they are also different in their personal approach to the black man and in their attitude toward the institution of marriage. A woman of the Post-Reconstruction Era, Lucy is a traditionalist regarding the Black woman's role in the family. She remains committed for twenty-two years to her marital vow to John, despite his years of infidelity and neglect of their seven children. Her speech in the early marriage years reveals genuine efforts to love and encourage John in his political and religious ventures, while her talk in the later years reflects her attempt to maintain the marriage by severely tongue-lashing him for his repeated sins of the flesh. On her deathbed, her emotional mother-to-daughter dialogue with Isie reveals a verbal re-awakening. She speaks of the consequences of having committed herself too fully in marriage to John, of having loved him too much, almost better than herself, and of having been his protective gourd vine too long. In the end, Lucy's insight affords her the opportunity to articulate perceptive words about the man she once loved, refusing to untie the binding love knot of marriage and union.

By contrast, Janie is a liberated woman of the Roaring-Twenties and nineteen-thirties generation of assertive Black women. She has no compunction or regret about rebelling from a pre-arranged and loveless marriage, particularly when it clashes with her own dreams and expectations as woman. Her desire for change and chance to keep in tune with her personal aspirations causes her to experiment with three men in marriage before she finally experiences total love and happiness. She is eventually able to articulate her feelings of love and contentment to Tea Cake, her ideal image of a husband, and later, in years of widowhood, to her trusted woman friend, Phoeby. For Janie, a happy marriage, springing from free choice, enables her to explore the speech process in harmony and love with an equally compatible mate. Marriage is freedom to be her verbal self while attempting to reach the limits of her grasp for dreams on the horizon. In a short-lived but fluently harmonious relationship with her spouse, Janie grows content, while her assertive sister, Lucy, grows discontent with a long term love relationship that eventually deteriorates into misery and heartache. The story of each woman's growth to an effective level of assertive individualism in marriage will be explored in detail with a study of the two major novels, *Jonah's Gourd Vine* and *Their Eyes Were Watching God.*

Chapters two through sixteen of *Jonah's Gourd Vine* chronicle the rise and fall of the Pearson marriage, beginning with the courtship ritual and marriage ceremony, and concluding with the last days of the ill-fated marriage wherein Lucy's fiery deathbed conversation with a sinful John serves as a symbolic dissolution of the union. Throughout the various stages of the relationship, Lucy's voice changes into an increasingly powerful force to be reckoned with. She is in a position to negotiate respect for herself as woman and individual from John, their children, his church congregation and the townsfolk. Persuasive influence and strong leadership qualities are the ingredients embedded in her assertive individualism.

As the years of the marriage pass, so does the power of Lucy's voice increase. By the end of the marriage, though in misery, and totally unhappy, she emerges as a strong talking woman who upholds her principles and ideals to the very end. Certainly she reigns as an assertive woman of endurance and high distinction in Hurston's art. Materially, she may have failed in a marriage gone sour, but spiritually and individualistically she prospered. From Hurston's perspective of Black womanhood, this is what counts. She endures the marriage by her mere verbal strength and basic humanistic qualities. The various stages of her marriage to John Pearson, from the good times to the bad moments, bear this out.

In the beginning courtship phase of the union between Lucy and John, verbal cohesion is significant. John first attempts to establish the correct rapport with Lucy who is a woman of words. He is only an over-the-creek Negro who lacks the reading, writing, and speaking skills that would make him her verbal and intellectual equal. To speak effectively to the well-educated Lucy, John, therefore, requires appropriately compatible words, for he knows that other girls "merely called for action, but with Lucy he needed words and words that he did not have" (63). Aware of her verbal gift and superiority over her suitor, young Lucy modifies her assertive voice into a mild one of instruction, counsel, and motivation. The intelligent and kind Lucy encourages John to refine his verbal skills in the context of the school and church where she excels. She advises him that he can speak pieces better than she: "You kin speak 'em better'n me" (63). Responding to her friendly coaching voice, John strives to develop an appropriate speech to speak his love and start the oral courtship ritual where they will be on equal verbal footing. He particularly aims to establish a tone that would not turn her away from him in "disgust" (64), but would rather make her "gasp and do him reverence" (65).

Much of the beginning courtship period, therefore, focuses on John's growing to a level of verbal maturity equal to that of Lucy, who because of schooling and other environmental factors, knows how to effectively express herself. John's heroic feat in killing the rattle snake so that he can safely carry Lucy across the creek without fear (66) draws them closer together in courtship and eventual verbal equality. After this deed, he feels more confident as they speak freely about her diminutive size up against his huge bulkiness: "Little ez you is nobody wouldn't keer how fur he hafta tote you. You ain't even uh handful," remarks John. Lucy holds her own in her response: "Ahm uh lil' piece uh leather, but well put t'gether, Ah thankee, Mist' John" (69). As well, their joint participation in other school and church affairs also strengthens the love ties of communication between them. Compatible talk in all aspects of their relationship is crucial.

The love relationship develops further after John becomes aware of the growing power of his own public oratory. Somehow John feels that he must be verbally competent before he can grow into a full union with Lucy. The inspiration for both his expressive maturity and new manhood is established in a confrontation with Ned, his stepfather. Ned, an over-the-creek sharecropper, threatens to whip John with trace chains for his philandering with Lucy—activities which have taken him away from work in the cotton fields. John's response to Ned finds him becoming verbally competent enough to defend his ground. With feet spread wide and a large rock drawn back to hurl at Ned, John talks defiantly with a verbal strength he thought he lacked: "Don't you vary! Dog damn yuh! Come uhnother step and Ah'll bust you wide open, wid dis rock. You kin cuff and kick Zeke and them around but Ah done promised Gawd and uh couple uhother men tuh stomp yo' guts out next time you raise yo' hand tuh me" (83).

John speaks even more fluently when he steps before a tree trunk and, through the use of figurative speech and personification, throws the character of Ned upon it. He is all word power as he speaks the dozens to lowrate Ned's character:

> You ole battle-hammed, slew-foot, box-ankled nubbin, you! You ain't nothin' and ain't got nothin' but whut God give uh billy-goat, and then round tryin' tuh hell-hack folks! Tryin' tuh kill somebody wid talk, but if you wants tuh fight,—dat's de very corn Ah wants tuh grind. You come grab me now, and Ah bet yuh Ah'll stop you from suckin' eggs. Hit me now! G'wan hit me! Bet Ah'll break uh egg in yuh! Youse all parts of uh pig! Don't you part yo lips tuh me no mo' jes' ez long ez heben is happy—do Ah'll put somethin' on yuh dat lye soap won't take off. You ain't nothin' but uh big ole pan of fell bread. Now dat's de wood wid de bark on it (85, 86).

Following this verbal demonstration of strength, John longs for Lucy and returns to the Pearson plantation for good. He is now a confident man who strives hard to match Lucy in the communication process. In church, he sings and prays and speaks pieces alongside of Lucy (92, 93). His oratorical powers are quickly recognized by all, including Lucy. He writes love letters and poetry to Lucy (93), as they equally engage in the oral ritual of old style courtship. Now John becomes the verbal aggressor as he courts Lucy and then voices a proposal of marriage in poetic speech. He is the master of persuasive talk as they knot a handkerchief from different ends (This is one of the typical pastimes of courters during the 1930s in Black folk culture). When the designs in the handkerchief are completed, they form a "love knot," the very bond of marital unity John hopes to establish for real in his courtship talk with Lucy. Lucy, a mistress of word power, pretends innocence as she purposely permits John the opportunity to talk his way into her heart with a proposal to take her hand in marriage:

> John: . . . which would you ruther be, if you had yo' ruthers—uh
> lark uh flyin', uh uh dove uh settin'?
> Lucy: Ah don't know whut you talkin' 'bout, John. It mus' be uh
> new riddle.
> John: Naw 'tain't Lucy. Po' me, Lucy. Ahm uh one winged bird.
> Dont leave me lak dat, Lucy.
> Lucy: Look, John, de knot is tied right, ain't it pretty?
> John: Yeah, Lucy iss sho pretty. We done took and tied dis knot,
> Miss Lucy, less tie uh 'nother one (124–125).

As the interchange draws to an end, John showers Lucy with more exaggerated love talk before making a final appeal for her hand in marriage:

> John: Lucy, Ah looked up intuh Heaven and Ah seen you among de
> angels right 'round dethrone, and when Ah seen *you*, mah
> heart swole up and put wings on mah shoulders, and Ah 'gin
> tuh fly 'round too, but Ah never would uh knowed yo' name if
> ole Gab'ull hadn't uh whispered it tuh me. (Extending his
> hands appealingly) Miss Lucy, how 'bout changin' from
> Potts tuh Pearson?
> Lucy: Yeah, John.
> John: When?
> Lucy: Whenever you ready fuh me. You know mo' bout dat den Ah
> do (125–126).

John and Lucy then marry with the understanding that both are verbal and spiritual equals in their union of love. John vows to hold up his end of the love knot by remaining true and loving to Lucy, by having her put her dependence in him as he props her up on every leaning side (131). Lucy loves John with a devotion and dedication that cause her to hold her end of the love union by leaving her prosperous home life and joining him in the house-servants' quarters of the Pearson plantation. She realizes, to her mother's chagrin, that property ownership and materialism do not necessarily make love and happiness.

As the marriage begins to take its course starting with the early years on the Pearson plantation grounds, Lucy performs her task as faithful and loving wife, while John in turn acts responsibly as a husband. Their peace and contentment and overall happiness are most indicative in their verbal communication. But, in due time, John sins and grows verbally arrogant, compelling Lucy to draw on fiery word power to assert herself vigorously against his infidelity with the hope that he will discontinue such a despicable act. Her words, however, have no immediate positive effect on John's misdeeds and infidelity. The marriage begins to disintegrate as misery becomes the root consequence of Lucy's assertive individualism—an avenue of what may be termed her constructive criticism to rectify John's wrongdoing.

With the marriage knot broken, the talk in the marriage now reaches a new level as it moves from love to critical dialogue about John's errant behavior and his repeated dismemberment of their symbolic love handkerchief. There is no cohesive verbal union between them as Lucy's language changes to communication bordering on hostility and frustration. She speaks her mind, constantly frailing him about his exploits with Big Oman and other women of the town in general. After he nearly drowns coming home from Big Oman's, Lucy confronts him about his sin in the eyes of his family and before God: "Ah'm so glad you ain't dead 'way from me and mah lil' chillun, and then again Ah hated tuh think 'bout you headed tuh judgment in yo' sins" (143). As well, she asserts herself regarding his possible need for freedom to go to another woman. Boldly, she states he's free to take his heart where he pleases, thus ending their marriage: "If you loves her de bes', John, you gimme our chillun and you go on where yo' love lie" (144). But John counters with his verbal strength intact. He articulates his love for her, attributing his weakness and violation of the marital love knot to "the brute beast in him" (144) and pleading for forgiveness. Lucy obliges even though she clearly senses that the marriage is falling apart because of John's wrongdoing. She's of the firm opinion that the two of them are "tied tuhgether by uh long cord string and youse at one end and Ahm at de other. Way off" (157).

Despite John's continued infidelity, Lucy remains a pillar of strength in the marriage even during pregnancy and childbirth. When the

strong, able-bodied John should be her helping hand, he is absent in sin
and her cries for help while in pain at childbirth are uttered (like
Walker's Celie's) to God: "Oh Gawd," Lucy screams out, "have mercy
on me! Have mussy in uh mos' puhticular manner. Have mussy on
mah ever-dyin' soul" (150)! No longer able to count on John's listening
ear and helping hand, Lucy presses on. Her inner hurt and loneliness do
not prevent her from upholding her end of the marriage partnership, as
when she supportively uses her talking skill to rescue John from jail
for assaulting her brother, Budd, in a fracas over a bed taken from their
home. She is faithful and strong as any wife is expected to be when her
husband is to be defended. Miraculously, three days after giving birth,
she leaves her sick bed to protect John from going to the chain gang,
pleading successfully before the judge to free John. Words are her
calling card, not money for bail. John is saved once again from his sins
because of her influence and assertive power in the community, with
both Black and white people. Her voice is respected and trusted. As
John's travails mount, her voice stands as moral and social authority
asserting honesty, truth and wisdom.

On the home front as well, she hopes that John will heed her
verbal authority. In a pleading voice, she asks that he be a man to his
wife and children, to show some spunk in, as she phrases it, "covering
de ground you stand on. Jump at de sun and eben if you miss it, you
can't help grabbin' hold uh de moon" (156). Once this tone is
maintained, she also cautions him with folk wisdom about his
vulnerability to the assaults of other people: "John you give mah folks
too much tuh go on. Ah wants mah husband tuh be uh great big man
and look over 'em all so's Ah kin make 'm eat up dey talk. Ah wants
tuh uphold yuh in everything, but you know John, nobody can't fight
war wid uh brick" (158).

John is allowed yet another opportunity at rebuilding his
crumbling marriage and also at establishing himself economically
without people trampling all over him as he is sidetracked by his
philandering when Alf Pearson (his presumed white father) provides
him monetary passage for a new start in the all-black town of
Eatonville, Florida. Although physically weak and frail, the morally
strong and loving Lucy remains by his side, despite the bad economic
times and his womanizing. The marriage now has a second chance to
heal the wounds of infidelity. John is ever mindful of Lucy's continued
love for him, as well as her verbal strength in articulating his sins.
Often frightened by her mighty tongue of truth, he acknowledges that

there is power in the mouths of women like his wife: "Dat piece uh red flannel she got between her jaws is equal tuh all de fists God ever made and man ever seen" (157). As the marriage disintegrates, John's words become more and more prophetic, as Lucy takes the verbal helm and repeatedly talks about John's sins. Indeed, she is the woman with the law in her mouth when she asserts her identity in the Pearson home.

Lucy's steadfast verbal might and commitment to the renewed marriage is tested when John begins love talk about their marital vow. Lucy is as verbally astute as ever as she takes on a carefree language demeanor and delves into signifying. She signifies (a way of verbally, but rather indirectly, hinting at an idea) to John about the possibility of her getting another man to take his place. She is so effective in outwitting him that he feels insecure in the talking game and threatens her with a killing if she attempts to break free of the marriage. The following dialogue is a return to the verbal, courtship ritual that originally united the two. Here, however, John is far the more aggressive and adamant in his speech about sealing a permanent love union with Lucy:

> John: Lucy, is you sorry you married me instead uh some big nigger wid uh whole heap uh money and titles hung on tuh him?
>
> Lucy: Whut makes you ast me dat? If you tied uh me, jus' leave me. Another man over de fence waitin fuh yo' job.
>
> John: Li'l Bit, Ah ain't never laid de weight uh mah hand on you in malice. Ain't never raised mah hand tuh yuh even when you gits mad and slaps mah jaws, but lemme tell you somethin' right now, and it ain't two, don't you never tell me no mo' whut you jus' tole me, cause if you do, Ahm goin' tuh kill you jus' ez sho ez gun is iron. Ah's de first wid you, and Ah means tuh be de last. Ain't never no man tuh breathe in yo' face but me. You hear me? Whut made you say dat nohow?
>
> Lucy: Aw, John, you know dat's just uh by-word. Ah hears all de women say dat.
>
> John: Yeah, Ah knows dat too, but you ain't tuh say it. Lemme tell you somethin'. Don't keer whut come uh go, if you ever start out de door tuh leave me, you'll never make it tuh de gate. Ah means tuh blow yo' heart out and hang fuh it.
>
> Lucy: You done—

John: Don't tell me 'bout dem trashy women Ah lusts after once in
  uh while. Dey's less dan leaves uh grass. Lucy do you still
  love me lak you useter?
Lucy: Yeah John, and mo'. Ah got mo' tuh love you fuh now.
John: Neb mine mah crazy talk. Jus' you hug mah neck tight. Ah'd
  sweat in hell fuh yuh. Ah'd take uh job cleanin' out de
  Atlantic Ocean jus' fuh you. Look lak Ah can't git useter de
  thought dat you married me, Lucy, and you got chillun by me
  (179–180).

The love ties between the two are once again in proper place with
each in equal love partnership and verbal harmony. Lucy assumes the
role of supportive wife and devoted mother. She is John's protective
shield, his gourd vine, as husband and wife now explore the unknown
in Eatonville. She is so dedicated to him that she "has the capacity to
spread carpets by his feet and break off the points of thorns" (268). It is
her intellectual expertise and articulate strength that provide direction for
John's successful rise in the town as a major public figure. It is her
wise voice that guides him on the importance of property ownership
and self-employment: "'Tain't nothin' lak being yo' own boss" (178).
Lucy is at his side, as well, when he takes on the pastorship of Zion
Hope, bringing primitive poetry to the pulpit and leadership to the
State Association of preachers. As the preacher's wife, she also wins
the respect of the congregation and town in her efforts to support John,
whom they call a woman-made man (184). It is her verbal ingenuity on
the public or community level in conversation and action before the
townsfolk that helps John to rise.

On the home front, Lucy is a preacher to John in her own right.
She relies on her persuasive talking skill as she coaches him on the
qualities of leadership necessary to remain on top. Folk wisdom is
evident in her talk about how he should handle church politics: "Don't
pump dem deacons so much. Dey'll swell up and be de runiation of
yuh. Much up de young folks and you got somebody tuh strain wid
dem old rams when dey git day habits on. You lissen tuh me. Ah
hauled de mud tuh make old Cuffy. Ah know whuts in 'im" (182). And,
on the dangers of intermixing leadership with friendship, she advises:
"Don't syndicate wid none of 'em, do dey'll put yo' business in de
street. Friend wid few. Everybody grin in yo' face don't love yuh.
Anybody kin look and see and tell uh snake trail when dey come across
it but nobody kin tell which way he wuz goin' lessen he seen de snake.

You keep outa sight, and in dat way, you won't give nobody uh stick tuh crack yo' head wid" (183).

As John's successes as mayor and preacher in the community mount, he returns to his old sin of infidelity, and verbal disharmony returns to the marriage. Lucy's assertive demeanor changes as the problems of the disintegrating marriage beset her. Like Delia and Missie Mae, Lucy's moment of epiphany unfolds in her assertive individualism. John continues his old ways. Again, Lucy is left alone in childbirth, and during crucial times when a child is ill and is in need of his assistance. But on this occasion, it is Lucy's heart that suffers the pains of John's unfaithfulness and child neglect. Gradually her love and admiration for him diminish. That the marriage is on the road to complete failure is quite obvious in the way they communicate. Lucy's feelings have changed, for "a little cold feeling impinged upon her antennae" (186) at the thought of John's involvement with more women. As the marriage falters, there develop in Lucy "times of cold feelings and times of triumph. Only the coldness grew numerous" (188). Becoming stoical as she copes with John's flaw, Lucy relies on her religion to give her strength to spiritually free herself from any blame for having caused John to stray. She surmises—to God, her only listening friend—"'Tain't mah fault, Lawd, Ahm jus' ez clean ez yo robes" (186).

As well, her verbal rapport with John changes as she fearlessly criticizes and scorns him. She signifies her displeasure when she sarcastically remarks that all he has to do is to "ack" (189) like a man and not love every woman he sees. Of the Hattie Tyson affair, Lucy scores an insulting knockout blow when she says to her arrogant husband: "John, you kin keep from fallin' in love wid *anybody,* if you start in time. You either got tuh stop loving Hattie Tyson uh you got tuh stop preachin! Dat's whut de people say" (192). This belligerent talk is effective as John grows ashamed of his sins and begs for forgiveness and Lucy's help, as he is on the verge of being cast out of his church as head preacher. In an about face, Lucy's verbal demeanor, again, becomes one of the protective wife, shielding her husband from danger. Advising John how to handle the members of his church who are trying to oust him for his adulterous behavior, Lucy speaks with a constructive voice, though her distrust of John has weakened their love knot: "Don't you go 'round dat church mealy-moufin 'round dem deacons and nobody else. Don't you break uh breath on de subjick. Face 'em out, and if dey wants tuh handle you in conference, go dere totin' uh high head and Ah'll be right dere 'long side of yuh" (193).

John succeeds at the church conference with Lucy's cautionary advice. Because of the forcefulness of her tongue, he is not dethroned. Similarly, her powerful talk advises him what sermon to preach so as to overcome the hostile folk in his congregation on Sunday mornings. Indeed, she is a knowledgeable person whose words articulate her perceptiveness and deep insight into the folly of human nature. Certainly, John could not survive without her powerful assertive talk as indicated, for example, in the following words of guidance: "You git yo' self out dey mouf and stay out of it, hear me? You preach uh sermon on yo' self, and you call tuh they remembrance some uh de good things you done, so they kin put it long side de other and when you lookin' at two things at de same time neither one of 'em don't look so big, but don't tell uh lie, John. If youse guilty you don't need tuh git up dere and put yo' own name on de sign post uh scorn, but don't say you didn't do it neither. Whut you say, let it be de truth. Dat what comes from de heart will sho reach de heart again" (196).

Although John's relationship with his church is temporarily mended by Lucy's guidance, their marriage is still in crisis. John returns yet again to his old ways, even as his child is gravely ill, and then, a while later, as Lucy herself is dying from tuberculosis. At this point, Lucy's verbal relationship with him at home changes into one of heated arguments as she reprimands him sternly for his sins. Toward the end of the novel, there is no chance of reconciliation between the two. Verbal animosity, as contrasted to the verbal amicability early in their marriage, is dominant as the relationship flounders seriously. Love is conspiciously absent as John verbally and physically retaliates against the frail and weak Lucy. She is not a woman prone to fighting (like a Big Sweet or Laura Lee), but her defensive mechanisms do help her endure and become victorious in her own right; for instance, her accusing eye and mighty tongue keep John at bay as she verbally conquers him before her death. The following dialogue illustrates the war of words and personal conflict between the two in the final days of the marriage. Lucy's speech is vibrant as she tussles with John and figuratively unties their love knot, once sealed with verbal cohesiveness and love. She perceives him as an unloving and uncaring husband and neglectful father:

Lucy: Know too, Ahm sick and you been home fuh de las' longest
and ain't been near me tuh offer me uh cup uh cool water uh ast
me how Ah feel.

John: Oh you sick, sick, sick! Ah hate tuh be round folks always
complainin', and then again you always doggin' me 'bout
sumpin'. Ah gits sick and tired uh hearing it!

Lucy: Well, John, you puts de words in mah mouf. If you'd stay
home and look after yo' wife and chillun, Ah wouldn't have
nothin' tuh talk about.

John: Aw, yes you would! Always jawin' and complainin'.

Lucy: If you keep ole Hattie Tyson's letters out dis house where
mah chillun kin git holt of 'em then you kin stop folkeses
mouf by comin' on home instid uh layin' 'round wid her in
Oviedo (203).

Lucy's poignant and perceptive voice angers John in his guilt as
the quarrel intensifies and John verbally retaliates against her with
language the least exemplary of his once well-mannered speech. He is
totally antagonistic against the physically defenseless Lucy and orders
her to hush her assertive mouth: "Shet up! Ah sick an' tired uh yo'
yowing and jawin'. 'Tain't nothin' Ah hate lak gittin' sin throwed in
mah face dat done got cold. Ah do ez Ah please. You jus' uh hold-back
tuh me nohow. Always sick and complainin'. Uh man can't utilize
hisself" (203). Despite his mean disposition, Lucy remains assertive
and strong; words are the only weapons she possesses as she eyeballs
John and addresses herself to his new perception of her as a nagging
wife. She cautions him with proverbial folk wisdom which John
haughtily scorns:

Lucy: Ahm glad tuh know dat, John. After all dese years and all dat
done went on dat Ah ain't been nothin' but uh stumblin'-
stone tuh yuh. Go 'head on, Mister, but remember—youse
born but you ain't dead. 'Tain't nobody so slick but whut they
kin stand uh 'nother greasin'. Ah done told yuh time and time
uhgin dat ignorance is de hawse dat wisdom rides. Don't git
miss-put on yo' road. God don't eat okra.

John: Oh you always got uh mouf full uh opinions, but Ah don't
need you no mo' nor nothin you got to say, Ahm uh man
grown. Don't need no guardzeen at all. So shet yo' mouf wid
me (204).

Rebellious for the first time in confrontation with her husband, Lucy does not heed his command to remain silent and she suffers as a result for talking a truth that arouses his guilt and shame with her insightful voice of wisdom. He grows physically violent as he directs the hand of his mighty strength at her in retaliation for her final verbal blow to his credibility:

> Lucy: Ah ain't goin' tuh hush nothin' uh de kind. Youse livin' dirty and Ahm goin' tuh tell you 'bout it. Me and mah chillun got some rights. Big talk ain't changin' whut you doin'. You can't clean yo' self wid yo' tongue lak uh cat.
> John: (Slaps Lucy's face with his hand) Ah tole you to hush.
> Lucy: De hidden wedge will come tuh light some day, John. Mark mah words. Youse in de majority now, but God sho don't love ugly (204–205).

This final dialogue between the two symbolically ends the marriage with Lucy maintaining her positive image as assertive woman, and John losing his verbal stature as loving husband before Lucy. Her wise voice and deep penetrating eyes—eyes that had the capacity to search his face and see all of his guilt—terminate their relationship as husband and wife. Her death, a few days later, confirms the reality of the marital break.

The silencing of Lucy's once supportive voice leaves John fending for himself, often against hostile forces from which he cannot verbally liberate himself as Lucy might have. He lingers in guilt, shame and torment as he attempts to repent for his sins and mistreatment of Lucy, but he still fails in his efforts at re-marriage with Hattie and then with the verbally strong Sally. His love of the flesh, now represented in the aggressive man-chaser and materialist, Ora Patton, leads to his final destruction—a demise which Lucy foreshadowed in her prophetic folk wisdom. At the end of the novel, it is her wise, assertive voice of truth that seems to symbolically reincarnate itself in the reader's ear and predict the path of a wayward John as he meets his violent fate in an automobile collision with a train. Surely, it can be said, nobody knew him but the perceptive and verbally fluent Lucy who spoke in tune with an Omnipotent God. Her assertive voice fostered his prosperous rise and predicted his most tragic fall. Throughout the novel, Lucy speaks with the voice of truth and authority in her mouth, although her marriage to

Chapter 12

Janie in *Their Eyes Were Watching God*[1]

Janie is the last of the long line of admirable assertive women worthy of discussion in Hurston's art. She is more in alignment with the dreams and aspirations of the contemporary Black American woman than any of Hurston's other assertive women. She is an independent-minded woman who eventually finds authentic love with a man who "gives her every consolation in the world" (10), including personal freedom and verbal contentment.

The triumphs, joys and sorrows, resulting from Janie's assertive individualism, her inclination to rebel against the constraints of traditional marriage and the material life that infringe on her personal happiness, are almost entirely recorded in the medium of the talk experience. It is predominantly her vibrant and active voice which characterizes the stylistic mode of *Their Eyes Were Watching God*. In fact, the talk motif in general is a dominant element in the novel as Janie's speech performance unfolds; throughout the novel, she has the law of verbal authority in her mouth as she articulates her oral history to Phoeby, her best friend of twenty years. Her rhetorical style is typical of a Black storyteller as she talks in confidence to a one-woman audience with the belief that her tongue is in her friend's mouth. She is divulging personal facts to a faithful friend and not to a public audience. Kinship is established with her listeners as the real circumstances of her personal life are verbally unfolded in a carefully crafted oral history of her life.

Through the talk experience with Phoeby, Janie gives understanding and clarity to a Black love saga spanning a twenty-five year period, and to her final unexpected re-appearance in Eatonville after several years of absence. Even though she is still a wealthy woman,

Janie returns to town dressed in muddy overalls, brogans and a dirty work shirt, and without the young man, ten years her junior, with whom she eloped. In this humble image, she first confronts the eyes and tongues of the town gossipers who are dumbfounded by such an unexplained appearance and by Janie's blatant effort not to provide a plausible explanation. Although their tongues wag maliciously, Janie, in typical Hurston fashion, remains free-spirited and unconcerned about what they think of her. She represents the gossipers to Phoeby as worthless talkers who cannot express the true reality of experience, diminishing them to the stature of "a lost ball in the high grass" (9). Thus she will invest her time telling the events and details of her story to a woman friend of equal verbal stature.

The opening and closing chapters mark the beginning and ending of Janie's talk experience. In each, Hurston projects Janie as a powerful storyteller who creates a provocative beginning and a dynamic ending to her sermon-like story on life and love. In addition to establishing a rapport between Janie and Pheoby, the latter, a hungry and attentive listener who gives Janie respect and encouragement to assert herself, Chapter One also sets forth the verbal atmosphere in which Janie is able to retell her story in confidence to Phoeby and to justify her unusual return to Eatonville. For Janie, the speech process on the back porch of her home is part of reality; it has significant meaning and purpose in the healing process. It is not a playful, chatty exercise in words between distant friends or strangers. It is rather the verbal recreation of existence, a means of articulating real experience in proper context. It is also a way to remember those things she wants never to forget; it is a healing process in overcoming and understanding the tragic and sorrowful. Her use of personal and truthful talk, here, is to be distinguished from the purposeless and evil talk of the sitters and gossipers—the Mouth almighties, she calls them (8)—who idle away time on Phoeby's porch, passing notions through their mouths about other people as they sit in judgment without the full experience of life to verify their talk. They are weak, inexperienced folk whose only sense of power comes from destructive talk, providing killing tools of life with their tongues. As Janie explains to Phoeby, in her criticism of the gossipers at the end of the narration, talking is useless without the experience to go along with it:

> Dem meatskins is *got* tuh rattle tuh make out they's alive. Let 'em
> consolate theyselves wid talk. 'Course, talkin' don't amount tuh

hill uh beans when yuh can't do nothin' else. And listenin' tuh dat kind uh talk is jus' lak openin' you' mouth and lettin' de moon shine down yo' throat. It's uh known fact, Pheoby, you got tuh *go* there tuh *know* there. Yo' papa and yo' mama and nobody else can't tell yuh and show yuh. Two things everybody's got tuh do fuh theyselves. They got tuh go tuh God, and they got tuh find out about livin' fuh they-selves (158–159).

Janie's talk becomes more self-revealing as she provides the experiential insight leading up to the death of Tea Cake. In conversation with Phoeby, she is now capable of re-living her experience in verbal drama. She grows capable of articulating her findings in philosophical figures of folk speech expression as she succinctly explains her whereabouts of the past years: "Ah been a delegate to de big 'ssociation of life. Yessuh! De Grand Lodge, de big convention of livin' is just where Ah been dis year and a half y'all ain't seen me" (10). As the chapters unfold, she entices Pheoby with the detailed verbal pictures which shape her speech performance.

Chapter Twenty is a companion piece to Chapter One. It marks the ending of Janie's talk about living and loving, about simultaneously finding independence and experiencing love. Her voice, at the end, is a matured one expressing contentment at having fulfilled her dreams, even though, with the death of her beloved Tea Cake, they were short-lived. She expounds instructive wisdom about life and love as she concludes her story to Pheoby on a positive note: "Now dat's how everything wuz, Pheoby, jus' lak Ah told you. So Ah'm back home again Ah'm satisfied tuh be heah. Ah done been tuh de horizon and back and now Ah kin sit heah in mah house and live by comparisons. Dis house ain't so absent of things lak it used tuh be befo' Tea Cake come along. It's full uh thoughts, 'specially dat bedroom" (158). And: "Love ain't somethn' lak uh grind-stone dat's de same everywhere and do de same thing tuh everything it touch. Love is lak de sea. It's uh movin' thing, but still and all, it takes shape from de shore it meets, and it's different with every shore" (158). As bearer of the word, Janie is an effective and persuasive talker. Her story has an impact on Pheoby who in turn voices praise of Janie and personal discontent in her own marriage to Sam: "Lawd! Ah done growed ten feet higher from jus' listenin' tuh you, Janie. Ah ain't satisfied wid mahself no mo'. Ah means tuh make Sam take me fishin' wid him after this. Nobody better not criticize yuh in mah hearin" (158).

Chapters Two through Nineteen comprise a separate sequence from Chapters One and Twenty in that they are the detailed core of Janie's poignant oral story. They capture her verbal disposition with the variety of other voices in her life—Johnny, Nanny, Killicks, Jody, Tea Cake, and the white court. With each, her language demeanor indicates a new aspect of her assertive individualism as she rebels against male oppression and materialism. In the trusting verbal rituals of courtship conversation with Tea Cake, her language dispositon changes again as she asserts a happy and satisfied voice.

As in the oratorical tradition of the Black storyteller or even of the African griot, Janie's singular personal voice powerfully shapes the chronology of those experiences which led to the fulfillment of her dream to achieve a harmonious and reciprocal relationship with a man. Hurston shows Janie's verbal growth from a girlish talker to an experienced adult speaker, and from a conforming wife to a rebellious woman in action and speech mannerism, significantly illustrating that Janie is indeed a folk person of the deep South in every respect. She is just as close to her rural vernacular roots as she is to nature, to the soil and local color of country life. Words and environment help inspire, instruct, and create her expressive mood in relating the dynamics of life, from birth through death. She grows in close union with nature and the man she loves as she excels in spiritual perception and verbal fluency.

The dual representation of nature as having a beautiful simplicity in the early years of her adolescent and marriage years to Killicks, and as having an awesome and destructive complexity during later years of marriage to Tea Cake, provide a pictorial vision of her word thought. Like nature, Janie's speech is increasingly beautiful and awesome in scope as she reaches spiritual maturity and contentment. Through nature, she understands and verbalizes her life from the perspective of such natural forces as trees, flowers, seeds, and storms. Soft, easy earthy phrases are employed to express herself, as in the case when she first envisions her whole life from the perspective of a "great tree in leaf with the things suffered, things enjoyed, things done and undone. Dawn and doom was in the branches" (11). And, the young adolescent stage of her development and bloom into adulthood is equated with springtime and budding of trees while her widowhood (brought about by the shock and horror of the hurricane and its aftermath) is equated with the serenity of night time and the eventual beauty and brightness of early daylight.

The story begins with the young adolescent stage of her development. She is closely in tune with nature as she gives the oral

history of her family roots and an account of her overwhelming
infatuation with springtime and the beginning of life she witnesses
with plants and trees in nature. Flower dust and pollinated air arouse her
own desire to experience life and marriage as she witnesses the
unfolding of an intense sensuality under a blossoming pear tree. Her
consciousness is aroused as she asserts herself in romantic and wishful
talk: "Oh to be a pear tree—any tree in bloom! With kissing bees
singing of the beginning of the world" (14)!

Infatuated with the beauty of life around her, Janie blindly becomes
a participant, fantasizing her own springtime of blooming flowers and
marriage. She selects Johnny Taylor as her potential mate by
permitting him to kiss her. She envisions her experience with him to
be a beautiful union to form life as she sees it in nature. Nanny
observes this act, however, and grows alarmed as she interprets it to be
a sign of Janie's dangerous sexual maturity: "Janie, youse got yo'
womanhood on yuh. So Ah mout ez well tell yuh whut Ah been savin'
up for up spell. Ah wants to see you married right away" (15).

Here, Janie's childish fantasy will draw her into real conflict with
Nanny on the issue of Black womanhood and marriage. Nanny (an
effective talker in her own right) becomes a very assertive and powerful
voice as she assumes the verbal rostrum and pleads her case to Janie
about the importance of security in marriage over love. Nanny sounds
persuasive as she tells the painful history of her own and her daughter's
sexual exploitation. She wants to protect Janie from becoming
entangled with a trashy and unworthy young man the likes of Johnny
Taylor who might use her body to "wipe his foots on" (15) or to kick
around "from pillar to post" (17) and consequently overwork her like a
"work-ox or brood sow" (18).

By marrying in Nanny's way, Janie will have a greater chance of
"picking from a higher bush and sweeter berry" (15) so as to not let any
man, Black or white, make a "spit cup" (21) out of her. The doctrine of
protection and survival for the Black woman, as perceived by Nanny, a
former slave, is explained in a most logical fashion: "Yo' Nanny
wouldn't harm a hair on yo' head. She don't want nobody else to do it
neither if she kin help it. Honey, de white man is de ruler of everything
as fur as Ah been able tuh find out. Maybe it's some place way off in
de ocean where de black man is in power, but we don't know nothin'
but what we see. So de white man throw down de load and tell de nigger
man tuh pick it up. He pick it up because he have to, but he don't tote
it. He hand it to his women folks. De nigger woman is de mule uh de

world so fur as Ah can see. Ah been prayin' fuh it tuh be different wid
you" (16). Nanny illustrates her point by providing Janie with an oral
history of her treatment by her slave master and mistress along with an
account of Janie's mother's exploitation by a Black man. All of
Nanny's dreams of sitting on a high chair of do-nothing like her
mistress were unfulfilled as a slave, as work and sexual exploitation
were the reality of her life. Indeed, she was the mule of the world in
several ways. As a result, her expectations are high for Janie to fulfill
her dream of what Black womanhood means. It means surviving and
protecting oneself against economic hardship, as Nanny explains when
she refers to the real significance of Janie's marriage to Logan Killicks:
"'Tain't Logan Killicks Ah wants you to have, baby, it's protection"
(31). It also means making a respectable name for oneself so that one's
"feathers won't always be crumpled by folks throwin' up things in
one's face" (21).

Janie grows submissive in accepting Nanny's wise folk talk as
truth, thereby forsaking her personal desire to find love or experience
marriage in her own self-designed way. In her estimation, old man
Killicks looks "lak some ole skull-head in de graveyard" (28) as he
desecrates her image of the pear tree and life, but she marries him
anyway, sixty acres of land and all, with the assumption that love will
eventually come to the marriage. But it never does. Janie never desires
him in a loving way; there is an absence of springtime and bloomtime
at their home which to her is a "lonesome place like a stump in the
middle of the woods where nobody had ever been. The house was absent
of flavor" (22).

After two months of life with Killicks, Janie returns to Nanny to
talk, to inquire about the absence of love in the marriage. Nanny's
response prompts a discussion centering on the romantic versus the
pragmatic perception of marriage for the Black woman. She provides a
treatise against Black women being blinded solely by love for a man
instead of a mutual economic partnership. She scolds Janie severely
about her rejection of Killicks and desires for a man merely to love: "If
you dont want him, you sho oughta. Heah you is wid de onliest organ
in town, amongst colored folks, in yo' parlor. Got a house bought and
paid for and sixty acres uh land right on de big road. . . . Lawd have
mussy! Dat's de very prong all us black women gits hung on. Dis love!
Dat's just whuts's got us uh pullin' and uh haulin' and sweatin' and
doin' from can't see in de mornin' till can't see at night. Dat's how

come de ole folks say dat bein' uh fool don't kill nobody. It jus' makes you sweat" (23).

On this occasion, however, Janie rebels during the grandmother-to-granddaughter talking experience and does not submit herself to Nanny's anti-love ideology. She asserts her own views as she rejects the notion that materialism and protection are the sole factors in a marriage relationship. She talks freely about her dislike of Killicks' looks in a childish and rather immature speech demeanor that finds her drawing on a mild form of the dozens to scorn and low-rate him and his prized land:

> Ah ain't takin dat ole land tuh heart neither. Ah could throw ten acres of it over de fence every day and never look back to see where it fell. Ah feel de same way 'bout Mr. Killicks too. Some folks never was meant to be loved and he's one of 'em. . . . Ah hates de way his head is so long way and so flat on de sides and dat pone uh fat back uh his neck. . . . His belly is too big too, now, and his toe-nails look lak mule foots. And 'taint nothin' in de way of him washin' his feet every evenin' before he comes tuh bed. 'Taint nothin' tuh hinder him 'cause Ah places de water for him. Ah'd ruther be shot wid tacks than tuh turn over in de bed and stir up de air whilst he is in dere. He don't even mention nothin pretty. . . . Ah wants things sweet wid mah marriage lak when you sits under a pear tree and think (23–24).

Janie maintains her dream of experiencing love with a man, even though she now realizes that marriage to Killicks, Nanny's ideal of a man, is not the same as love. She matures in her thoughts as her first dream to select her own lovemate dies, while the reality of Nanny's intrusion on her independence is all around her as she grows miserable as Killick's wife. Nanny's over-protectiveness has made her stray from the road to fulfillment through love.

Life with Killicks, the economically prosperous Black man, is an unhappy one lacking love and consummation of the marriage union in courtship talk or word rhymes of affection. There is increasing disunity and verbal disharmony as Janie is relegated to her place in the kitchen, clad in an apron. Dissatisfaction with Killicks and her oppressed state are therefore demonstrated in Janie's speech disposition as she comes to the realization that his perception of marriage is no different from Nanny's. As she sees it, "He don't take nothin' to count but sow-belly and corn-bread" (29). Words of verbal discord multiply as she asserts

herself in rebellion against Killicks' command that she labor, work and
sweat in the fields just like his first wife did, in fact become his mule.
The antagonism between the two is apparent in the following
interchange where Janie's maturity of speech exhibits itself in non-
conformity to Killicks' work instructions:

> Killicks: If Ah kin haul de wood heah and chop it fuh yuh, look lak
>   you oughta be able tuh tote it inside. Mah fust wife never
>   bothered me 'bout choppin' no wood nohow. She'd grab dat
>   ax and sling chips lak uh man. You done been spoilt rotten.
> Janie: Ah'm just as stiff as you is stout. If you can stand not to
>   chop and tote wood Ah reckon you can stand not to git no
>   dinner. 'Scuse mah freezolity, Mist' Killicks, but Ah don't
>   mean to chop de first chip (25).

Working to keep the peace and to maintain a degree of verbal
equality in the talking game, Killicks accepts Janie's smart reply
because he realizes early that she is a strident verbal warrior who can
hurt him deeply with her talk. His only other means of cutting her
down to size, to a level of talk that will damage her pride and ego, is to
draw on the dozens by talking of her family background and illegitimate
birth. He remarks to her of her sordid past, "'Tain't too many mens
would trust you, knowing yo' folks lak they do" (29), and criticizes her
for her pompous disposition to act like white folks since she had the
distinction of being "born in a carriage that had no top to it" (28) and
reared by her mama in "the white folks' back yard" (28). He lands a
final insult to her fatherless background and personal pride by
suggesting that he has done her a favor by marrying a person of her
questionable family and economic background: "'Tain't no mo' fools
lak me. A whole lot of mens will grin in yo' face, but dey ain't gwine
tuh work and feed yuh. You won't git far and you won't be long, when
dat big gut reach over and grab dat little one, you'll be gald to come
back here" (29).

Killicks' belittling talk (a mild form of playing the dozens by
insulting Janie's mother and family heritage) has no overt influence on
Janie's behavior; in fact, the verbal disharmony between the two
intensifies as Janie speaks for her independence more so than she does
for the protection Killicks offers. Killicks becomes more domineering
as he instructs her a second time to vacate the kitchen and to work and
plow the fields, but Janie remains defiant. Her assertive individualism

gradually surfaces in opposition to Killicks' commands, as the following dialogue indicates:

> Killicks: Janie! Come help me move dis manure pile befo' de sun gits hot. You don't take a bit of interest in dis place. 'Taint no use in foolin' round in dat kitchen all day long.
> Janie: You don't need mah help out dare Logan. Youse in yo' place and Ah'm in mine.
> Killicks: You ain't got no particular place. It's where ever Ah need yuh. Git uh move on yuh, and dat quick (29).

Janie evens the score, however, by employing her own mild form of the dozens to neutralize Killicks' authority. She offers a voice that reveals insight into his motives for demanding that she work in the field and earn her keep: "Mah mama didn't tell me Ah wuz born in no hurry. So whut business Ah got rushin' now? Anyhow dat ain't whut youse mad about. Youse mad cause Ah don't fall down and wash-up dese sixty acres uh ground yuh got. You ain't done me no favor by marryin' me. And if dat's what you call yo' self doin', Ah don't thank yuh fuh it. Youse mad 'cause Ah'm tellin' yuh whut you already knowed" (29).

Shamed and weakened by the truth of Janie's bold tongue, Killicks is verbally inadequate to respond in kind to Janie's words. Instead, he orders her to hush her talk, otherwise he will use physical force to silence her for good: "Don'y you change too many words wid me dis mawin', Janie, do Ah'll take and change ends wid yuh! Heah, Ah just as good as take you out de white folks' kitchen and set you down on yo' royal diasticutis and you take and low-rate me! Ah'll take holt uh dat ax and come in dere and kill yuh! You better dry up in dere! Ah'm too honest and hard-workin' for anybody in yo' family, dat's de reason you don't want me! Ah guess some low-lifted nigger is grinnin' in yo' face and lyin' tuh yuh. God damn yo' hide" (29–30)!

Janie realizes the futility of her marriage to Killicks. Without love, affection and springtime beauty, there is no reason for remaining in a relationship founded on mere property and work. She longs for physical and emotional attachment in a harmonious marriage. Jody Starks, an outsider who passes the Killicks' place on the big road, seems to be a possible alternative to Killicks. His confident, citified way of talking seems to convince her that with him her dream of love and marital bliss might be fulfilled. He talks in courtship rhymes of affection and tenderness as he expresses his concept of womanhood to her: "You

behind a plow! You ain't got no mo' business wid uh plow than uh
hog is got wid uh holiday! You ain't got no business cuttin' up no seed
p'taters neither. A pretty doll-baby lak you is made to sit on de front
porch and rock and fan yo' self and eat p'taters dat other folks plant just
special for you" (27).

Janie is fascinated by his flattery and future plans to be a Big Voice
with her reaping the benefits. Although he does not "represent sun-up
and pollen and blooming trees" (28), he speaks of far horizons and
change and chance. It is his talk, though, which eventually wins her
over to elopement. She senses the possibility of a romantic union and
verbal compatability between them. In the following dialogue, Jody
effectively woos Janie. He resembles the suitor of the old-time
courtship rituals trying to infatuate the girl of his eye with exaggerated
love talk:

> Jody: Janie, if you think Ah aims to tole you off and make a dog
> outa you, youse wrong, Ah wants to make a wife outa you.
> Janie: You mean dat, Joe?
> Jody: De day you puts yo' hand in mine, Ah wouldn't let de sun go
> down on us single. Ah'm uh man wid principles. You aint
> never knowed what it was to be treated lak a lady and Ah wants
> to be de one tuh show yuh.
> Janie: But s'posin'.
> Jody: Leave de s'posin and everything else to me. Ah'll be down
> dis road uh little after sunup tomorrow mornin' to wait for
> you. You come go wid me. Den all de rest of yo' natural life
> you kin live lak you oughta. Kiss me and shake yo' head.
> When you do dat, yo plentiful hair breaks lak day (28).

A feeling of change and chance and newness comes over Janie as she
abandons Killicks for Jody, a man of words with whom she can grow in
love and verbal harmony. She leaves Killicks' place facing the freshness
of the morning air and the beauty of flowers around her as she joins in
union with Jody, a man she selects to fulfill her dream of being loved.
A new Janie emerges as she embarks on a road that implies the
necessity of a new language: "From now on until death she was going
to have flower dust and springtime sprinkled over everything. A bee for
her bloom. Her old thoughts were going to come in handy now, but
new words would have to be made and said to fit them" (30).

Although Janie starts her second marriage with great expectations, over a twenty year period her life with Jody as Mrs. Mayor of Eatonville, "the bellcow and the other women the gang" (37), grows to be an oppressive one. The "bloom and springtime" tempo of their relationship gradually disappears in the absence of authentic love and a shared social life. Jody grows increasingly domineering with the "bow-down command" (42) he exhibits as a Big Voice in both home and community. Consequently, Janie's assertive voice is silenced and her freedom curtailed as Jody shapes her into his man-made image of a showcase doll to be seen and not heard. She is to sit on high as Queen of his storeporch and do nothing more.

Jody's expectations of Janie as wife sitting on a pedestal of do-nothing are obviously clear early on in the marriage when he is formally welcomed and acknowledged by the townsfolk for his contributions to the town. According to his perspective of life, Janie, as Mrs. Mayor, is not to be a participant in public talk on the storeporch. He takes the center of the verbal floor, refusing an invitation for Janie to speak with the announcement to the townsfolk that "She's uh woman and her place is in de home" (39). Janie is alarmed and turns cold as Jody disregards her freedom of talk—one of the main ingredients necessary to the harmony of their marriage. She also complains that this restrictive social status infringes on their marriage partnership: "It keeps us in uh kinda strain . . . it's jus' looks lak it keeps us in some way we ain't natural wid one 'nother. You'se always off talkin' and fixin' things, and Ah feels lak Ah'm jus' markin' time. Hope it soon gits over" (41).

As Jody's ambitious drive and oppression of Janie continue, she endures in her unhappy state. His self-centeredness and refusal to listen to her opinion or to demonstrate his love for her in words, rather than through economic progress, take their toll on Janie. She grows distant and lonely in the marriage. She reasons that there is no point fighting with Jody. "It just wasn't in him" (48) to change and see things her way. She wisely chooses to hold her tongue for a while just to keep the peace in the marriage because she tells herself "Ah hate disagreement and confusion, so Ah better not talk. It makes it hard tuh git along" (50).

Jody's economic and verbal authority also oppresses Janie as she begins working in the store, a place which gives her "a sick headache" (48). As Mrs. Mayor, head clerk of his store, Janie is ordered by Jody to wear a head rag over her beautiful mane of hair and to refrain from participating in the oral rituals of the common folk on the store porch. A gifted storyteller and talker in her own right, Janie desires to participate in the lying sessions and the courtship episodes of the mule talkers, but Jody has forbidden her to do so because the folk are of a lower socio-economic class than she. He cannot see what a woman of Janie's stature would want to be "treasurin' all dat gum grease from folks dat don't even own de house dey sleep in. "'Tain't no earthly use. They's jus' some puny humans playin' round de toes uh Time" (47).

The mule talkers' talk—in which they make crayon enlargements of life through word power—is what interests Janie, not their social status in the town. As well, she observes the hypocrisy of Jody's orders to refrain from the people's talk rituals while he himself enjoys them with his "big heh, heh laughs" (47). Such disparity causes a change in Janie's heretofore submissive voice. She finds it necessary to begin to assert herself about the inequalities around her. Love talk—the expressive language she has longed for since her adolescent years—will be far distant from the type of language she will articulate in her marriage relationship with Jody, an oppressive voice.

As Jody's oppression mounts, encompassing Janie's sixteenth through thirty-sixth birthdays, she gradually grows verbally rebellious and non-conformist as she engages both Jody and the storeporch talkers in public talk. She displays a behavior strictly forbidden for years by Jody. When she discovers, for example, the mule-baiting carried out against Matt Bonner's old mule, she voices her feelings aloud as she grows angry at the sight of a helpless beast of burden (almost like a woman with an oppressive husband) being treated and tortured by mighty men who have no regard for weak creatures: "They oughta be shamed uh theyselves! Teasin' dat poor brute beast lak they is! Done been worked tuh death; done had his disposition ruint wid mistreatment, and now they got tuh finish devilin' 'im tuh death. Wish Ah had mah way wid 'em all" (49–50).

Janie's perceptive assertive talk influences Jody, as he purchases the mule from Bonner on pretense of taking it out of its misery. But the true fact is Janie's poignant words have left their mark on his guilty conscience. She again takes the public speaking platform as she ironically mocks Jody for his gesture of freeing the mule: "Jody, dat wuz uh mighty fine thing fuh yuh tuh do. 'Taint everybody would have thought of it, 'cause it ain't no everyday thought. Freein' dat mule makes uh mighty big man outa you. Something like George Washington and Lincoln. Abraham Lincoln, he had de whole United

States tuh run so he freed de Negroes. You got uh town so you freed uh mule. You have tuh have power tuh free things and dat make you lak uh king uh something" (51).

Janie now goes public with the assertion of her talking voice, rather than privately sharing it with Jody in a loving marriage conversation, the likes of Missie and Joe, perhaps. Even the storeporch talkers or big liars, though mistaking the ironic meaning directed at Jody, are attracted by her verbal fluency. Hambo acknowledges her easy flow of words when he compliments Jody: "Yo wife is uh born orator, Starks. Us never knowed dat befo'. She put jus' de right words tuh our thoughts" (51). Jody bites down hard on his cigar and does not speak a word to his wife, although he pretends in public face to beam at the praise. Desiring to keep Janie a verbal weakling under his control, Jody is obviously displeased with Janie, jealously drawing apart from her rather than joining her in a public verbal union of their togetherness as man and wife.

Jody's anger at Janie's growing verbal empowerment is also evident when he prevents her from participating with him and the townsmen in the oral ritual of exaggerated talk accompanying the dragging-out ceremony for Matt Bonner's dead mule. He argues that it is a "mess of commonness" (53) in which he instructs her not to participate, overlooking the fact that she desires to laugh, play and speak in good humor with the folk. While sharing laughter and words of play is Janie's idea of having sunshine in a marriage, Jody desires dominating and controlling her freedom of speech. Unexpectedly defiant, she scolds him for his short-sightedness and narrow perspective on life and pleasure: "Everybody can't be lak you, Jody. Somebody's bound tuh want tuh laugh and play" (55). Thus her way of countering Jody's oppression is to attack him with ridicule and criticism. Anger and discontent kindle her fiery talk as the marriage relationship grows soar. To combat Janie's assertive momentum, Jody (in reality, no verbal match for her in the talking game) must finally resort to physical violence as a remedy for controlling this assertively strong woman.

As her speech becomes more expressive of unhappiness and misery as Mrs. Mayor, Janie is physically abused by Jody. He will not tolerate her defiant assertive voice and threatens to even the score by "boxing her jaws" (55) if she doesn't hush. At this stage of the marriage, the war between the two becomes more pronounced, even in the store where they increasingly argue over business-related matters before the customers—shrewd listeners who want to hear and see who will, in fact, be the victor in the dramatic war of words between husband and wife. Janie, and not Jody, begins to speak with the law of moral authority in her mouth. She becomes the assertive wife in battle with an oppressive husband. This is not a mock battle of love and play fights like Missie and Joe; instead, it is a real battle of hate and contempt, the likes of the vicious battle between Delia and Sykes. The verbal law articulated by the generally good assertive wife prevails, often to the detriment of the evil and unloving husband.

The episode in *Their Eyes Were Watching God* in which Janie misplaces an invoice brings the verbal battle between the two to a climax before the male storytellers. Jody aims to shame her before the customers by reminding her of his mental superiority. He contends that Janie must obey him—let him do the thinking in the marriage. But Janie, unwilling to be outdone in this talking performance before the men, begins openly to defy him:

> Jody: Ah done told you time and time agin tuh stick all dem papers
>   on dat nail! All you got tuh do is mind me. How come you
>   can't do lak Ah tell yuh?
> Janie: You sho love to tell me whut to do, but Ah can't tell you
>   nothin' Ah see!
> Jody: Dat's cause you need tellin'. It would be pitiful if Ah didn't.
>   Somebody got to think for women and chillun and chickens
>   and cows. I god, they sho don't think none theirselves.
> Janie: Ah knows uh few things, and womenfolks thinks
>   sometimes too!
> Jody: Aw naw they don't. They just think they's thinkin'. When
>   Ah see one thing Ah understands ten. You see ten things and
>   don't understand one" (62).

From this acrimonious moment to the end of the marriage, the relationship between Jody and Janie crumbles in word battles before the townsfolk, masters and judges of Black folk talk in all of its varied styles. Not long after the above exchange, Janie reveals her independent folk wisdom when she talks with displeasure about the mistreatment of Mrs. Tony Robbins by Jody and the other men. She thrusts herself into their conversation with an ironic criticism of men and their overwhelming sense of power and authority over women: "Sometimes God gits familiar wid us womenfolks too and talks His inside business. He told me how surprised He was 'bout y'all turning out so smart after

Him makin' yuh different; and how surprised y'all is goin' tuh be if you ever find out you don't know half as much 'bout us as you think you do. It's so easy to make yo'self out God Almighty when you ain't got nothin' tuh strain against but women and chickens" (65). His male ego rankled by the barb, Jody can muster no response but to call Janie "too moufy" (65) and interrupt her fluency by sending her off to fetch the checkerboard so the men can play.

Although the springtime image of her marriage to Jody has faded, Janie's inner desire to eventually find a man who could love and make summertime out of lonesomeness has not. She exhibits a stoic external face to Jody and the outside world, while internally she "was saving up feelings for some man she had never seen. She had an inside and outside now and suddenly she knew how not to mix them" (63). She becomes emotionally indifferent to Jody and his material wealth, resigning herself so that "she receives all things with the stolidness of the earth which soaks up urine and perfume with the same indifference" (66).

With the passage of time, the antagonism reaches a new level where Jody employs the dozens to ridicule Janie's physical appearance as she ages. He hopes to draw attention from his own aging and sagging body because Janie still holds her youth in spite of her age. This style of verbal play, which will eventually result in the most intense moments of verbal warfare in the marriage, sets up a serious confrontation between the two in public view. It will bring their marriage to an end, as Janie defends her womanly ground by exposing Jody's waning virility to public scrutiny. Talking in the family, as the dozens of insults is defined by the folk, will lead to dire consequences for Jody as he challenges Janie to a verbal duel in which she, the bold and daring assertive woman of fiery temperament, emerges the victor.

The dramatic battle of Jody at war with Janie is performed in open view and it is initiated when Jody complains about the haphazard way Janie cuts a piece of chewing tobacco: "Don't stand dere rollin' yo' pop eyes at me wid yo' rump hangin' nearly to yo' knees!" (68). Janie abruptly confronts the insult as she does something she hasn't done before. She takes the floor or stage and talks directly to Jody's face: "Stop mixin' up mah doings wid mah looks, Jody. When you git through tellin' me how tuh cut uh plug uh tobacco, then you kin tell me whether mah behind is on straight or not" (68). Jody is dumbfounded at the harshness of Janie's response: "Wha—whut's dat you say, Janie? You must be out yo' head" (68). But because he continues talking on the subject of her looks and her womanhood, Janie plays her own version of the dozens of personal insult with devastating effect on Jody's masculine prestige before the menfolk:

> Janie: Ah'm nearly forty and you'se already fifty. How come you can't talk about dat sometimes instead of always pointin' at me?
>
> Jody: T'aint no use in gettin' all mad, Janie, 'cause Ah mention you ain't no young gal no mo'. Nobody in heah ain't lookin' for no wife outa yuh. Old as you is.
>
> Janie: Naw, Ah ain't no young gal no mo' but den Ah ain't no old woman neither. Ah reckon Ah looks mah age too. But Ah'm uh woman every inch of me, and Ah know it. Dat's uh whole lot more'n you kin say. You big-bellies round here and put out a lot of brag, but 'tain't nothin' to it but yo' big voice. Humph! Talkin' bout me lookin old! When you pull down yo' britches, you look lak de change uh life (68–69).

Jody has no time to recover from Janie's knock-out verbal punch landing squarely on his declining manhood, as the response of the gathered men helps to solidify the resounding force of its impact. "Great God from Zion!. . . . Y'all really playin' de dozens tuh night," (69) gasps Sam Watson, as Jody tries to absorb the shock, hoping his ears are fooling him. But the other talkers intercept his verbal escape route and make sure he gets the full meaning of Janie's message. They appear to be on Janie's side as they talk tauntingly to Jody, urging him on for an equal reply. "You heard her, you ain't blind," remarks Walter, whiie Lige commiserates, "Ah ruther be shot with tacks than tuh hear dat 'bout mahself" (69).

Jody now realizes the power of Janie's scorn against his vanity before the townsmen—folks economically inferior to him, but strong human beings who will laugh at his loss of vanity in front of his wife. His only recourse for combatting Janie's powerful talk is not a verbal one, but rather a physical one, for he strikes her with all his might and drives her from the store. His wordless action reveals that for once in the marriage, Janie is able to talk to Jody in a way he understands, in a way that demonstrates he is no longer the dominating Big Voice. Only through the ridicule and insult of the dozens is she able to strike through to an overly ambitious man who "worships de works of his own hands" (74).

Janie's act of verbal defiance causes the marriage to disintegrate into separation. Although Jody avoids Janie for the next months, her assertive tongue still finds a way to reach him and scold him for his oppressive behavior throughout the marriage. As Jody becomes sick and lingers close to death, Janie is determined to air her grievance—to, in the folk's way of expression, "put her foot on his doorstep" in a direct face-to-face conversation. Jody will not escape her verbal wrath through death. Although he aims to order Janie away from his deathbed for fear she is hoodooing him, he is virtually powerless as she defies him and speaks her mind. She reprimands him for his selfish and domineering character in a firm and mean voice: "Ah knowed you wasn't gointuh lissen tuh me. You changes everything but nothin' don't change you—not even death. But Ah ain't goin' outa here and Ah ain't gointuh hush. Naw, you gointuh listen tuh me one time befo' you die. Have yo' way all yo' life, trample and mash down and then die ruther than tuh let yo' self heah 'bout it. Listen, Jody, you ain't de Jody Ah run off down de road wid. You'se whut's left after he died. Ah run off tuh keep house wid you in uh wonderful way. But you wasn't satisfied wid me de way Ah was. Naw! Mah own mind had tuh be squeezed and crowded out tuh make room for yours in me" (74).

In characteristic behavior, Jody instructs Janie to hush, to shut up, but Janie remains steadfast in her tongue-lashing of him to the bitter end. The last minutes of his life are filled with Janie's words about the meaning of living and sharing—aspects of the marriage experience which he overlooked during their twenty year relationship with him sitting in the ruling chair: "You got tuh die tuh find out dat you got tuh pacify somebody besides yo' self if you wants any love and sympathy in dis world. You ain't tried tuh pacify *nobody* but yo' self. Too busy listening tuh yo' own big voice. . . . All dis bowin' down, all dis obedience under yo' voice—dat ain't whut Ah rushed off down de road tuh find out about you" (74–75).

With the death of Jody, Janie's mean assertive voice dies as well. There is another side to her assertive individualism. A new Janie emerges after Jody is laid to rest. Spiritually, she returns to her old adolescent self again, loving her freedom and desiring to undergo the springtime existence of life she observed as a girl under the blossoming pear tree. Removal of the headrag—which Jody had forced her to wear to cover her beautiful hair—symbolically represents her passage away from life as Mrs. Jody Starks to a new experience as a free woman of property and wealth still remembering her dream to love and to be loved. Her love of language and conversation also finds her adopting a new verbal rapport with customers entering her store. It is this verbal flexibility in her nature which creates an amicable union upon her first meeting with the final man in her life, Tea Cake, who becomes her springtime, her blossoming pear tree, her horizon, and the bright lightning rod of inspiriation and spirituality.

Tea Cake's friendly verbal mannerisms and laughable disposition set him apart from Jody and Killicks and leave a lasting impression on Janie as their courtship relationship develops and finally culminates in marriage. His friendly speech communication on entering the store, as well as his unselfish inclusion of her in the checkers game, have an impact on Janie. She feels like a woman again in the presence of a man: "She found herself glowing inside. Somebody wanted her to play. Somebody thought it natural for her to play. That was even nice. She looked him over and got little thrills from every one of his good points. Those full, lazy eyes with the lashes curling sharply away like drawn scimitars. The lean, over-padded shoulders and narrow waist. Even nice!" (81).

It is perhaps Tea Cake's skill with words which demonstrates his character and his respect for Janie and eventually unites them in courtship and then marriage. A man close to his cultural roots and simple ways of life, Tea Cake is such a pleasant and humorous voice that he has the ability to strike an acquaintance with Janie before revealing his name. It is long after they have acted like they were old friends engaging in an enlivened game of checkers that Janie suddenly announces she does not know his name. His infectious personality and pleasing speech delight her fancy as she inquires about his identity:

Janie: Mr, er—er—You never did tell me whut yo' name wuz.
Tea Cake: Ah sho didn't. Wuzn't expectin' fuh to be needed. De name mah mama gimme is Vergible Woods. Dey call me Tea Cake for short.
Janie: Tea Cake! So you sweet as all dat?
Tea Cake: Ah may be guilty. You better try me and see (83).

The happy dialogue leads Tea Cake on to engage in courtship play and exhibit his dramatic mannerisms, his irresistible grin, and natural showmanship. Jokes and laughter draw them close in merriment as Janie bursts out in praise of him with her repeated admonishment of "You crazy thing!" (85). She also grows to identify with him so that he suddenly seems no stranger but rather the ideal man she has longed for since her days under the pear tree and Nanny's intrusion on her dreams of finding a blossom for her pear tree with the reality of a marriage to old man Killicks. Together, she and Tea Cake are verbally harmonious talkers who communicate pleasant words of springtime and bloomtime. They assert their shared love and affection for each other in the manner of Missie and Joe.

As the courtship between the two unfolds, Janie and Tea Cake jointly participate in oral rituals and social activities. She is an active verbal partner in love talk in which they express admiration for each other. When he praises her hair with the acknowledgment that "it's so pretty. It feels lak underneath uh dove's wing next to mah face" (87), Janie responds by drawing on nature to create a glowing description of Tea Cake. To her thinking and creative imagery, he "looked like the love thoughts of women. He could be a bee to a blossom—a pear tree blossom in the spring. He seemed to be crushing scent out of the world with his footsteps. Crushing aromatic herbs with every step he took. Spices hung about him. He was a glance from God" (90). United in love and affection, Janie and Tea Cake also present a cohesive social front, interesting as a team in work and play. Consider, for example, the following description of their unity—a far cry from Janie's social isolation from her previous husbands: "Tea Cake and Janie gone hunting. Tea Cake and Janie gone fishing. Tea Cake and Janie gone to Orlando to the movies. Tea Cake and Janie gone to a dance. Tea Cake making flower beds in Janie's yard and seeding the garden for her. Chopping down the tree she never did like by the dining room window. All those signs of possession. Tea Cake in a borrowed car teaching Janie to drive. Tea Cake and Janie playing checkers; playing coon-can; playing Florida flip on the store porch all afternoon as if nobody else was there. Day after day and week after week" (93).

A strong marriage founded on love and verbal compatability further unites the two in the love game. Janie now marries the man she wants on the basis of feeling and communication, of verbal cohesion. Property and money are of little significance, and neither is the age disparity between them a major matter of concern, for Tea Cake has shown her where "It's de thought dat makes de difference in ages. If people thinks de same they can make it all right" (96). She intends to partake of everything her husband does in the arena of language and music, too, so as to unify their marriage and generate the happiness and delight of springtime feelings.

They embark on a new life away from Eatonville in the fertile lands of the Everglades. Tea Cake becomes the source of verbal regeneration as Janie carries with her new thoughts and new words. Tea Cake has "taught her the maiden language all over" (97) and she is anxious to experience his style of marriage. Her wifely duties of labor are fondly cherished. She lives and works alongside of him on the muck in happiness over their simple carefree life. Participation in the oral rituals of song and talk, originating on the porch of their house, the unauthorized social center of the job, comes naturally for Janie as Tea Cake encourages her full participation as their house on the muck in the Everglades becomes a magnet, the unauthorized center of the work camp. Tea Cake, a far contrast to the oppressive Killicks and dictatorial Jody on the storeporch, becomes an admired man of the people as he engages in Black cultural rituals of song, talk, and dance. A man of musical perfection with his guitar in the Quarters or in the jook, Tea Cake, full of laughter in work or play, is the center of joy. Janie fondly participates with the folk in the singing of the humorous dozens songs when the folk on the muck gather at their house to stuff courage in each other's ears when the hurricane approaches. This dozens song is one of cheer and laughter, one far removed in tone from the hostile and personally-inflamed dozen blow Janie levelled at Jody years earlier in her second marriage:

> Yo' mama don't wear no Draws
> Ah seen her when she took 'em Off
> She soaked 'em in alcoHol
> She sold 'em tuh de Santy Claus
> He told her 'twas aginst de Law
> To wear dem dirty Draws (129).

In community and home, their love prevails in words and action for a peaceful two years, enabling Janie to grow more philosophical about life as they encounter danger and the prospect of death during the hurricane. A matured Janie voices no regrets for her simple, but loving and fulfilling life with Tea Cake: "If you kin see de light at daybreak, you dont keer if you die at dusk. It's so many people never see de light at all. Ah wuz fumblin' round and God opened the door" (131). She clings to him out of love as they both weather the cruel elements of nature and watch the power of God's will unfold before them.

The love bond in the marriage is finally tested when Janie is attacked by a mad dog (perhaps symbolic of that mad man of a husband, Jody, who also tried to attack Janie's assertive individualism). The heroic Tea Cake, a striking contrast to the evil and domineering Jody, risks his life to rescue Janie who in turn praises this demonstration of his love and defense of her: "You was twice noble tuh save me from dat dawg.... He wuzn't nothin' all over but pure hate" (137). In saving Janie's life, Tea Cake is bitten and eventually contracts rabies, grows mad, and finally attacks Janie with a gun. Out of self-defense, Janie shoots him, thus igniting "the meanest moment of eternity" (158), a great day of sorrow in her life. Tea Cake, the son of Evening Sun, dies by her own hand. For loving her, he pays the ultimate price with his life, as does Janie in suffering the loss.

Even though she is saddened by the violent end of her splendid love relationship with simplistic and loving Tea Cake, Janie does not become mired in grief. Her vibrant assertive voice makes it possible for her to re-live her brief love story, explaining in detail the love she and Tea Cake shared, as well as describing for her listener the hostile white court of law which accused her of willful murder. Her talk is convincing to the court, however, as she wins her freedom to bury Tea Cake's body, but not her memories. Through him, she fulfills her dream of a strong love relationship with a man and intends to keep it alive through the process of oral narrative.

Her assertive voice strengthens her will and endurance as she recreates her fond memories in words to Pheoby, her close friend. In widowhood the talk experience becomes for her a kind of healing process that is most indicative of her race's historical reliance on the Black oral tradition to add perspective and substance to survival. She strengthens her link to the natural world of rural Florida by recreating another springtime existence, planting a package of her dead husband's garden seeds. Through nature and words, through natural and authentic talk, Janie survives as she traces her verbal roots from innocence with Killicks to maturity with Tea Cake. Oral rituals of talk and song will afford her peace and contentment as she pulls in her "horizon" (159). However temporary, Janie does have the experience of expressing the love she had longed in her youth under the pear tree. Her assertive individualism experienced its harsh evil moments in verbal conflict with Killicks and Jody, but it also underwent the process of true love in the good moments of marital bliss with Tea Cake.

The reliance on natural verbal ability was also a main ingredient in the individuality and survival of the other seven diverse women of words previously discussed—Lucy, Delia, the Harlem domestic, Daisy, Missie, Laura Lee and Big Sweet. Like Janie, they are all guided to an understanding of the human experience through the talking process. Words are their tickets to survival, as are weapons of fists or cold steel, if required. In the Hurston tradition of Black womanhood and assertive individualism, they are capable of backing up their fiery word power with physical force on occasion, hence their folkloric proclamation, "Don't say no more than you back can stand."

In their folk world, the experience of talking and fighting becomes their survival medium for negotiating and gaining self-respect and, in the case of Janie, for experiencing reciprocal love. No other select group of Black folk women rises to the occasion of personal survival and defiant independence like the women who populate the artistic landscape in Hurston's fiction, folklore, and drama. They are "spunky" and noble heroines with creative verbal talents which all contemporary Black women should emulate in intra-familial, intra-racial and inter-racial experiences. To be a woman of courage and an individual of noble, fighting spirit is to assert one's identity and beliefs like these women, or even like Hurston herself, without fear of the consequences. They all talk with a bold spirit of mind and body which gives them a sense of empowerment with the law of authority in their mouths.

At best, the assertive woman's total being is existence made possible through the talking (and when necessary, fighting) process. It alone bears the spirit and heartbeat of a life of spunk and nobility whereby the assertive woman indeed speaks with the law of truth and moral authority in her mouth. Hurston's fiction, folklore, and drama illustrate the dynamics of assertive individualism which is the Black woman's most endearing quality in private and public life. Her beauty is in the execution of her talking tongue to articulate the essence of her inner identity. The final test of humanity rests in her assertive folk voice, the main jewel and singing stone of her heroic existence as talker and fighter who is prepared to say no more with her mouth than her back could physically stand. Indeed, Hurston's assertive woman has the law of authority in her verbal folk wisdom and in her genuine spunk for direct action when she proclaims that "Ah got de law in mah mouf" (MM, 162).

Notes

Introduction

1. Ernest Kaiser, "Recent Books," *Freedomways,* Second Quarter, 1978, 118.

Chapter 1

1. Zora Neale Hurston, *Dust Tracks on a Road* (New York: Lippincott, 1971), 187. All additional references from this source will appear in the text with page number citations and the abbreviation *DTOR.*

2. References appearing in the text are to the 1965 Fawcett primer reprint edition (New York: Lippincott, 1937). The abbreviation *TEWWG* will accompany page number citations from the novel.

3. Zora Neale Hurston, *Mules and Men* (New York: Harper & Row, 1970), 187. References from this edition of the book are cited in the text in parentheses and with page numbers and the abbreviation *M&M.*

4. Zora Neale Hurston, *Jonah's Gourd Vine* (New York: Lippincott, 1971), 157–158. Other references from the novel will appear with parentheses in the text with the abbreviation *J'sGV,* followed by page number citation.

5. Robert Hemenway, "Are You a Flying Lark or a Setting Dove?" in *Afro-American Literature: The Reconstruction of Instruction,* edited by Dexter Fisher and Robert Stepto (New York: Modern Language Association, 1979), 145.

6. Roger D. Abrahams, "Negotiating Respect: Patterns of Presentation Among Black Women," *Journal of American Folklore,* Vol. 88, 1975, 62.

7. Robert Hemenway, "Are You a Flying Lark or a Setting Dove?" 146.

Chapter 2

1. *Ms.*, May 1974, Vol. 2, No. 1, 65–70, 195.
2. *J'sGV*, 228–229, 245, 253. John's beating of Hattie is the most vicious that we find in Hurston's fiction, with the exception perhaps of Sykes' domestic violence against Delia in "Sweat."
3. Zora Neale Hurston, "John Redding Goes to Sea," *Stylus*, 1 (May, 1921), 11–22. Reprinted in *Opportunity*, 4 (Jan., 1926), 16–21.
4. Hurston's male characters, such as Bentley, Muttsy, Mah Honey, Jelly and Sweet Back, are also fanatically color struck. See "Magnolia Flower," "Muttsy," *Mules and Men* and "Story in Harlem Slang."
5. Zora Neale Hurston, "Color Struck." *Fire!!,* 1 (Nov., 1926), 7–15. Reprinted in *The Portable Harlem Renaissance Reader,* edited by David Levering Lewis. New York: Penguin Books, 1994, 703–719.
6. "Color Struck" in *The Portable Harlem Renaissance Reader,* 707.
7. References taken from this novel are to the 1939 edition (Philadelphia: Lippincott). The abbreviation *MMM* will precede each page number reference.
8. Throughout her art, Hurston is concerned about the leadership qualities of assertive women. Big Sweet, Lucy, Sally, and Leafy Lee, for example, represent admirable and positive role models of leadership, while Miriam serves as a contrasting symbol of poor leadership qualities due to ineffectiveness and lack of self-motivation. Hurston also expresses, at length, her ideas on the question of strong leadership in the Black race. It is more in her fiction that she suggests a Black woman may also be a strong leadership force among Blacks, while in the socio-political essays such as "The Pet Negro System," "I Saw Negro Votes Peddled," "A Negro Voter Sizes Up Taft," and "Crazy for This Democracy," she merely sets forth her philosophical points on the subject without being specific as to who might best fulfill her guidelines on leadership.
9. References in the text concerning this novel are to the 1948 edition (New York: Scribner). Page citations appear in parentheses with the abbreviation *SOS*.

Chapter 3

1. See David Levering Lewis. *The Portable Harlem Renaissance Reader.* New York: Penguin, 1994, 695.
2. Ralph Ellison, "Introduction" to *Invisible Man.* (New York: Vintage/Random House, 1989), ix.

3. *The Color Purple.* (New York: Washington Square Press, 1983), 53.

4. Zora Neale Hurston, "Uncle Monday," was published as part of Hurston's series, "Characteristics of Negro Expression," in *Negro: An Anthology*, edited by Nancy Cunard (London: Wishart, 1934), 39–46. "Uncle Monday" is reprinted in *Zora Neale Hurston: The Complete Stories*, edited by Henry Louis Gates, (New York: Harper Collins, 1995), 106–113.

Chapter 4

1. "Characteristics of Negro Expression," in *Negro* edited by Nancy Cunard (New York: Unger Publishers, 1970), 30.

Chapter 6

1. Zora Neale Hurston and Dorothy Waring, *Polk County: A Comedy of Negro Life on a Sawmill Camp, with authentic Negro Music, in Three Acts.* Play is available on microfilm through Library of Congress, Washington, D.C.

2. Hurston and Waring, *Polk County,* 1, 1, 32.

Chapter 7

1. Zora Neale Hurston, "The Conscience of the Court," *Saturday Evening Post,* Vol. 222 (March 18, 1950), 112–122. Page citations in the text pertaining to this story are from this source.

2. Like Rosa Parks, whose assertive woman's voice gave credence to the Civil Rights Movement of the late fifties and then the sixties, Black maids have been widely known throughout the South and North for their spontaneity in speaking up for their rights—particularly in white homes where they work and make it clear that they will not be addressed as though they were beasts of burden or mules of the world. Hurston worked as a domestic worker to gain experience about the intricate workings of the job and even planned to write a book about Black domestics, although the plan never materialized. For more contemporary accounts of domestics and their assertive individualism in the Jim Crow South and urban North, see the story of Dorothy Bolden who worked for years as a maid in Georgia, and then organized maids and founded a pioneer labor organization for domestic workers called National Domestic Workers, Inc. Read the portrait of her life as a maid in Nancy Seifer's *Nobody Speaks for Me!: Self-Portraits of American Working Class Women* (New York: Simon and Schuster, 1976),

136–178. Bolden recounts the details of her employer ordering her arrest for having boldly talked back to her in self defense. Also read in the same book the life of Carolyn Reed, an assertive domestic servant for twenty years and her efforts to professionalize the craft of domestic work while serving as a member of the U.S. National Committee on Household Employment.

3. See Hurston's "The Pet Negro System," *American Mercury*, Vol. 56 (May, 1943), 593–600.

4. Langston Hughes. *The Ways of White Folks.* (New York: Knopf), 1979.

5. Observe in "The Pet Negro System" Hurston's admiration of whites who have what she calls "culture and a sense of class, dignity and respect" about themselves in their treatment of Blacks, as opposed to her revulsion of the "poor white trash" (such as those she depicted in *Seraph on the Suwanee*) who are ignorant and inhuman in inter-racial relations.

6. In the autobiography, *Dust Tracks on a Road* and the folklore anthology, *Mules and Men,* Hurtson calls the imaginative, highly exaggerated art of storytelling the experience of making colorful, crayon enlargements of the simplisitc Southern folk experience that encompasses more laughter and humor than it does tears and tragedy. Also see Robert Hemenway's reference to the term under a chapter heading entitled "Crayon Enlargements of Life" in *Zora Neale Hurston: A Literary Biography,* 218–246.

Chapter 8

1. All page citations in the text regarding this story are taken from *I Love Myself When I Am Laughing And Then Again When I Am Looking Mean and Impressive*, edited by Alice Walker (New York: The Feminist Press, 1979), 208–218.

2. See Hurston's recording of the folktale, as told by Mathilda Moseley, about the power of women in always taking advantage of men, in *Mules and Men*, 49–54.

3. For more examples of old time Southern courting rituals, see Frank D. Banks and Portia Smiley, "Old-Time Courtship Conversation," in *Mother Wit from the Laughing Barrel*, edited by Alan Dundes (New Jersey: Prentice Hall, 1973), 251–257.

Chapter 9

1. Reference citations are taken only from Act 3 of the play which appears in *Drama Critique*, Vol. 7, No. 2 (Spring, 1964), 103–197.

2. Page references occuring in the text are taken from the July, 1942 edition of *American Mercury*, Vol. 55, 84–96.

3. For a critical denouncement of this urban, street corner style of communication by which Black men compete amongst themselves for acquaintance with women, see James Roland's "Street Corner Communication," *Dawn Magazine*, Vol. 2, No. 10 (New York: Afro-American Company, Inc.), October, 1974, 12.

Chapter 10

1. All citations for this story are taken from *I Love Myself When I am Laughing. . .*, edited by Alice Walker (New York: The Feminist Press, 1979), 197–207.

2. Hurston is fascinated by snakes that are indigenous to the Floridian terrain, and for many of her male characters, a test of manhood and "spunk" is demonstrated often in feats with snakes. A snake in this story is a symbol of power, torment and eventual destruction for the despicable Sykes, while it denotes more admirable qualities of strength and power in the demonstration of manhood and nobility for such characters like John Pearson of *J'sGV*, Moses of *MMM*, Uncle Monday of "Uncle Monday," and Jim Meserve of *SOS*.

3. In a sketch of "Tippy," Sykes Jones' dog, Hurston presents a tale about Tippy who has the bad habit of sucking eggs. See "The Eatonville Anthology," in *The Messenger*, September–November, 1926.

Chapter 11

1. Page reference citations used in discussion of the character of Lucy and Janie are taken from *J'sGV* (New York: Lippincott, 1971) and the Fawcett primer reprint of *TEWWG* (New York: Lippincott, 1965).

Chapter 12

1. Page reference citations employed in the discussion of Janie's character are cited from the Fawcett Primer reprint of *TEWWG* (New York, Lippincott, 1965).

Selected Bibliography

Primary Sources

Books

Jonah's Gourd Vine. Philadelphia: J. B. Lippincott, 1934. Reprinted with an introduction by Larry Neale, Philadelphia: J.B. Lippincott, 1971. Reprinted by Harper & Row, Publishers, Inc., 1990.

Mules and Men. Philadelphia: J. B. Lippincott, 1935. Reprinted, New York: Negro Universities Press, 1969. Reprinted, with an introduction by Darwin Turner, New York: Harper and Row, 1970. Reprinted by Harper & Row, Publishers, Inc., 1990.

Their Eyes Were Watching God. Philadelphia: J.B. Lippincott, 1937. Reprinted, Greenwich, Conn.: Fawcett Publications, 1965. Reprinted by Negro Universities Press, 1969. Reprinted, Urbana: University of Illinois Press, 1978. Reprinted by Harper & Row, Publishers, Inc., 1990.

Tell My Horse. Philadelphia: J.B. Lippincott, 1938. The European version of this book appeared under the title, Voodoo Gods: An Inquiry into Native Myths and Magic in Jamaica and Haiti. London: J.M. Dent & Sons Ltd., 1939. Reprinted by Harper & Row, Publishers, Inc., 1990.

Moses, Man of the Mountain. Philadelphia: J.B. Lippincott, 1939. Reprinted, Chatham, New Jersey: Chatham Bookseller, 1974. Reprinted by Harper & Row, Publishers, Inc., 1991.

Dust Tracks on a Road. Philadelphia: J.B. Lippincott, 1942. Reprinted, with an introduction by Darwin Turner, New York: Arno Press, 1969. Reprinted with an introduction by Larry Neal, New York: J.B. Lippincott, 1971. Reprinted by Harper and Row, Publishers, Inc., 1991.

Seraph on the Suwanee. New York: Charles Scribner's Sons, 1948. Reprinted, Ann Arbor, Michigan: University Microfilms, 1971. Reprinted, New York: AMS Press, 1974. Reprinted by Harper Collins Publishers, 1991.

Mule Bone: A Comedy of Negro Life. Complete play reprinted by Harper Collins Publishers, 1991.

156   *Selected Bibliography*

Other Publications

"*Under the Bridge,*" "*American Visions,*" December/January 1997, 14–20.

"John Redding Goes to Sea." *Stylus 1* (May, 1921), 11–22. Reprinted in *Opportunity,* 4 (Jan., 1926), 16–21.

"Drenched in Light." *Opportunity,* 2 (Dec., 1924), 371–374.

"Spunk." *Opportunity,* 3 (June, 1925), 171–173. Reprinted in *The New Negro,* edited by Alain Locke, 105–11. New York: Albert and Charles Boni, 1925.

"Magnolia Flower." *Spokesman,* July, 1925, 26–29.

"The Hue and Cry about Howard University," *Messenger,* 7 (Sept., 1925), 315–19, 338.

"Muttsy." *Opportunity,* 4 (Aug., 1926), 7–15.

"The Eatonville Anthology." *Messenger,* 8 (Sept., 1925), 315–19, 338.

"Muttsy." *Opportunity,* 4 (Aug., 1926), 7–15.

"The Eatonville Anthology." *Messenger,* 8 (Sept., Oct., Nov., 1926), 261–62, 297, 319, 332.

Color Struck: A Play. (Nov., 1926), 40–45.

"Sweat." *Fire!!,* (Nov., 1926), 40–45.

The First One: A Play. In Ebony and Topaz, edited by Charles S. Johnson, 53–57. New York: National Urban League, 1927.

"Cudjo's Own Story of the Last African Slaver." *Journal of Negro History,* 12 (Oct., 1927), 648–63.

"How It Feels to Be Colored Me." *World Tomorrow,* 11 (May, 1928), 215–216.

"Dance Songs and Tales from the Bahamas." *Journal of American Folklore,* 43 (July–Sept., 1930), 294–312.

"Hoodoo in America." *Journal of American Folklore,* 44 (Oct.–Dec., 1931), 317–418.

"The Gilded Six-Bits," *Story,* 3 (Aug., 1933), 60–70.

"Characteristics of Negro Expression." In *Negro: An Anthology,* edited by Nancy Cunard, 39–46. London: Wishart, 1934. Reprinted in *Zora Neale Hurston: The Sanctified Church* with an introduction by Toni Cade Bambara, Berkeley, California: Turtle Island Press, 1983.

"Race Cannot Become Great Until It Recognizes Talent." *Washington Tribune,* Dec. 29, 1934.

"Fannie Hurst." *Saturday Review,* October 9, 1937, 15–16.

"Stories of Conflict." *Saturday Review,* April 2, 1938, 32.

"Now Take Noses." In *Cordially Yours,* 25–27. Philadelphia: J.B. Lippincott, 1939.

"Cock Robin, Beale Street." *Southern Literary Messenger,* 3 (July, 1941), 321–323.

"Story in Harlem Slang." *American Mercury,* 55 (July, 1942), 84–96.

"Lawrence of the River." *Saturday Evening Post,* Sept., 5, 1942, 18, 55–57. Condensed in *Negro Digest,* 1 (June, 1943), 47–49.

"The Pet Negro System." *American Mercury,* 56 (May, 1943), 593–600. Condensed in *Negro Digest,* 1 (June, 1943), 37–40.

"High John De Conquer." *American Mercury,* 57 (Oct., 1943), 450–458.

"Negroes without Self-Pity." *American Mercury*, 57 (Nov., 1943), 601–603.

"The Last Slave Ship." *American Mercury,* 58 (Mar., 1944), 351–358. Condensed in *Negro Digest*, 2 (May, 1944), 11–16.

"My Most Humiliating Jim Crow Experience." *Negro Digest*, 2 (June, 1944), 25–26.

"The Rise of the Begging Joints." *American Mercury*, 60 (Mar., 1945), 288–294. Condensed in *Negro Digest*, 3 (May, 1945).

"Crazy for This Democracy." *Negro Digest,* 4 (Dec., 1945), 45–48.

"Thirty Days Among the Maroons." *New York Herald Tribune Weekly Book Review*, Jan., 12, 1947, 8.

Caribbean Melodies for Chorus of Mixed Voices and Soloists. With accompaniment for piano and percussion instruments. Arranged by William Grant Still. Philadelphia: Oliver Ditson, 1947.

Review of *Voodoo in New Orleans* by Robert Tallant. *Journal of American Folklore*, 60 (Oct.–Dec., 1947), 436–438.

"Conscience of the Court." *Saturday Evening Post*, March 18, 1950, 22–23, 112–22.

"I Saw Negro Votes Peddled." *American Legion Magazine*, 49 (Nov., 1950), 12–13, 54–57, 59–60. Condensed in *Negro Digest*, 9 (Sept., 1951), 77–85.

"What White Publishers Won't Print." *Negro Digest*, 8 (Apr., 1950), 85–89.

"Mourner's Bench, Communist Line: Why the Negro Won't Buy Communism." *American Legion Magazine*, 50 (June, 1951), 14–15, 55–60.

"A Negro Voter Sizes Up Taft." *Saturday Evening Post,* Dec., 8, 1951, 29, 150.

"Zora's Revealing Story of Ruby's First Day in Court." *Pittsburgh Courier*, Oct. 11, 1952.

"Victim of Fate." *Pittsburgh Courier,* Oct. 18, 1952.

"Ruby Sane." *Pittsburgh Courier*, Oct. 18, 1952.

"Ruby McCollum Fights for Life." *Pittsburgh Courier*, Nov. 22, 1952.

"Bare Plot against Ruby." *Pittsburgh Courier*, Nov. 29, 1952.

"Trial Highlights." *Pittsburgh Courier,* Nov. 29, 1952.

"McCollum-Adams Trial Highlights." *Pittsburgh Courier*, Dec. 27, 1952.

"Ruby Bares Her Love." *Pittsburgh Courier*, Jan. 3, 1953.

"Doctor's Threats, Tussle over Gun Led to Slaying." *Pittsburgh Courier*, Jan. 10, 1953.

"Ruby's Troubles Mount." *Pittsburgh Courier*, Jan., 17, 1953.

"The Life of Mrs. Ruby J. McCollum," *Pittsburgh Courier,* Feb. 28, March 7, 14, 21, 28, April 4, 11, 18, 25, and May 2, 1953.

Manuscripts of Significance in Library Collections

"Back to the Middle Ages: Becoming a Peasant in the United States." Columbia University, Rare Book and Manuscript Library.

"Book of Harlem." James Weldon Johnson Collection, Yale.

"The Chick With One Hen." James Weldon Johnson Collection, Yale.

"The Emperor Effaces Himself." James Weldon Johnson Collection, Yale.

"The Florida Negro." (Florida Federal Writers' Project) Florida Historical Society Papers, University of South Florida Library.

"Folklore" in "The Florida Negro" manuscript in the Archive of Folk Song, Library of Congress, Washington, D.C.

Herod the Great. (Biography) in Hurston Collection, Rare Books and Manuscripts, University of Florida Library at Gainesville.

"The Lost Keys of Glory." Columbia University, Rare Book and Manuscript Library.

Mule Bone: A Comedy of Negro Life. (Written in collaboration with Langston Hughes in 1930). Hurston Collection, Rare Books and Manuscripts, University of Florida Library at Gainesville. Act 3 was published in *Drama Critique*, Spring, 1964, 103–107. Full Text of Play Reprinted by Henry Gates. New York: Harper Perennial, 1991.

Polk County: A Comedy of Negro Life on a Sawmill Camp, with Authentic Negro Music. Play in three acts with Dorothy Waring, 1944. James Weldon Johnson Collection, Yale, and Library of Congress, Washington, D.C.

Unpublished copyright typescripts of newly discovered Hurston plays are housed in manuscript division of the Library of Congress, Washington, D.C. Included are the following works: *"Woofing," "Poker," "Forty Yards," "Lawing and Jawing," "Cold Keener, a revue, "De Turkey and de Law, a comedy in three acts.*

Secondary Sources

Abrahams, Roger D. *Deep Down in the Jungle.* Chicago: Aldine Publishing Co., 1963.

———. "Negotiating Respect: Patterns of Presentation Among Black Women,"*Journal of American Folklore,* 88 (1975), 58–80.

———. *The Men-of-Words in the West Indies.* Baltimore: John Hopkins University Press, 1983.

Bailey, Pearl. *The Raw Pearl.* New York: Harcourt Brace, 1968.

———. *Talking to Myself.* New York: Harcourt Brace, 1971.

———. *Hurry Up, America, and Spit.* New York: Harcourt Brace, 1976.

Baker, Houston. *Black Literature in America.* New York: McGraw-Hill, 1971.

———. *Long Black Song: Essays in Black American Literatue and Culture.* Virginia: University Press of Virginia at Charlottesville, 1972.

———. *Singers of Daybreak: Studies in Black American Literature.* Washington, D.C.: Howard University Press, 1974.

Baldwin, James. *Go Tell It on the Mountain.* New York: Knopf, 1953.

Barksdale, Richard and Kinnamon, Kenneth. *Black Writers of America*. New York: Macmillan Company, 1972.

Barton, Rebecca. *Witnesses for Freedom: Negro Americans in Autobiography*. New York: Harper, 1948.

Beckford, Ruth. *Katherine Dunham*. New York: Marcel Dekker, 1979.

Bell, Roseann and Guy-Sheftall, Beverly and Parker, Bettye. *Sturdy Black Bridges*. New York: Doubleday, 1979.

Bennett, Lerone. *Before the Mayflower*. Baltimore: Penguin, 1962.

Bergman, Mort and Bergman, Peter. *The Chronological History of the Negro in America*. New York: American Library, Inc., 1969.

Berry, Faith. *Langston Hughes: Before and Beyond Harlem*. Connecticut: Westport Lawrence Hill and Co., 1983.

Birmingham, Stephen. *Certain People: America's Black Elite*. Boston: Little Brown and Co., 1977.

Black Scholar. "Black Anthropology, 1," Vol. 2, No. 7, Sept. and Oct. 1980.

———. "Black Anthropology, 2," Vol. 2, No. 8, Nov. and Dec. 1980.

Black World. "The Harlem Renaissance Revisited," Vol. 20, No. 1, Nov. 1970.

Blake, Emma. "Zora Neale Hurston, Author and Folklorist," *Negro History Bulletin*, Vol. 29, No. 7, 1966, 149, 150 and 165.

Bloom, Harold. *Major Black American Writers Through the Harlem Renaissance*. NewYork: Chelsea House Publishers, 1995.

———. *Zora Neale Hurston* (Modern Critical Views; Modern American Literature Series). New York: Chelsea House, 1986.

———. *Their Eyes Were Watching God* (Modern Critical Views; Modern American Literature Series). New York: Chelsea House, 1987.

Boas, Franz. *Race, Language and Culture*. New York: Free Press, 1940.

Bone, Robert. *The Negro Novel in America*. New Haven, Connecticut: Yale University Press, 1965.

———. *Down Home*. New York: G.P. Putnam's Sons, 1975.

Bontemps, Alberta. *The Old South and Other Stories of the Thirties*. New York: Cornwall Press, 1973.

Bontemps, Arna and Hughes, Langston. *The Book of Negro Folklore*. New York: Dodd Mead, 1958.

Bontemps, Arna. *The Harlem Renaissance Remembered*. New York: Dodd Mead, 1972.

Bordelon, Pam. "New Tracks on Dust Tracks: Toward a Reassessment of the Life of Zora Neale Hurston." *African American Review*, Spring 1997, 5–21.

Botkin, B. A. *A Treasury of Southern Folklore*. New York: Crown Publishers, 1949.

Boulware, Marcus. *The Oratory of Negro Leaders*. Westport, Connecticut: Negro University Press, 1969.

"Boys 10 Accuse Zora." *Baltimore Afro-American* 11, October 23, 1948.

Brewer, J. Mason. *Juneteenth: Tone the Bell Easy*. Austin, Texas: Texas Folklore Society, 1932.

————. *Negrito: Negro Dialect Poems of the Southwest.* San Antonio: Naylor, 1933.

————. *Aunt Dicy Tales.* Austin: Privately Published, 1956.

————. Dog Ghosts and Other Texas Negro Folk Tales. Austin: University of Texas Press, 1958.

————. *American Negro Folklore.* Chicago: Quadrangle Books, 1968.

Bridgman, Richard. *The Colloquial Style in America.* New York: Oxford University Press, 1966.

Bronz, Stephen. *Roots of Negro Racial Consciousness.* New York: Libra Publishing, Inc., 1964.

Brown, Claude. *Manchild in the Promised Land.* New York: The New American Library, Signet, 1965.

Brown, H. Rap. *Die Nigger Die.* New York: The Dial Press, 1969.

Brown, Sterling. *Southern Road.* Boston: Beacon Press, 1932.

Burke, Virginia. "Zora Neale Hurston and Fannie Hurst as They Saw Each Other," *College Language Association Journal,* Vol. 20, June 1977, 435–47.

Butcher, Margaret Just. *The Negro in American Culture.* New York: Signet, 1956.

Butterfield, Stephen. *Black Autobiography in America.* Amherst: University of Massachusetts Press, 1974.

Butts, Hugh F. and Haskins, Jim. *The Psychology of Black Language.* New York: Harper and Row, 1973.

Byrd, James W. "Zora Neale Hurston: A Novel Folklorist," *Tennessee Folklore Society Bulletin* #21 (1955), 37–41.

————. *J. Mason Brewer.* Austin, Texas: East Texas State University, Steck-Vaughn Company, Publishers, 1967.

Calverton, V.F., ed. *Anthology of American Negro Literature.* New York: The Modern Library Publishers, 1967.

Cantarow, Ellen. "Sex, Race, and Criticism: Thoughts of a White Feminist on Kate Chopin and Zora Neale Hurston," *Radical Teacher,* September 1978, 30–31, 32–33.

Carruth, Ella Kaiser. *The Story of Mary McLeod Bethune.* New York: Archway, 1969.

Chapman, Abraham. *Black Voices.* New York: New American Library, 1968.

Chesnutt, Charles W. *The Wife of His Youth and Other Stories.* Ann Arbor: University of Michigan Press, 1968.

————. *The Conjure Woman.* Ann Arbor: University of Michigan Press, 1972.

Christian, Barbara. *Black Feminist Criticism.* New York: Pergamon Press, 1985.

Clarke, John Henry. *Harlem, U.S.A.* Berlin: Seven Seas Books, 1964.

Clemens, Samuel L. *Adventures of Huckleberry Finn.* Boston: Houghton Mifflin Company, Riverside Editions, 1958.

Cohen, Henning and Dillingham, William. *Humor of the Old Southwest.* Boston: Houghton Mifflin, 1964.

Cooke, Michael G. *Afro-American Literature in the Twentieth Century.* New Haven: Yale University Press, 1984.

Courlander, Harold. *Negro Folk Music U.S.A.* New York: Columbia University Press, 1963.

————. *A Treasury of Afro-American Folklore.* New York: Crown Publishers, Inc., 1976.

Cruse, Harold. *The Crisis of the Negro Intellectual.* New York: William Morrow and Co., 1967.

Cunningham, Virginia. *Paul Laurence Dunbar and His Song.* New York: Dodd, Mead & Co., 1947.

Dance, Daryl. "Shuckin' and Jivin' ": *Folklore from Contemporary Black Americans.* Bloomington: Indiana University Press, 1978.

Dannett, Sylvia. *The Negro Heritage Library.* Chicago: Educational Heritage Inc., 1966.

Davis, Arthur P. *From the Dark Tower.* Washington: Howard University Press, 1974.

————. *The New Negro Renaissance.* New York: Holt, Rinehart and Winston, 1975.

Demby, William. *Beetlecreek.* New York: Rinehart, 1950.

————. *The Catacombs.* New York: Pantheon, 1965.

Dillard, J. L. *Black English: History and Usage in the U.S.* New York: Random House, 1972.

Dixon, Thomas. *The Leopard Spots, a Romance of the White Man's Burden.* New York: Doubleday, 1902.

————. *The Clansman.* New York: Doubleday, 1905.

Dorner, Jane. *Fashion in the Twenties and Thirties.* London: Ian Allan Ltd., 1973.

Dorson, Richard. *American Negro Folktales.* Greenwich, Connecticut: Fawcett Premier Book, 1956.

————. *American Folklore.* Chicago: University of Chicago Press, 1959.

————. *African Folklore.* New York: Doubleday, 1972.

Douglass, Frederick. *Narrative of the Life of Frederick Douglass, An American Slave.* New York: Doubleday, 1963.

DuBois, W.E.B. *The Souls of Black Folk.* New York: The New American Library, Signet Classics, 1969.

Dunbar, Paul. *The Complete Poems of Paul Laurence Dunbar.* New York: Dodd Mead, 1913.

Dundes, Alan. *Mother Wit from the Laughing Barrel.* New Jersey: Prentice-Hall, 1973.

Dunham, Katherine. *Journey to Accompong.* New York: Holt and Company, 1946.

Duster, Alfreda. *Crusade for Justice: The Autobiography of Ida B. Wells.* Chicago: University of Chicago Press, 1970.

Ellison, Ralph. *Invisible Man.* New York: Signet Books, 1952.

Emanuel, James. *Langston Hughes: A Biography.* New York: Twayne Publishers, 1967.

Emanuel, James and Gross, Theodore, eds. *Dark Symphony: Negro Literature in America.* New York: The Free Press, 1968.

Epstein, Samuel. *Harriet Tubman*. Champaign, Illinois: Garrard Publishers, 1968.

Fanon, Frantz. *Black Skin, White Masks*. New York: Grove Press, 1967.

Farb, Peter. *Word Play: What Happens When People Talk*. New York: Bantam, 1973.

Faulkner, William. *The Sound and the Fury*. New York: Random House, 1929.

————. *Three Famous Short Novels*. New York: Vintage Books, 1961.

Fauset, Arthur. *Black Gods of the Metropolis*. Philadelphia: University of Pennsylvania Press, 1944.

Federal Writers' Project of the WPA for the State of Florida. *Florida: A Guide to the Southernmost State*. New York: Oxford University Press, 1939.

Feldman, Susan. *African Myths and Tales*. New York: Dell, 1963.

Finnegan, Ruth. *Oral Literature in Africa*. New York: Oxford University Press, 1970.

Fire I!! Vol. 1, No. 1, Liechtenstein, Switzerland: Kraus, 1968.

Fisher, Dexter and Stepto, Robert. *Afro-American Literature: The Reconstruction of Instruction*. New York: Modern Language Association of America, 1979.

Fisher, Rudolph. *The Walls of Jericho*. New York: Arno Press, 1928.

Flanagan, John and Hurdson, Arthur. *Folklore iin American Literature*. New York: Row, Peterson & Co. 1958.

Ford, Nick Aaron. *The Contemporary Negro Novel*. Maryland: McGrath Publishing Co., 1968.

Forten, Charlotte. *The Journal of Charlotte Forten*. New York: Collier Books, 1953.

Foster, Herbert. *Ribbin', Jivin', and Playin' the Dozens*. Cambridge, Massachusetts: Ballinger Publishing Co., 1974.

Franklin, E. Franklin. *Black Bourgeoisie*. New York: Collier Books, 1957.

Franklin, John Hope. *Three Negro Classics*. New York: Avon Books, 1965.

Fry, Gladys-Marie. *Night Riders in Black Folk History*. Knoxville: University of Tennessee Press, 1975.

Fullinwider, S.P. *The Mind and Mood of Black America*. Homewood, Illinois: 1919.

Gaines, Ernest J. *Catherine Camier*. New Jersey: Chatham Bookseller, 1964.

————. *The Autobiography of Miss Jane Pittman*. New York: Bantam Books, 1971.

Gates, Henry Louis. *Black Literature and Literary Theory*. New York: Methuen, 1984.

————. *The Signifying Monkey: A Theory of African-American Literary Criticism*. New York: Oxford University Press, 1988.

————. *Zora Neale Hurston: Critical Perspecties, Past and Present*. New York: Amistad, 1993.

————. *Zora Neale Hurston: The Complete Stories*. New York: Harper Collins Publishers, 1995.

Gayle, Addison. *Black Expression*. New York: Weybright and Talley, 1969.

————. *The Black Aesthetic*. New York: Doubleday, 1972.

————. *The Way of the New World.* New York: Doubleday, 1976.

Giles, James. "The Significance of Time in Zora Neale Hurston's *Their Eyes Were Watching God,*" *Negro American Literature Forum,* Vol. 6, 1972, 52–54.

Glenn, Robert. *Black Speech: Black Rhetoric, A Guide to Afro-American Communication.* New York: Scarecrow Press, 1976.

Gloster, Hugh. "Zora Neale Hurston, Novelist and Folklorist." *Phylon,* Vol. 4, 1943, 153–159.

————. *Negro Voices in American Fiction.* New York: Russell and Russell, 1965.

Goldstein, Rhoda. *Black Life and Culture in the U.S.* New York: Crowell, 1971.

Gonzales, Ambrose. *The Black Border: Gullah Stories of the Carolina Coast.* Columbia, South Carolina: The State Company, 1922.

Green, Elizabeth. *The Negro in Contemporary American Literature.* College Park, Maryland: McGrath Publishing Co., 1928.

Greene, J. Lee. *Time's Unfading Garden: Anne Spencer's Life and Poetry.* Baton Rouge: LSU Press, 1977.

Greenfield, Eloise. *Rosa Parks.* New York: Crowell, 1973.

Gross, Seymour and Hardy, John E. *Images of the Negro in American Literature.* Chicago: University of Chicago Press, 1966.

Guy, Rosa. *A Measure of Time.* New York: Holt, Rinehart, 1983.

Haley, Alex. *Roots.* New York: Doubleday & Co., 1976.

————. "A Black American's Search for his Ancestrel African Roots," *Ebony,* August, 1976, 100–107.

Hamilton, Virginia. *M.C. Higgins, The Great.* New York: Dell, 1974.

Hannerz, Ulf. *Soulside: Inquiries into Ghetoo Culture and Community.* New York: Columbia University Press, 1969.

Hansberry, Lorraine. *A Raisin in the Sun.* New York: Random, 1959.

Harris, Joel Chandler. *Uncle Remus, His Songs and Sayings.* New York: Appleton and Company, 1890.

————. *The Favorite Uncle Remus.* Boston: Houghton Mifflin, 1948.

Haskins, James. *Barbara Jordan.* New York: The Dial Pres, 1977.

————. *The Cotton Club.* New York: Random House, 1977.

Helmick, Evelyn. "Zora Neale Hurston." *The Carrell,* Vol. 11, June–Dec., 1970, #1 and 1, 1–20.

Hemenway, Robert. *The Black Novelist.* Columbus, Ohio: Charles Merrill, 1970.

————. "Folklore Field Notes from Zora Neale Hurston," *Black Scholar,* Vol. 7, No. 7, April 1976, 39–47.

————. "Are You a Flying Lark or a Setting Dove? in Dexter Fisher and Robert Stepto, *Afro-American Literature: The Reconstruction of Instruction.* New York: Modern Language Association, 1979, 122–153.

————. *Zora Neale Hurston: a Literary Biography.* Chicago: University of Illinois Press, 1977.

Henderson, David. *"Harlem Anthropology."* (A poem for the late Zora Neale Hurston), *Saturday Review of the Arts,* September, 1972, 40.

Henderson, George. *Ollie Miss.* Chatham, New Jersey: Chatham
    Bookseller, 1935.
Henri, Floretti. *Black Migration: Movement North, 1900–1920.* New York:
    Doubleday, 1975.
Hernton, Calvin. "The Sexual Mountain and Black Women Writers," *Black
    Scholar,* July and August, 1985, 1–11.
Hill, Lynda. *Social Ritual and the Verbal Art of Zora Neale Hurston.*
    Washington: Howard University Press, 1996.
Himes, Chester. *The Quality of Hurt.* New York: Doubleday, 1972.
Holloway, Karla. *The Character of the Word: The Texts of Zora Neale
    Hurston.* Westport: Greenwood, 1987.
Holt, Rackham. *Mary McLeod Bethune.* New York: Doubleday, 1964.
Howard, Lillie P. *Alice Walker and Zora Neale Hurston: The Common Bond.*
    Westport: Greenwood, 1993.
————. "Zora Neale Hurston: Just Being Herself," *Essence,* Nov. 1980,
    101, 156, 160–166.
————. *Zora Neale Hurston.* Boston: Twayne, 1980.
————. "Marriage: Zora Neale Hurston's System of Values," *College
    Language Association Journal,* XXI, December 1977, 256–268.
Huggins, Nathan. *Harlem Renaissance.* New York: Oxford University Press,
    1971.
Hughes, Carl. *The Negro Novelist, 1940–50.* New York: Citadel Press,
    1953.
Hughes, Langston. *The Big Sea.* New York: Hill and Wang, 1940.
————. *Laughing to Keep From Crying.* New York: Henry Holt, 1952.
————. "My Most Humiliating Jim Crow Experience," in *Langston Hughes
    Reader.* New York: George Braziller, Inc., 1958, 488–489.
————. *The Book of Negro Folklore.* New York: Dodd Mead, 1958.
————. *The Best of Simple.* New York: Hill and Wang, 1961.
————. *Not Without Laughter.* New York: Collier-Macmillan, 1969.
————. *The Best Short Stories by Negro Writers.* Boston: Little Brown &
    co., 1967.
————. *The Ways of White Folks.* New York: Knopf, 1979.

Huie, William Bradford. *The Crime of Ruby McCollum.* London: Jarrolds,
    1957.
Hull, Gloria and Scott, Patricia and Smith, Barbara. *All the Women Are
    White, All the Blacks are Men, But Some of Us Are Brave.* New York:
    The Feminist Press, 1982.
Hunter, Kristin. *The Survivors.* New York: Scribners, 1975.
Hurst, Fannie. *Imitation of Life.* New York: Perma Books, 1933.
————. Review of *Jonah's Gourd Vine. The Spectator,* Vol. 154, 1935, 25.
————. "Zora Neale Hurston: A Personality Sketch," *Yale University
    Library Gazette,* Vol. 35, 1960, 17–22.
Jackson, Blyden. "Some Negroes in the Land of *Goshen,*" *Tennessee
    Folklore Society Bulletin,* Vol. 19, 1953, 103–107.
Jackson, Bruce. *The Negro and His Folklore in Nineteenth Century
    Periodicals.* Austin: University of Texas Press, 1967.

————. *Get Your Ass in the Water and Swim Like Me.* Cambridge, Massachusetts: Harvard University Press, 1974.
Jackson, Irene. "Black Women and Afro-American Folk Song Tradition." *Sing Out!* Vol. 25, No. 2, 1976, 10–14.
James, Charles. *From the Roots.* New York: Dodd Mead, 1970.
James, Roland. "Streetcorner Communication," *Dawn Magazine,* Oct. 26, 1974, 12.
Johnson, Barbara. "Metaphor, Metonymy and Voice in *Their Eyes Were Watching God,"* in Henry Gates, *Black Literature and Literary Theory.* New York: Methuen, 1984.
————. "Thresholds of Difference: Structure of Address in Zora Neale Hurston," *Critical Inquiry,* Vol. 12, Autumn 1985, 278–289.
————. A *World of Difference.* Baltimore: John Hopkins University, 1987.
Johnson, Charles. *Ebony and Topaz: A Collectanea.* New York: National Urban League, 1927.
Johnson, James Weldon. *Along This Way.* New York: Viking Press, 1938.
————. *God's Trombones.* New York: Viking Press, 1969.
Jones, LeRoi (Amiri Baraka). *Blues People.* New York: William Morrow, 1963.
————. *Dutchman and the Slave.* New York: William Morrow, 1964.
————. *Home: Social Essays.* London: MacGibbon & Kee, 1968.
Jordan, Barbara and Hearon, Shelby. *Barbara Jordan: A Self-Portrait.* New York: Doubleday, 1979.
Jordan, June. *Fannie Lou Hamer.* New York: Crowell, 1972.
————. "On Richard Wright and Zora Neale Hurston: Notes Toward A Balancing of Love and Hatred," *Black World,* Vol. 23, No. 10, August 1974, 4–10.
Jordan, Milton. "African Kingdom in South Carolina," *SEPIA,* Vol. 24, No. 4, April 1975, 17–25.
Kearns, Francis. *The Black Experience.* New York: Viking Press, 1970.
Keckley, Elizabeth. *Behind the Scenes.* New York: Arno, 1968.
Kellner, Bruce. *Carl V. Vechten and The Irreverent* Decades. Norman: University of Oklahoma Press, 1968.
————. *Keep-A-Inchin' Along: Selected Writings of Carl Van Vechten about Black Art and Letters.* Connecticut: Greenwood Press, 1979.
Kennedy, Randall. "Looking for Zora," *New York Times Book Review,* Dec., 30, 1980, 8, 17.
Keyes, Jean. A *History of Women's Hairstyles, 1500–1965.* London: Methuen & Co., 1967.
Kilson, Marion. "The Transformation of Eatonville's Ethnographer," *Phylon,* Vol. 33, No. 2, Summer, 1972, 112–119.
Kochman, Thomas. *Rappin' and Stylin' Out.* Urbana: University of Illinois Press, 1972.
Kunitz, Stanley. *Twentieth Century Authors.* New York: H.W. Wilson, 1942.
Larsen, Nella. *Passing.* New York: Collier Books, 1971.

Lamolinara, Guy. "Zora Neale Hurston Playscripts Found in the Library of Congress." *The Library of Congress News, (Public Affairs Office),* April 24, 1997, PR97-75, ISSN 0731-3527.

Lee, Valerie Gray. "The Use of Folktalk in Novels by Black Women Writers," *CLA Journal,* Vol. 23, No. 3, March, 1980, 266–272.

Lerner, Gerda. *Black Women in White America.* New York: Vintage Books, 1972.

Lester, Julius. *Black Folktales.* New York: Grove Press, 1969.

Levine, Lawrence. *Black Culture and Consciousness.* New York: Oxford University Press, 1977.

Lewis, David Levering. *The Portable Harlem Renaissance Reader.* New York: Penguin, 1995.

Liebow, Elliot. *Tally's Corner.* Boston: Little Brown, 1967.

Locke, Alain. *The New Negro.* New York: Albert and Charles Boni, 1925.

Logan, Rayford. *The Negro in American Life and Thought.* New York: The Dial Press, 1954.

Loggins, Vernon. *The Negro Author: His Development in America to 1900.* New York: Columbia University Press, 1931.

Lomax, Alan and Cowell, Sidney. *American Folk Song and Folklore (A Regional Bibliography).* New York: Progressive Education Association, 1942.

Lomax, Alan. "Zora Neale Hurston: A Life of Negro Folklore," *Sing Out!* Vol. 10, Oct.–Nov., 1960, 12–13.

Lord, Albert. *The Singer of Tales.* Cambridge: Harvard University Press, 1964.

Love, Theresa. "Zora Neale Hurston's America," *Papers on Language and Literature,* Vol. 12, No. 4, Fall, 1976, 422–437.

Lowe, John. *Jump at de Sun: Zora Neale Hurston's Cosmic Comedy.* Urbana: University of Illinois Press, 1994.

Lyons, Mary E. *Sorrow's Kitchen: Life and Folklore of Zora Neale Hurston.* New York: Scribners, 1990.

MacCann, Donnarae and Woodard, Gloria. *The Black American in Books for Children.* New Jersey: Scarecrow Press, 1985.

McDonogh, Gary. *The Florida Negro: A Federal Writers' Project Legacy.* Jackson: University Press of Mississippi,1993.

McIlwaine, Shields. *The Southern Poor-White.* New York: Cooper Square Publishers, 1970.

McKay, Claude. *Home to Harlem.* New York: Pocket Books, 1965.

McKissack, Patricia. *Zora Neale Hurston: Writer and Storyteller.* Hillside, N.J.: Enslow Publishers, 1992.

Major, Clarence. *Dictionary of Afro-American Slang.* New York: International Publishers, 1970.

———. *The Dark and Feeling.* New York: Third Press, 1974.

Malcolm X (with the assistance of Alex Haley). *The Autobiography of Malcolm X.* New York: Grove Press, 1964.

Margolies, Edward. *Native Sons.* Philadelphia: Lippincott, 1968.

Marks, Donald. "Sex, Violence, and Organic Consciousness in Zora Neale Hurston's *Their Eyes Were Watching God*," *Black American Literature Forum*. Winter 1985, Vol. 19, No. 5, 152–157.

Martin, Jay. *A Singer in the Dawn*. New York: Dodd Mead and Company, 1975.

Martin, Jay and Hudson, Gossie. *The Paul L. Dunbar Reader*. New York: Dodd Mead and Company, 1975.

Mason, Rufus Osgood. *Telepathy and Subliminal Self (An Account of Recent Investigations Regarding Hypnotism, Automatism, Dreams, Phantasms and Related Phenomena)*. New York: Henry Holt & Co., 1897.

Massaquoi, Hans. "Alex Haley in Juffure," *Ebony*, July 1977, 36–42.

Matthiessan, F.O. *American Renaissance*. New York: Oxford University Press, 1962.

Miller, Ruth. *Black American Literature*. California: Glencoe Press, 1971.

Mitchell, Henry. *Black Preaching*. New York: Lippincott, 1970.

Mitchell, Loften. *Voices from the Black Theatre*. New Jersey: James T. White & Co., 1975.

Morrison, Toni. *The Bluest Eye*. New York: Simon and Schuster, 1970.

Mullen, Bill. *Revolutionary Tales: African American Women's Short Stories from the First Story to the Present*. New York: Dell, 1995.

Nathiri, N.Y. *Zora! Zora Neale Hurston: A Woman and Her Community*. Orlando, Fla.: Sentinel Communicatons Co., 1991.

Naylor, Gloria. *The Women of Brewster Place*. New York: The Viking Press, 1980.

Neal, Larry. "Eatonville's Zora Neale Hurston: A Profile," *Black Review*, Nol. 2. New York: William Morrow, 1972, 11–24.

Nicholas, Charles. *Arna Bontemps-Langston Hughes Letters, 1925–1967*. New York: Dodd Mead, 1980.

Noble, Jeanne. *Beautiful, Also Are The Souls of My Black Sisters*. New Jersey: Prentice-Hall, 1978.

O'Brien, John. *Interviews with Black Writers*. New York: Liverright, 1973.

Ortiz, Victoria. *Sojourner Truth, A Self-Made Woman*. Philadelphia: Lippincott, 1974.

Ostendorf, Berndt. *Black Literature in White America*. New Jersey: Barnes & Noble Books, 1982.

Page, Thomas Nelson. *The Negro: The Southerners' Problem*. New York: Scribner, 1904.

———. *The Old South*. New York: Chautauqua Press, 1919.

Parker, Dorothy. "Arrangement in Black and White," 41–47, in *The Viking Portable Dorothy Parker*. New York: The Viking Press, 1966.

Patterson, James T. *Mr. Republican: A Biography of Robert A. Taft*. Boston: Houghton Mifflin, 1972.

Patterson, Lindsay. *An Introduction to Black Literature in America From 1748 to the Present*. New York: Publishers Company, Inc., 1970.

Payne, Ladell. *Black Novelists and The Southern Literay Tradition*. Athens: University of Georgia Press, 1981.

Pelton, Robert. *Voodoo Secrets From A to Z.* New York: Barner Press, 1973.

Perry, Margaret. *Silence to the Drums: A Survey of the Literature of the Harlem Renaissance.* Westport, Connecticut, 1976.

Peterkin, Julia. *Green Thursday.* New York: Knopf, 1924.

———. *Black April.* New York: Bobbs-Merrill, 1927.

———. *Scarlet Sister Mary.* New York: Grosset & Dunlop, 1928.

———. *Roll, Jordan Roll.* New York: Ballou Publishers, 1931.

———. *Bright Skin.* Indianapolis: Bobbs-Merrill, 1932.

Peters, Pearlie. "Women and Assertive Voice in Hurston's Fiction and Folklore," *The Zora Neale Hurston Forum,* Vol. VI, Number 2, Spring 1992, 11–31.

———. "The Resurgence of Dorothy West as Short-Story Writer," *ABAFAZI: The Simmons College Review of Women of African Descent,* Fall/Winter, 1997.

Petry, Ann. *The Street.* New York: Pyramid Books, 1961.

Pettigrew, Thomas F. *A Profile of the Negro American.* Princton, New Jersey: D.Van Nostrand, 1964.

Pierpont, Claudia Roth. "A Society of One: Zora Neale Hurston, American contrarian," *The New Yorker,* February 17, 1997, 80–86.

Pinckney, Darryl. "In Sorrow's Kitchen," *New York Times Review of Books,* Vol. 25, No. 20, December 21, 1978, 55–57.

Plant, Deborah. *Every Tub Must Sit on Its Own Bottom: The Philsophy and Politics of Zora Neale Hurston.* Urbana: University of Illinois Press, 1995.

Pondrom, Cyrene N. "The Role of Myth in Hurston's *Their Eyes Were Watching God,"* American Literature, Vol. 58, No. 2, May 1986, 181–202.

Porter, A.P. *Jump At De Sun: The Story of Zora Neale Hurston.* Minneapolis: Carolrhoda Books, 1992.

Poussaint, Alvin. "A Negro Psychiatrist Explains the Negro Psyche," *New York Times,* August 20, 1967, Section 6, 52.

———. "Problems of Light Skinned Blacks," *Ebony,* Feb., 1975, 85–91.

Pratt, Theodore. "A Memoir: Zora Neale Hurston: Florida's First Distinguished Author," *Negro Digest,* Feb., 1962, 52–56.

Pryse, Marjorie and Spillers, Hortense. *Conjuring: Black Women, Fiction and Literary Tradition.* Bloomington: Indiana University Press, 1985.

Puckett, Newbell N. *Folk Beliefs of the Southern Negro.* New York: Negro University Press, 1968.

Rampersad, Arnold. *The Life of Langston Hughes, I, Too, Sing America,* Vol. 1, 1902–1941. New York: Oxford University Press, 1986.

Ramsey, Priscilla. "A Study of Black Identity in Passing Novles of the Nineteenth and Early Twentieth Centuries," *Studies in Black Literature,* Vol. 7, No. 2, Spring 1976, 1–7.

Rawlings, Margaret. *The Yearling.* New York: Scribners, 1938.

Rayson, Ann. "The Novels of Zora Neale Hurston," *Studies in Black Literature,* Vol. 5, No. 3, Winter 1974, 1–10.

————. "*Dust Tracks on a Road*: Zora Neale Hurston and the Form of Black Autobiography," *Negro American Literature Forum,* Vol. 7, 1973, 39–45.

Redding, Saunders. *On Being Negro in America.* Indianapolis: the Bobbs-Merrill Company, 1951.

Rediger, Pat. *Great African Americans in Literature.* New York: Crabtree Publishing Company, 1996.

Reed, Carolyn. "The Housemaid Who Rose to Lead a National Cause: Carolyn Rogers," *Toronto Star,* March 19, 1980, C9.

Render, Sylvia Lyons. *The Short Fiction of Charles W. Chesnutt.* Washington: Howard University Press, 1974.

Robinson, Wilhelmena. *Historical Negro Biographies: International Library of Negro Life and History.* New York: Publishers Company Insurance (auspices of the Association of Negro Life and History), 1967.

Rosenberg, Bruce. *The Art of the American Folk Preacher.* New York: Oxford University Press, 1970.

Rosenblatt, Roger. *Black Fiction.* Cambridge: Harvard University Press, 1974.

Roses, Lorraine Elena and Ruth Elizabeth Randolph. *Harlem's Glory.* Massachusetts: Harvard University Press, 1997.

————. *Harlem Renaissance and Beyond.* Massachusetts: Harvard University Press, 1990.

Sanfield, Steve. *The Adventures of High John the Conqueror.* New York: Orchard Books, 1989.

Schuyler, George. *Black No More.* Maryland: McGrath Publishing Co., 1969.

Scruggs, Charles. "Alaine Locke and Walter White: Their Struggle for Control of the Harlem Renaissance," *Black American Literature Forum,* Vol. 14, No. 3, Fall, 1980, 91–100.

Sebestyan, Ouida. *Words by Heart.* New York: Bantam, 1981.

Seifer, Nancy. *Nobody Speaks for Me.* New York: Simon and Schuster, 1976.

Sidran, Ben. *Black Talk.* New York: Holt, Rinehart & Winston, 1971.

————. Talking Black. Mass.: Newberry House, 1976.

Skeeter, Sharyn. "Black Women Writers: Levels of Identity," *Essence,* May, 1973, 58–59, 76, 89.

Smitherman, Geneva. *Talkin' and Testifyin': The Language of Black America.* Boston: Houghton Mifflin, 1977.

Southerland, Ellease. "The Novelist-Anthropologist's Life and Works: Zora Neale Hurston," *Black World,* Vol. 23 No. 10, August 1974, 20–31.

Spaulding, Henry Bruce. *Encyclopedia of Black Folklore and Humor.* New York: Jonathan David Publishers, 1972.

Sterling, Dorothy. *Black Foremothers.* New York: The Feminist Press, 1979.

Stuckley, Sterling. *Paul Robeson: The Great Forerunner.* New York: Dodd Mead and Company, 1965.

Szwed, John. "An American Anthropologist Dilemma: The Politics of Afro-American Culture," in Hymes, Dell. *Reinventing Anthropology.* New York: Random House, 1969.

———. *Afro-American Anthropology.* New York: Free Press, 1970.

Tallant, Robert. *Voodoo in New Orleans.* New York: Macmillan Co., 1946.

Tally, Thomas. *Negro Folk Rhymes: Wise and Otherwise.* New York: Macmillan Co., 1922.

Tate, Claudia. *Black Women Writers at Work.* New York: Continuum, 1983.

Taylor, Clyde. "Black Folk Spirit and The Shape of Black Literature," *Black World,* Vol. 21, No. 19, August 1972, 31–40.

Taylor, Mildred. *Roll of Thunder, Hear My Cry.* New York: Bantam, 1978.

———. *Let the Circle Be Unbroken.* New York: Bantam, 1981.

Thurman, Wallace. *The Blacker the Berry.* New York: Macmillan, 1970.

Tischler, Nancy. *Black Masks: Negro Characters in Modern Southern Fiction.* University Park, Pennsylvania: State University Press, 1969.

Tolson, Melvin. *Harlem Gallery.* New York: Collier, 1965.

Toomer, Jean. *Cane.* New York: Harper and Row, 1923.

Torrence, Jackie Seals. *The Importance of Pot Liquor.* Little Rock, Arkansas: August House, 1994.

Turner, Darwin and Jean Bright. *Images of the Negro American.* Boston: D.C. Heath, 1965.

Turner, Darwin. "The Negro Novelist and the South," *Southern Humanities Review,* I (1967), 21–29.

———. *Black American Literature: Essays and Fiction.* Columbus, Ohio: Merrill, 1969.

———. *Theory and Practice in the Teaching of Literature by Afro-Americans.* Urbana, Illinois: National Council of Teachers of English Educational Resources Information Center, 1971.

———. *In a Minor Chord.* Carbondale: Southern Illinois University Press, 1971.

Turner, Kenneth. *Negro Collectors of Negro Folklore: A Study of J. Mason Brewer and Zora Neale Hurston.* Master Thesis, East Texas State College, Commerce, Texas.

Turner, Lorenzo Dow. *Africanisms in the Gullah Dialect.* Chicago: University of Chicago Press, 1949.

Van Vechten, Carl. *Nigger Heaven.* New York: Harper & Row, 1926.

Walker, Alice. *In Love and Trouble.* New York: Harcourt Brace Jovanovich, 1967.

———. *The Third Life of Grange Copeland.* New York: Harcourt Brace Jovanovich, 1970.

———. "In Search of Zora Neale Hurston," *Ms.* Vol. 3, No. 9, March 1975, 74–76, 78–79, 85–89.

———. *The Color Purple.* New York: Harcourt Brace Jovanovich, 1982.

———. *In Search of Our Mothers' Gardens.* San Diego. Harcourt Brace Jovanovich, 1983.

Walker, Margaret. *For My People.* New Haven, Conn: Yale University Press, 1942.

———. *Jubilee.* Boston: Houghton Mifflin, 1966.

Walker, S. Jay. "Zora Neale Hurston's *Their Eyes Were Watching God: Black Novel of Sexism*," *Modern Fiction Studies*, Vol. 20, 1974–75, 519–527.

Wall, Cheryl. *Zora Neale Hurston: Sweat*. New Brunswick, New Jersey: Rutgers University Press, 1997.

———. *Women of the Harlem Renaissance*. Bloomington: Indiana University Press, 1995.

———. *Zora Neale Hurston. Folklore, Memories and Other Writings*. New York: Library of America, 1995.

———. *Zora Neale Hurston. Novels and Stories*. New York: Library of America, 1995.

———. "Zora Neale Hurston: Changing Her Own Words," in Fleischmann, Fritz. *American Novelist Revisited: Essays in Feminist Criticism*. Boston: G.K. Hall, 1982.

Walter, Mildred Pitts. *Because We Are*. New York: Lothrop, Lee & Shepard, 1983.

———. *Trouble's Child*. New York: Lothrop, Lee & Shepard, 1985.

Walters, Raymond. *Negroes and The Great Depression*. Connecticut: Greenwood Publishing Co., 1970.

Ward, Jerry and John Oliver Killens. *Black Southern Voices*. New York: Penguin, 1992.

Washington, Joseph. *Black Religion*. Boston: Beacon Press, 1964.

Washington, Mary Helen. "Zora Neale Hurston: The Black Woman's Search for Identity," *Black World*, Vol. 21, No. 10, August, 1972, 68–75.

———. *Black Eyed-Susans*. New York: Doubleday Anchor Books, 1975.

———. *Midnight Birds*. New York: Doubleday Anchor Books, 1980.

———. *Invented Lives (Narratives of Black Women, 1860–1960)*. New York: Doubleday Anchor Books, 1987.

Waters, Ethel. *His Eye Is On The Sparrow*. New York: Pyramid Books, 1972.

Watson, Steven. *The Harlem Renaissance*. New York: Pantheon Books, 1995.

Wheatley, Geoffrey. "Doctors Acknowledge Witch Doctors' Skill," *Toronto Star*, June 29, 1978.

Whitlow, Roger. *Black American Literature*. Chicago: Nelson Hall, 1973.

Willis, Susan. *Specifying: Black Women Writing the American Experience*. Madison: University of Wisconsin Press, 2987.

Wilson, J.L. "Man and Mule on the Plow." *The Shreveport Times*, August 27, 1972, 9-F.

Witcover, Paul. *Zora Neale Hurston, Author*. New York: Chelsea House, 1991.

Woodson, Carter. *A Century of Negro Migration*. Washington, D.C.: The Association for the Study of Negro Life and History, 1918.

———. *Negro Orators and Their Orations*. Washington: D.C.: Association Publishers, 1925.

———. *The Rural Negroes*. Washington, D.C.: The Association for the Study of Negro Life and History, 1930.

Wolfe, George C. *Spunk: Three Tales by Zora Neale Hurston.* New York: Theatre Communications Group, Inc., 1991.

Wright, Ellen and Fabre, Michel. *Richard Wright Reader.* New York: Harper & Row, 1978.

Wright, Richard. *Uncle Tom's Children.* New York: Harper & Row, 1936.

———. *Black Boy.* New York: Harper & Row, 1937.

Wright, Sarah. *This Child's Gonna Live.* New York: Delacorte Press, 1969.

Young, James. *Black Writers of the Thirties.* Baton Rouge: Louisiana State University Press, 1973.

Yannuzzi, Della. *Zora Neale Hurston: Southern Storyteller.* Springfield, New Jersey: Enslow Publishers, 1996.

Yates, Janelle. *Zora Neale Hurston: A Storyteller's Life.* Staten Island, New York: Ward Hill Press, 1991.

Young, James. *Black Writers of the Thirties.* Baton Rouge: Louisiana State University Press, 1973.

Index

Harris, Patricia Roberts, 17
Hattie Tyson, 19, 20, 122, 124,
125
Hemenway, Robert, 13, 14

"I Saw Negro Votes Peddled", 81
Isie, 18

Jaine (Killicks Starks Woods), 5,
6, 8, 12–15, 17–19, 21, 30,
33–34, 69, 88, 91, 113–14,
127–48
Jelly, 101–102, 104
Jim Allen, 38
Jim Meserve (Arvay's husband),
18, 28, 29
Jim Presley, 53–55
Joe (Jody) Starks, 12, 13, 14,
136–39, 141, 142–48
Joe Banks, 13, 89–95, 98
Joe Kanty, 19
Joe Wiley, 44
Joe Willard, 35, 37, 38, 39, 41,
43, 48–49, 51, 53–55
John Pearon, 5, 8, 15, 19, 20,
113–26
John Redding, 23–24
"John Redding Goes to Sea", 24
Johnnie Mae, 13
Johnny Taylor, 130, 131
Jonah's Gourd Vine, 5, 19, 88,
114
Jordan, Barbara, 17

Kennedy, Florence, 17
"kissing friends", 6, 34, 66, 69
Kitty Brown, 23–24

Larkins, 44, 48
Laura B, 68–69, 76
Laura Lee Kimble, 5, 9, 10, 14,
18, 33, 81, 82–88, 148
Leafy Lee, 13, 17, 25, 34, 59–
60, 67–72, 73, 76–78
Lena, 19
Logan Killicks, 8, 12, 13, 130,
132–36, 144–46

Lonnie, 13, 25, 37, 58–61, 64–
66, 71–76, 78
Lorraine, 29
loud talking, 4, 48, 51, 63
Lucy (*Mules and Men*), 19, 25,
48–51, 54–55
Lucy Pearson, 5, 8, 12, 14, 15,
17, 18–21, 30, 33–34, 88,
113–26, 148

Mack, 42–43, 49, 63
mambo of Haiti, 18
Mathilda Moses, 13
Mattie Redding, 23, 24
Minnie Foster, 23, 24
Missie May, 8, 13, 18, 33, 88–
95, 98, 104, 122, 148
Miz' Celestine Clairborne, 82,
85–87
Moses, 27
Moses, Man of the Mountain, 26
Mother Catherine, 18
mouth stones, 33–34
Mrs. Bertha, 37
Mrs. Tony Robbins, 140
Mrs. Turner (Janie's nemesis),
27
Mrs. Turner (*TEWWG*), 60
mulatto experience, 26, 32, 65
Mules and Men, 20, 21, 35, 37,
45, 57, 62, 63
My Honey, 13, 25, 42–43, 59–
60, 65–67, 70–71, 78

Nanny, 18, 130–33, 145
Ned (Amy's husband), 8, 9, 10
Ned (John Pearson's stepfather),
116
"negotiating respect", 14, 31,
52, 88
Negro courtship ritual, 7, 14, 94
non-verbal communication
techniques
body stance, 4
eyeballing, 4, 46
hand gesturing, 4
hip swaying, 4
walking style, 4